T3-BNI-299

CHANGING BRITAIN
Social Diversity and Moral Unity

A Study for the Board for Social Responsibility

CHURCH HOUSE PUBLISHING

Church House, Great Smith Street, London, SW1P 3NZ

ISBN 0 7151 6572 0

Published 1987 for the General Synod Board for Social Responsibility by Church House Publishing

© *The Central Board of Finance of the Church of England 1987*
This publication may not be reproduced either in whole or in part whether for sale or otherwise by any method without written permission which should be sought from the Legal Adviser to the General Synod, Church House, Great Smith Street, London, SW1P 3NZ.

The Board for Social Responsibility is an advisory committee of the Church of England General Synod. Its functions are to promote and co-ordinate the thought and action of the Church in matters affecting the lives of men and women in society.

THIS STUDY is the work of a group set up by the Board. It is offered as a contribution to debate because its contents are thought likely to prove of interest. It is not intended to represent the policy of the Board for Social Responsibility itself.

HN
39
.G7
C45
1987

Cover design by Bill Bruce. Photograph by Michael Langford.

Contents

Contents

Foreword

'Although the signs have been there for some time for those who have eyes to see, it is now becoming clear to all that we are moving into a new and unprecedented type of society; and because we tend to be a traditional and conservative people, we are almost totally unprepared for what is bound to come.'

With those words I prefaced an invitation to church bodies and secular institutions to contribute their views to the Board about what goals are needed for our future society. A debate on the subject was also held in the General Synod on 19th November 1985. The distinguished Committee chaired by the Archbishop of York and set up by the Board for Social Responsibility then met to write their own report, bearing in mind the views the Board had gathered from these sources.

I am glad to commend to the General Synod, and indeed to the world at large, the result of their thinking. I hope that it will be regarded as a foundation document about the values needed for the era that lies ahead.

✠ HUGH BIRMINGHAM

St Joseph's Day 1987

Members of the Group

The Most Reverend John S. Habgood, Archbishop of York (Chairman)

Sir Peter Baldwin, KCB, Chairman of the South-East Thames Regional Health Authority

The Revd Myra Blyth, Secretary of the Youth Unit of the British Council of Churches

The Revd John Mahoney SJ, F. D. Maurice Professor of Moral and Social Theology, King's College London

Professor A. H. Halsey, Director of the Department of Social and Administrative Studies, University of Oxford

Miss Brenda Harrison, Inspector for Religious Education, Cambridgeshire

Sara Maitland, writer and broadcaster

Canon Ronald Preston, Emeritus Professor of Social and Pastoral Theology, University of Manchester

The Revd Michael Atkinson, Research Officer in the General Synod Board for Social Responsibility (Secretary)

Sir Michael Quinlan, KCB, Permanent Secretary in the Department of Employment attended as as observer.

The Group also benefited in the earlier period of its work from the presence of Mr Ronald Butt, writer and journalist, and Mr Peter Phillips, Chairman of AB Electronic Products Group PLC, but their other commitments made it impossible for them to attend the Group's later meetings.

Preface by the Archbishop of York

Questions about the future shape of British society can be answered in various terms. Some people see them as essentially questions about the distribution of power within this country. They are conscious of the extent to which both the possession of power, and the lack of it, can distort human perceptions. They bring to every practical issue the uncomfortable query, who stands to gain by what course of action? Some, indeed, take their analysis of power to its logical conclusion. They know, or think they know, what they want, and their main concern is to gain the power to achieve it.

Other people claim that it is no longer sensible to think of British society as if it could be changed simply from within. The world is one, and Britain as a trading nation with a long overseas history and a new commonwealth within its shores, is therefore inevitably caught up in the ebb and flow of world events. The shape of British society has to be set within a world context, and it may well be that Britain can discover a new sense of purpose only insofar as our understanding of our changed role in the world matches reality.

Others approach general questions about the shape of society with highly specific issues in mind. What is to be done about unemployment, or in support of family life, or against racism, or about a hundred-and-one other issues which make up the familiar agenda of the socially conscious?

In contrast to all these approaches, we have chosen to concentrate in this study on values. It may at first sight seem far removed from the concerns just listed. The danger inherent in writing about values is of lapsing into large vague abstractions. Everybody loves justice and peace, but to try to spell out in practice what they entail is much more difficult and leads to all the familiar disagreements. Yet values, expressed or unexpressed, underlie all moral and political action. And sometimes apparently insoluble practical problems can only be tackled by exposing the conflicts of value contained within them. This then is our justification for attempting a cool look at some of the value conflicts in present day British society. The bitterest political struggles wear their ideological labels openly and explicitly. But even small disagreements can often be traced back to shifts and differences of emphasis within value systems which all might claim to share. It is possible to avoid the dangers of abstraction, therefore, by constant reference back to the social and political realities within which value systems operate, but it would be beyond the scope of this study to go on from our general analysis to offer specific guidance on concrete issues. That is a task for more specialised working parties with more circumscribed briefs, aided we hope by some of the signposts we have tried to erect. Ours is a strictly limited exercise.

We have two reasons for limiting ourselves to Britain, without attempting to explore any of the difficult questions about our existing links with other nations and our future international role. First, what we say about values can, we believe, have a general application outside our own society. Second, in any analysis a choice has to be made between limiting the field of study, and so risking distortion by elimination of the wider context, or using as wide a perspective as possible, thereby running the risk of unmanageable complexity. We have deliberately chosen to do the former, in the hope that what we learn about ourselves as a society by looking inwards will help rather than hinder the next essential stage in seeing ourselves against a world backcloth.

Even so, the ground we have attempted to cover is huge. This wide brief given to us by the Board for Social Responsibility to report on 'Goals for our Future Society' was set out in a document containing hundreds of questions touching almost every aspect of public life. The large response to the study document circulated by the Board was evidence that many people are anxious about what is happening in British society. No doubt in every age there have been fears of apparently uncontrollable change, but there are new questions to be asked about the basis of response to such change in a society which is beginning to become self-conscious about its degree of moral and social diversity.

In trying to give some guidance towards appropriate responses we have chosen to present our argument in a way which we hope makes it accessible to people of different religious convictions, or none at all. If our society is to make any progress towards the moral unity referred to in the title of this study, a broad approach seems unavoidable. We could have contented ourselves with addressing a clear Christian message to any who might care to listen, and we do not underestimate the value of such statements from faith to faith. Our choice of a different method reflects our concern to say things which we believe have validity for the whole of our society.

That Britain is changing is a fact, which may or may not be congenial to those caught up in the changes. That Britain can be changed in ways which would be for the good of all involved in it and with it, is a hope whose realisation is going to need conscious commitment. We offer this study as a stimulus to that commitment and as a preliminary survey of some of the first essential steps.

It remains for me to thank those who have contributed so much to it, whether as members of the working party or as respondents to the original *Goals for our Future Society* document. Not all original members of the Working Party were able to stay the course, partly because the whole exercise proved more demanding and time-consuming than was anticipated. I want especially to thank our Secretary, Michael Atkinson, and Kathleen Sheen and Doreen Butland, who patiently and expertly produced draft after draft as we tried to clarify our thoughts and reduce the massive documentation to reasonable dimensions.

John Ebor:
Spring 1987

CHAPTER ONE
Stability and Change

1. We belong to a very old society. Leaving their refuges in central and southern Europe, our distant ancestors came north, following the retreating glaciers of the last ice age, long before the period, some six thousand years ago, when the land bridge between Britain and the rest of Europe was broken at the Straits of Dover. This great climatic and geological event did to the human population of our islands exactly what it did to the vegetation and the animal life: it produced, in the shape of the North Sea and the English Channel, an obstacle to further invasions – not a complete one, of course, but enough to ensure that the invaders tended to arrive in small numbers, and, having arrived, to stay. Compared with our European neighbours, the model of our society is thus that of a deposit continually enriched, rather than a flux of peoples arriving and departing with relative frequency and ease. This may seem rather a long way back to begin the account of British society today, but there does seem to be a 'set' to our history that was established early and whose consequences influence our society to this day when people are moving socially and geographically much more than we have been used to.

2. On the world scale the British have been a remarkably stable and successful nation, however tempting it is today to think otherwise. Britain has been able to grow and sustain a large population on a small piece of territory, and to do so at levels of affluence which left sufficient surplus in the economy to permit it to dominate increasingly vast tracts of the earth's surface for some hundreds of years. On the scale of history that performance had few, if any, rivals, until the present century. British influence, if not power, is not inconsiderable even now.

3. This stability and success seems in many eyes to be under threat. The Board for Social Responsibility's document *Goals for our Future Society* elicited long lists of ills requiring remedies. To gain perspective and to acquire an accurate 'fix' of our situation on some kind of mental map, they must initially be set aside. The purpose of this chapter is a swift characterisation of some basic features of our society. Such a programme can easily be 'downbeat' from the beginning. It is the things which we dislike which crowd upon our notice, and the 'upbeat' factors are taken for granted. So it is useful to begin with a picture of what is, in world terms, an old, stable, large and successful culture.

1

Some Basic Characteristics of Britain Today

4. The impression of Britain as a country which is basically socially stable is borne out by studies conducted by the European Value Systems Study Group (EVSSG) which had the heroic task of describing the moral condition of contemporary Europe. Professor Halsey and Professor Mahoney, both contributors to the present study, were also members of the EVSSG.

5. Professor Halsey's contribution to the first of EVSSG's published volumes was to comment on EVSSG's achievement and its limitations, and to suggest some possible directions for its further development. He summarises the main conclusions of the EVSSG as they relate to Britain:

> In the light of variations across Europe the broad and unsurprising impression is of a people culturally close to the countries of Northern Europe, diverging generally towards Scandinavia and away from Latin Europe. Britain occupies this position with respect to satisfaction with life, the perceived trust among the young towards the old, psychological well-being, job satisfaction, contentment with the financial condition of one's household, willingness to fight for one's country in case of war, belief in the first three Commandments and acceptance of the Commandments against stealing and bearing false witness, belief in God and conception of self as a religious person.[1]

The average scores for values with a conventionally secular connotation descend from Scandinavia through Northern Europe to Latin Europe. The explicitly religiously-phrased values run in the opposite direction. Britain lies neatly along the trend in the position that our geographical location might suggest. But there are a number of characteristics in which Britain at the time of the survey seemed to buck the trend.

> They are the most optimistic . . . about the future and about the promise of science and the use of technology in that future. They are more proud of their nationality, think of themselves as having more pride in their work, more satisfied with their personal health, more approving of any future increase in respect of authority, more inclined to see themselves as to the right in politics, and, most conspicuously, more likely to choose personal freedom as against social equality if forced to do so.[2]

They are 'markedly more moralistic' than any other Europeans about honouring parents and recognising the force of the Commandments against murder, adultery, envy and desire.

---

[1] Mark Abrams, David Gerard and Noel Timms eds. *Values and Social Change in Britain* (Basingstoke, Macmillan, 1985) pp. 11-12.
[2] Abrams et al. *Values*, p. 12.

6. The sample used by EVSSG was too small to provide any useful description of the views of British Jews, Muslims, Buddhists, Hindus and Sikhs, though these minority groups occupy an important place in British society. Halsey fills out the EVSSG information with material from a study by Bowker, who noted abounding commonalities between the five faiths and Christianity, namely, the centrality of prayer to religious practice, the significance of individual life as a balance of virtue and vice determining a fate beyond death, the insignificance of individual life in the pages of eternity, the rootedness of religious belief in family continuity, and the ultimate belief in one God. This last, Halsey believes, 'seems capable of translation into a common ethical creed of love, hope and charity binding a nation and extending towards all, even all creation'.[1]

7. The European Values study thus suggests that there is a strong moral and ethical tradition in Britain, that the values underlying British society are relatively tough ones. Stability compared with the rest of Europe does not rule out feelings within the British population that there is within Britain considerable instability. People are not usually very conscious of living their lives on the large European scale. It is the things nearer home which are most immediate and maybe most threatening. Expressions of emotional unrest are frequent in Britain these days. Some of the features of British society which give rise to anxiety and concern are now examined.

Recent Economic and Social Transformations

8. In a population of fifty million people which includes much diversity, even minority views and feelings can be held by quite large numbers of people. So evidence of both stability and instability may be valid. Social changes, diverse yet interlinked, may feel threatening despite the strength of moral traditions. Feelings of complexity and resulting insecurity may arise and anxiety may remain about their power to cause alarm. People often express alarm about the morality and stability of others around them, even though in response to questionnaires their own personal stability seems assured. The experience of rapid, wide and continuing change can be unnerving, and can put the moral tradition under strain. Change can become so threatening that people can no longer even communicate their fears about it to one another, and feel isolated in them. What are these changes that cause such apprehension?

---

[1] Abrams et al. *Values* p. 16.

9. The domestic sphere, the economic sphere and the state are social realities that govern the conditions of people's lives. In the past the three seemed to exist separately from each other. Men worked for wages in the productive economy. Women, especially once they were married, were confined to administering the home and raising children. Except in times of war the state seemed pretty remote from these spheres, but by the beginning of this century it has taken on some power in 'protecting' and 'controlling' both the economy and the family and some role in redistributing a certain amount of resources from household to household.

10. The 'pure' division between these basic social institutions no longer obtains. The state, compared with earlier practice, now increasingly intervenes in exchanges between the domestic and the economic spheres, as well as directly into both. Taxation has increased, and money is redistributed in larger amounts, though not always to such a degree as to counteract the even larger movements in market wages which widen the gap between those in work and those without it. Women increasingly enter the paid economy and bear fewer children. Families break up and re-form more frequently by divorce and remarriage. Men are drawn more into household work than they were. The traditional role of the parent and the neighbour has undergone subdivision and has been supplemented by a variety of state agents – doctors, nurses, teachers, police, social workers, and so on. The state produces both goods and services within the formal economy. Education is made compulsory by the state, and is being increasingly extended. Part time and voluntary education, for young people and adults, has greatly increased. Hours, weeks and years of work have reduced. Holidays have increased and they are now 'paid'. Retirement lasts longer than it used to, and the retired are supported substantially by the state. Finally, universal adult suffrage – still no more than 60 years old – alters the relationship of the individual (whether at home or at work) to the state.

11. Not everyone welcomes these trends, but they are real and raise important questions. If social relations need not be static, the possibility of altering them more deliberately in a preferred direction begins to suggest itself and the simple pattern of earlier ages disappears. Today's labour market has to take account of the need for longer and more vocational education. Work has to be reorganised to meet at each stage in their lives the needs of women, who now make up about 40 per cent of the employed population. Then, as longevity increases, policy about retirement age and the funding of old-age pensions becomes more

of a question. Within the family itself, what does the increased avail-ability of technological aids to household work do to the division of labour between men and women? There is general interest in steady non-inflationary economic growth, and in the more flexible and efficient use of labour. New relations between the state, family and community raise new questions about the shape of welfare. There is no widespread wish for a total dismantling of state support for the welfare functions which in times past were once mainly left to the family, and especially to women.

12. A good example of a shift in the balance of state, family and work, and how it creates problems, is the policy of offering as much care as possible within the community, rather than in hospitals and residential establishments. The policy had several origins. It was hoped that individual needs could be met sensitively and flexibly. It was also to some extent a reaction against 'bureaucratic centralisation' and special-isation. The hope was that services would be more efficient, saving professional overlap and reducing management costs. But the process of implementing the new ideas has often been problematic for all involved – in some cases no fewer than seven government departments have to co-ordinate their changes of policy. The position in local government is no simpler. For the individual clients and their families the difficulties can be considerable. 'Care in the community' depends on a degree of local, even personal, knowledge which no single agency possesses, or can probably now ever possess. There is rarely anyone who 'knows' a situation so completely as, in an earlier era, the minister, the schoolmaster, the doctor or the squire knew it. The gossip circle is weak, or may no longer exist. More information is on official records, but it may not create more knowledge. Much of it is lost to view in files and on tapes or discs and is not generally accessible. Conditions in which effective 'care in the community' could be provided can be imagined, but they call for interest, knowledge, time, and willingness in the population, as well as adequate financial and emotional support.

13. Those who deliver services are not always well placed to know where service is needed. The only people who do are the families and the neighbours of those who are in need. Care in the community will not succeed without a greater sense of neighbourliness and social unity. Given that, it stands a better chance of doing what caring is supposed to do. The Christian understanding of the duty to 'love one's neighbour' is obviously relevant here. But the point is that for some people, and at least for a time, the shift back to a more neighbourly kind of society can be threatening.

Social Division

14. Societies have always been divided along the lines of ethnicity, sex and class. These divisions are strong in Britain today, though opinions differ as to whether they are becoming more, or less, significant. Certainly they do not matter less to those personally affected by them. Over and above these features, which are fairly easily observed, there is however a greater reality which is sometimes unnoticed, concealed or ignored.

15. Ever since Disraeli coined the phrase 'two nations' in 1845 it has periodically been revived as an apt description of society. One hears it again today. What it indicates is not divisions as such in society (which might be haphazard) but rather the way in which several important divisions stack up into a single major divide, so that many characteristics on one side distinguish that side from the other. The claim is that society is now more deeply polarised than for a long time between a majority – David Sheppard's 'comfortable Britain', relatively secure and prosperous, in employment at wage or salary levels which increase at beyond the rate of inflation – and 'the other Britain'. This 'other Britain' is a minority overall (but sometimes locally present in large numbers) which, though generally maintained as to its real purchasing power, has in recent years not matched the steady increase in living standards secured by the more fortunate majority. The evidence is there in official statistics, and also among the findings of the Archbishop of Canterbury's Commission on Urban Priority Areas (ACUPA) published in *Faith in the City*.[1] It was earlier provided by the 'Diamond' Commission.[2]

16. On family income, it is clear that even after receiving all the benefits to which they are entitled and which they actually claim, the bottom fifth of all families now have a share of the national 'cake' which is *less* than it was ten years ago. By contrast the top fifth, even after taxation, have increased their share. The relative difference in final incomes between the one whole group and the other is, as in many other countries, no less than six-fold. Individual cases display much greater differences. Where wealth as distinct from income is concerned, there is no change from its historic concentration within a small 'rich' minority of the population. At the bottom end of the social scale there is recent evidence of increased mobility both upwards and downwards.

---

[1] London, Church House Publishing, 1985.
[2] Royal Commission on the Distribution of Incomes and Wealth 1974-9.

Unemployment (about which more is said shortly), and the low income and life-chances that go with it, in 1986 ran at an average rate across the country of eleven to twelve per cent. Of the three million or so individuals whom this represents, over a million had been unemployed for more than a year. Thus a new, large, substratum has become established at the bottom of the economy, which is heavily recruited from unskilled young people, the older manual workers and people in ethnic minorities. Those who enter it, with its ensuing deprivations, often find it very difficult to escape.

17. Social divisions cluster not just around individuals or their families but also in distinct geographical areas. This is due to reinforcing factors *between* different causes of division, and cumulative effects *within* any particular one. This factor is noted in the studies made by the Economic and Social Research Council and utilised in *Faith in the City*. They permit a 'gradient of advantage' to be constructed, and some areas or neighbourhoods score consistently at the bottom of this gradient, no matter which index of disadvantage is used. The result is a polarisation, involving a

> triple process of decision: by individuals competing for advantage in jobs, housing, schools and services; by governments offering mortgage relief (to home owners) but withholding investment from blighted districts; and by enterprises rationally investing where consumer power is greatest and growing.[1]

Only the most competitive people in such a situation can move, leaving the spent cityscape to carry a heavy concentration of the old, the sick and the lowly in skill or in spirit. It is hard to see any natural factors at work restoring balance.

18. Differences in ethnic origin create major social divisions in Britain as elsewhere. Most established societies view new members with some suspicion, and unfortunately Britain from the 1950s did not welcome West Indians, Pakistanis and Kenyan Asians and make them feel at home even though in many cases they had been actively recruited to work here. The problem was exacerbated by racial prejudice, now compounded by perceived competition for jobs, and because time cannot remove ethnic differences new generations of British-born black people suffer in a similar fashion to their forebears.

---

[1] *Faith in the City*, paras 1.43, 1.46.

Further Sources of Division

19. The presence of black people is only one source of pluralism in present-day Britain. Another aspect of that pluralism lies in the diversity of beliefs and values associated with liberal democracy. In Britain, liberal ideas began to emerge in the late eighteenth and early nineteenth centuries as a challenge to the existing powerful conservative tradition. These ideas were in turn challenged, from the late nineteenth century onwards, by different forms of democratic socialist thinking. This already complex picture became further compounded with the advent of Marxism and of the various right-wing movements which represented a reaction to Marxism.

20. Some social divisions in Britain are of long standing. They persist, even though they change somewhat in character. Such would be the divisions of class, and of wealth or poverty. What is felt to be new is the depth of the division between much of the urban area of the North and most of the South. Also people now seem to have a heightened sensitivity about all social divisions. There has also been an intensification of the generation gap through the emergence of a highly self-conscious and socially visible youth culture. There are many people now who are conscious of a sharpening of political conflict rooted in apparently incompatible political philosophies.

21. Whilst ethnic, cultural, political and economic differences are difficult enough to reconcile, perhaps the most fundamental and intractable differences are those which lie in the field of beliefs and values. These will be taken up in the next chapter.

An Extended Example – Unemployment

22. As stated earlier, unemployment is now a major source of social division. For very many of those who responded to *Goals for our Future Society* it is *the* major social problem. But though there may be widespread agreement about its seriousness, and even agreement about preferred social policies, this does not necessarily bring with it agreement about what should actually be done. In this section we take unemployment as an illustration of the difficulty of deciding such practical questions. Its purpose is to look as objectively as possible at the factors in the situation which might influence prospects for the future. But readers must not miss what is said elsewhere about unemployment being a major social evil, containing a huge potential for personal misery and social disruption unless one means or another is found for reducing or alleviating it.

23. To lose work is in some measure to feel discarded by society. If all around have lost their work too, all, as a group, feel that they have been dispensed with by the nation. The factors which have made life so difficult for young people who have never had a job impinge also upon those who possess a skill which in middle life becomes obsolete, so that they fear never to work again. Similarly affected are those who are unskilled and who lose their job in a region of high unemployment. The experience of personal futility and meaninglessness, of being where the action isn't, corrodes deeply into self-respect and personality. Many of the unemployed feel that the costs, in low standards of living and lack of personal satisfaction, of the failure of British society as a whole to solve economic problems, are being concentrated upon them; and no human system of values can acquiesce in this on so large a scale. However, a lot more must be said and especially about whether the current general magnitude of unemployment must be accepted as a permanent mark of the British social scene, and as such adjusted to by making long-term structural and economic arrangements.

24. By international standards, the United Kingdom's proportion of working-age people who are 'economically active' (in a paid job or wanting one) is extremely high – almost top of the major league; we are therefore in effect setting ourselves a stiff employment target. We rank high also, but not so markedly, in the proportion of the population which actually has a paid job. Our relatively high unemployment rate reflects the difference in our standing as between the two proportions.

25. A combination of two main factors – demographic rise in working-age population, and the attraction of more people (chiefly women) into the workforce – has increased the total workforce by over a million in the past decade. The importance of the second factor in the 1990s cannot be predicted for sure, but the first factor will tail off by about 1990. To that extent, the 'running-fast-to-stand-still' problem that has weighed on us in the last two or three years (so that substantial net growth in jobs, many, however, part-time, has accompanied a continuing slight rise in unemployment) should be eased.

26. 'Unemployment' is an imprecise concept amid the wide diversity of real-life situations. There is no single precisely-measurable definition neatly corresponding to what ordinary people probably think they mean by it. But late in 1986 the unemployment rate as officially defined was around eleven to twelve per cent. Meanwhile the real incomes of the majority had on average continued to rise steadily right through the recession and the unemployment surge.

27. The total figures mask a wide variety of continuing shifts in composition – for example employed/self-employed, manufacturing/ service, manual/non-manual, male/female, full-time/part-time, regional, and (among the unemployed) long-term/short-term. These changes in the workforce are aggravated by the sharp decline in some of our former major industries.

28. To gain perspective, it is worth casting the mind back a century or so. Suppose it had been forecast then that, partly for technological reasons

(a) agricultural employment (though not the agricultural industry and its output – a distinction perhaps worth remembering today in the context of manufacturing) was going to collapse;

(b) domestic-service employment was going to collapse;

(c) the horse-drawn transport industry was going to collapse.

Many of us might well have inferred that Britain faced major and permanent catastrophe in employment; whereas employment, both absolute and as a proportion of population, actually rose during the period of these changes. So the inference would have been quite wrong. Why? For a combination of overlapping reasons; for example;

(i) it would have underrated the capacity of the new technologies, as their applications progressively spread far beyond what could have been specifically foreseen, to generate extra jobs both directly and indirectly;

(ii) it would have underrated the effect of the world-wide expansion of markets, as more and more countries developed more and more fully, with higher investment and greater wealth;

(iii) it would have underrated the adaptive power of the economy generally, and of individuals (for example, people would probably have been very sceptical of the proposition that virtually everyone can quite easily be trained to drive a motor car acceptably);

(iv) it would have underrated the scope that existed for shifting, through real advances in productivity, the balance between work and leisure, towards shorter working hours/week/year/life.

29. Within the constraints imposed by our environment the scope of human aspirations can appear limitless. As more basic needs like minimum food and shelter are fulfilled, attention turns to second-order and third-order preferences, *ad infinitum*. People's desires for those goods and services which human effort can provide sometimes tend, unless specifically prevented, to expand to occupy available capacity to

meet them. No-one today argues that current employment levels cope with everything that it would be useful or desirable to do.

30. One can see various specific reasons for fearing that employment-restoring adaptation may be less easy for Britain now than in the past. For example, we no longer have the protected Imperial market; the industrial competition from other countries is now far stiffer; there are some severe regional differences in our employment pattern. We also have now a much denser institutional pattern – many more laws and institutions (trade unions, professional associations, environmental groups and the like). Some of these, for all their merits in other respects, can affect the speed and scope of our economic adjustment, at a time moreover when the mounting pace of world change requires from us more flexibility, not less. But there are points on the other side of the comparison too (like vastly improved educational and transport infrastructure, and the huge expansion of world trade); and in any event it is not clear why we should simply accept any of the difficulties as inherently constituting an insuperable obstacle to repeating past success in adaptation. In short, past experience suggests that even though we may have to undertake demanding efforts, there is no plausible basic reason why we should now resign ourselves to a deterministic pessimism about future employment, whether based on beliefs about the effects of technology, overseas competition or otherwise. It points, if anything, the other way.

31. Look also at other countries. The USA, Japan and Sweden, to take three conspicuous 'free-world' examples, have kept unemployment far lower than we have. We cannot reasonably convert ourselves into carbon copies of any of these; but the encouraging point is that they are not carbon copies of one another. There is no one socio-economic model which we must achieve, or else fail – we do not have to become Japanese; becoming flexible and efficiently-productive Britons should suffice, especially given our exceptional record for inventiveness. It is surely a counsel of despair to regard this as somehow a contradiction in terms.

32. The world of work is in continuous change, not just making sporadic jumps from one plateau to another. Adjustment is quite inescapable; the question is whether it is made well or badly. Over three million unemployed people is one form of adjustment, but it is for many reasons a bad one. There is almost certainly no simple recipe for a better one. The shortcomings which cumulatively and progressively have led us to this one are diverse, and the components of improving upon it are

sure to be equally diverse. It follows almost inescapably that we need a mix of improvements which, taken individually, or over a short time, may seem marginal or inadequate to the total scale of the problem. Most big secular socio-economic changes have been achieved by processes which, in discrete snapshot form, would have seemed too weak; the key has been substantially sustained movement in a substantially consistent main direction.

33. A mix of factors to move us gradually in the direction of a better form of adjustment might for instance include: more relevant education, better preparation for working life (going with later entry to the main work-force), more flexible patterns of work and working life, lower unit labour-costs, less short-term investment policies, changed management attitudes about training and about keeping close to the work-force, greater participation by employees, more self-employment, better help and more constructive incentive to the unemployed, and more stimulus to job-multiplying enterprise.

34. There are limited signs of success in several such directions, though difficult judgments about resource priorities remain – for all major partners in the economy. Sustaining the pace and direction of change to remove the causes of poor adjustment needs to be balanced against the short-term relief of urgent hardship among its victims.

35. The disappearance from the economy of many of the old-fashioned unskilled manual jobs creates a particular set of problems. At one period these amounted maybe to a half of all jobs. But the change need not be cause for despair. It should be entirely possible to continue and indeed accelerate the raising of skill levels among the population generally. Even for the substantial minority for whom this may remain difficult there can still remain work available. There are many forms of service in society crying out to be provided and which could use their obvious human qualities.

36. Though the direction of various particular trends, like falling manufacturing employment and rising skill demands, can be clearly enough seen, long term prediction is weak in the employment field overall (as in most others). Very few people in 1975 would have achieved a good forecast, even in the broadest terms, of unemployment in 1985; and we should beware of supposing that we can now do much better for 1995 and beyond. The difficulty is not mainly that we lack skill in reading the stars: the truth is that in large measure the answer is

not there to be read, for it depends upon what we in Britain as a society and as a wealth-creating economy choose to do. Acting on particular assumptions about outcomes risks slanting the outcome itself; one of the surest ways of translating into fact the possibility of unemployment at over three million in the long term would be to assume that it is certain to happen. Another would be to assume that it is certain not to. We need to recognise the possibility realistically, so that we are not paralysed into astonished unreadiness if it happens – but also, and more importantly, so that we can work to maximise the likelihood of avoiding it.

37. It is most dispiriting to read the predictions of the kind of futurologist who assumes that what is to come is determined and forecastable, usually by simply projecting forward from present trends. Hope is excluded from such a prediction, and will to change is sapped. If 'whatever will be, will be' there is no point even in regretting it. On such arguments, of course, the present is merely the 'natural' result of the past, and the world and the whole human venture within it takes on the character of the outworking of some simple but gigantic machine. Such may be the perspective of some world views. But the moral of rejecting such a determinism, in the context of the present economic and employment situation, is this: that if the future is open, and therefore uncertain, the only way to plan for it must be *flexibly*. That calls for both personal courage, and for encouragement from others around. It also calls for structural and institutional arrangements such that the burden of social change is not borne simply by a small number of vulnerable individuals. Otherwise, people will be defensive, and necessary change will not come.

Loss of Vision – the Danger

38. This discussion of unemployment has, it is hoped, illustrated the danger to which lack of vision may lead. The assumption that only one thing can be done, or that nothing at all can be done, is both dispiriting to any morally sensitive society as a whole, and oppressive to those groups in society which, by the accidents of birth or history, find themselves at an initial disadvantage. Parts of British society are undoubtedly depressed and unable to see a way out. Others are highly prosperous and expanding, especially where new 'high' technologies are taking root. Even in some of the most economically depressed areas new visions about more supportive forms of society and of social co-operation have grown.

39. The Grubb Institute in its response to the *Goals* document referred generally to a 'turning away from the language of vision and dream, except at the level of the individual and his or her own personal aspirations'. The Institute went on to relate this to a lack of leadership, a 'reluctance or inability of people to acknowledge or work with their *representativeness*: the extent to which in what they experience, feel and do they are representing anyone or anything other than themselves'. While this may be true for some, for others passivity is a response they have not freely chosen, but which is forced upon them by events over which they have little control. They experience this as a painful deprivation. As a result, to many people the ideas of 'our nation' or 'our society' make little sense these days other than as vague abstractions. These are no longer living ideas referring to a reality which, even though it is invisible, has sharp mental boundaries within which all the residents have a clear feeling of belonging together. Many people seem to have little live sense of being embedded within the society or nation whose formal citizenship they possess, nor of themselves being in any sense representative of it, with responsibility for its current state or its future prospects. Leaders in society, at many levels, thus find themselves unable to mobilise the real resourcefulness of the people who work with or for them.

40. In the psychology of individuals such feelings of aimlessness, actual deprivation and impoverishment can be crippling: the person ceases to act (thus denying one of the most human of characteristics) or begins to act irrationally, that is, in ways that may be emotionally satisfying in the short term but that do not address the real problems which return with ever greater force. Britain must 'come to itself', address itself and describe itself unemotionally and rationally. To do that it needs to honour all its parts and to celebrate such activities as it seems to do rather well. Societies cannot 'snap out' of some destructive or inhibiting frame of mind, any more than individuals can, unless large numbers of people can find something to take pride in and value, as a proof or first-fruits of possible other success yet undreamed. The plight of such sectors of society as are unable to do this must be taken as a burden onto the consciences of all.

41. It remains a fact that some people are more productive than the rest, while others can make very little material contribution to the well-being of the whole. In the case of the young, the sick and the old this is obvious enough, but, apart from them, one might reasonably expect that useful talent will be distributed in varying degrees across the population. There is a responsibility accordingly upon the holders of

power to use it to make wealth not simply for themselves. Otherwise those who are weaker will become dependent in the worst possible sense. The powerful need to use a proportion of their ability to create capital of a kind in which the others can share without incurring blame or guilt.

The Churches and Social Divison

42. It would be foolish to deny that churches have made their own contributions to social division. The Church of England could not and should not dissociate itself from such a condemnation. Churches must be regarded, and must accept themselves, as being *within* the situation and *not external* to it. There is a legitimate dogmatic assertion which all churches make, that they are parts of something nobler, greater, eternal and of God, but the contrary truth should not be lost sight of, that they have their 'treasures in earthen vessels' and that as long as history endures they will never totally fulfil the role that they claim. Christians both proclaim something unique about their hopes (and some degree of present realisation of those hopes) and live as members of societies as they find them. They share a common world with everyone else.

43. The churches themselves are thus both potential major sources for easing of the problems arising from pluralism and also hampered in performing that function by being in addition part of the problem. For instance, in Britain the emergence of political liberty was the fruit of ecclesiastical animosity. Political toleration came about in large part as a result of the fact that minority churches struggled, in the end successfully, for freedom of worship, freedom of speech and freedom of association. Tolerant pluralism was born out of this success. But the churches are now having to pay the penalty of that success. The divisions and rivalries between them have played a part in the weakening of the hold of Christian beliefs on the British people. Moreover, the Church of England in particular is less well-placed and well-equipped than it might otherwise have been to play the roles traditionally assigned to it – namely, to act as a unifying force and symbol of national unity and as a source of values.

44. One correspondent suggests that the churches are part of the problem in a further sense. Social and economic divisions commonly run not *within* congregations so much as *between* one congregation and the next. Each denomination also has to some degree its own tradition of comment upon society. More broadly, much of the style with which the churches address themselves to social issues is determined by the

ambience of the surrounding culture and by what they consider 'possible' or 'sayable' within that ambience. He concludes that 'the class nature of our own churches and church bodies – of all denominations – should be analysed'. The 'Mission Audit' being carried out in many Church of England parishes, in the wake of the *Faith in the City* report, lends itself to being used to make such an analysis.[1] Only if some such activity takes place can the churches play any creative part in attempting to bridge the divisions in society, or be clear that 'the theological priority is to overcome the feelings of powerlessness and to assist the poor to take responsibility for their own lives'. A study like the present one can only speak out of the experience of the church from which it comes. As far as the Church of England is concerned, the picture here painted is accurate enough, though many exceptions could be quoted.

45. In a rather different sense, the authors of the Grubb Institute submission saw the churches as part of the problem. They argued that 'part of our present situation is due to the failure of the Church to enable those whom it represents and to whom it ministers to sustain . . . a Christian vision of the aims of society and interpret it in the context of the challenges of secular life'. They saw the widespread attitude of what they term 'resourceless dependence' as feeding on 'the loss of "worthy vision" – something to fight for that is able to arouse commitment, release energy, encourage risk, justify sacrifice' and, despite their strictures on the Church, they looked to religion as 'the institution and activity of society which historically has represented and generated vision'.

46. A more jaundiced reading of history will attribute to the church, especially the Church of England, a share of responsibility for the perverse nationalism and jingoism of which the English at their worst have been guilty. If the Church is part of the problem it has little to contribute to the rest of society unless it can offer an example by the way in which it deals with that problem itself. The final chapter of this study takes this observation a little further.

---

[1] *Faith in the City: An Audit for the Local Church* (London, General Synod Board for Mission and Unity, n.d.).

CHAPTER TWO

A Basis for Values

47. It is all very well . . . to make allowance for variegated moralities, to refuse to judge other people; but still when we hear about someone tormenting a child, betraying a friend, driving recklessly, or spreading malicious rumours, we are coming across something which we are bound to say bluntly is wrong. . . . Extenuating circumstances may indeed extenuate, but they do not make conduct of these kinds a matter of choice.[1]

48. This study is concerned to establish an ethical base, a moral approach, upon which many people can take their stand. Such a value-system will underlie and underpin more elaborate and detailed moral judgements and ethical programmes. It begins from an explicitly Christian base, but others may find their way to similar conclusions, whatever their own personal starting-point and routes. Lady Oppenheimer argues that there *is* a basic morality about which *most* people agree but on the surface there appears to be a high degree of moral pluralism.

49. When questions of ethics are raised, it is common to find that people disagree about them. But there is more than one possible reason for disagreement. People may share a common frame of moral reference, but differ in their understanding of how it applies to a particular case under discussion. Or they may have quite different understandings of what moral discourse and judgement is. A common frame of moral reference permits reasoned moral discussion to take place, even though it frequently happens that agreement is not reached owing either to different perceptions of facts, or to different weights being assigned to different values within the one system of values. But where there is *no* shared moral framework, then all that is left is a 'dialogue of the deaf'. Disagreements can then be settled only by force. Basil Mitchell invents a hypothetical *Times* correspondence series to illustrate both kinds of situation.[2] He takes as his example a claim that moral standards have declined. Some writers will dispute the facts, or the basis of their compilation. If the facts are agreed, people may still

---

[1] H. Oppenheimer *The Hope of Happiness – A Sketch for a Christian Humanism* (London, SCM Press, 1983) p. 49.
[2] B. Mitchell *Morality, Secular and Religious – The Dilemma of the Traditional Conscience* (London, Oxford University Press, 1986) p. 2f.

differ as to whether or not they constitute a decline. Past restraint may have been occasioned more by fear than by morality, for example. Even if it be agreed that morals have declined some may still argue that that is a price worth paying for a greater degree of freedom. Individual morality may be subservient to a corrupt system, and be deemed relatively unimportant in comparison. And so on. But it may also be argued that morals are completely subjective, or socially conditioned, and that to speak of their decline makes literally no sense. Finally, writes Mitchell, some may say that science has not yet discovered the appropriate morality for our time, and so it is premature to make judgements about decline.

50. Mitchell's example is fictional but it carries some ring of truth. There is some evidence of such a breakdown in the shared moral framework. However, Dorothy Emmet concludes her *The Moral Roots of Democracy* by writing about the British bureaucratic tradition as she has been able to observe it. She believes that a lot of its customs and traditions are easily defended on moral grounds, and she believes that there is a much greater shared sense of morality at large in our society than Mitchell's example would suggest.[1] She finds the British system of social administration imbued with a sense of the respect which ought to be given to interests which have a broad base and can be expressed with conviction, a sense of the importance of fairness and of the indefensibility of unfairness, and a sense of the need to inform the whole bureaucratic process with some generosity of spirit. As she describes it, public life in Britain is *not* a 'dialogue of the deaf': it *does* incorporate shared moral values and a shared frame of moral reference.

51. The European Value Systems Study Group (see paragraph 4ff) seems to have shown that people in the United Kingdom hold moral views which are quite close to those expressed in the last seven of the Ten Commandments – honouring parents, avoiding murder, adultery, theft, falsehood, envy and lust – even though they are less agreed on the more purely 'religious' Commandments to honour only one God, to refrain from taking God's name in vain and to keep the Sabbath.[1] This might suggest that British society is living on a deposit of religious values which are slowly but surely being exhausted. It could equally be claimed that it provides evidence of a level of *human* morality – a

---

[1] D. Emmet *The Moral Roots of Social Democracy* (London, The Tawney Society, 1985).

[1] Abrams et al. *Values.*

morality widely accepted across groups with divergent religious beliefs or with none – which has been articulated for centuries, for which various philosophical explanations have been provided, and below which most people most of the time would not be disposed to sink, and which is regarded as more or less self-evident. Normal social life, particularly at the person-to-person level, suggests that there is a good deal of truth in this view, but a moral consensus needs clearer articulation and a stronger ground on which to stand. The Christian tradition teaches such a stronger ground which those who are not Christians will not completely share. However, the content of different traditions may coincide to a remarkable degree, even though the source of the obligation felt and the commitment given may differ.

52. The common ground is extensive, as the EVSSG study suggests. Notions of fairness and justice and concern for the other person are at its heart. It goes on to affirm that every person counts, either because people are made in God's image according to Christian belief, or because in humanist terms they are all rational creatures, or because 'nature' has made them basically alike. It asserts the basic reliability of established social customs and calls for rationality, consistency and fairness in administrative and other social structures. It needs some infusion with the warmth of unselfish goodwill. But at the heart of this attitude is an assertion of the central value of persons. An illustration is the growing world-wide acknowledgement of fundamental human rights even though there is a good deal of disagreement as to how they are to be given effect. It should be remembered though, that this growth is neither inevitable nor automatic. Insights gained in one generation can fail to become appropriated to the same degree by the next. In many parts of the world their possession is still precarious.

53. From this point of view, the Ten Commandments can be seen as an early attempt to inculcate, under divine sanction, the protection and promotion of certain values which are fundamental to the fulfilment of individuals living in community: religion, relaxation, care for the elderly, respect for innocent life, for marriage, freedom, reputation, possessions. They are not arbitrary divine impositions, but rather the way that a particular culture has understood divine concern for the human creatures, the people, whom God is in process of forming. Since the Renaissance there have been various attempts to delineate what would count as, or contribute to, human flourishing and similar lists of basic values have been suggested. They may be regarded as so many attempts at a kind of 'identikit' of common humanity, making sense of morality in terms of what seems fitting for human fulfilment. Lady

Oppenheimer, whose study in this field has already been quoted, believes that to build a more substantive personalism upon such a foundation, is a 'delicate', though promising, exercise. This 'substantive personalism' – a valuation of persons which involves much more than simply accepting people as they are – is easier to affirm than to prove. It can best be established, she believes, by 'making affirmations cautiously, building up a structure, in the hope that it will so to speak prove itself when the edifice actually stands up, not like a card house but like a building to be lived in'. Happily, people often *do* make more than the most simple affirmations about each other, and these do very often 'stand up'.

54. Theologians in many of the churches support this view. For instance the 'dignity of the human person' is the concept which lies behind the Humanum Studies of the World Council of Churches and much of the Second Vatican Council's positive teaching on ecumenism, religious freedom and conscience and life in society. It is not a static concept, however. Moral codes, or human identikits, have a dynamic element to them, as history uncovers or recovers apparently fresh aspects of what it is, desirably, to be human. One might illustrate this from many instances of resistances to political oppression such as the whole civil rights movement.

55. How far people realise their individual potential as persons depends partly upon their moral sensitivity and understanding. Christians have their own view about this, based on their particular religious self-understanding and on their observations of people around them, but it is difficult to give any content to the sense of person without taking into account the presence of other persons with whom one is in relationship. *Interrelatedness* seems to be integral to the development of the promise contained in the concept of personhood. For the development of personhood however this very interrelatedness requires a further condition, that of *freedom*. It is possible to be related to other persons in ways that inhibit freedom, one's own or theirs. To that degree, personhood is stunted. Personhood, for its flourishing, seems to require other persons in a relationship which is typified by freedom and is expressed in mutuality, in equality of respect, and in solidarity.

56. Morality, thus understood, is essentially a matter of respect for persons and the necessary conditions for their flourishing. The implications of this in practice leave plenty of scope for disagreement, and it is not hard to see how moral confusions arise in a time when there have been many changes in the understanding of human life and its

physical and social environment. The claims of moral relativism and subjectivism derive their plausibility from this confusion. The fact that people of goodwill may differ deeply from one another about what is right or wrong, so runs the argument, is proof that in the end moral choices are no more than expressions of opinion, or at best are totally conditioned by social circumstances. This is not the place to attempt a full-scale refutation of this argument for moral relativism, except by pointing out that it proves too much. To have no criteria for judging one culture better than another, to acquiesce, say, in torture in a society where it is socially accepted, is in the end to lose one of the most distinctive characteristics of morality, namely its ability to challenge the accepted order of things in the name of some higher obligation. If, on the other hand, persons are the focus of value, then despite disagreements which may occur in actual moral judgements, there remains a reference point, an ultimate criterion, which transcends all particular fashions, circumstances and social assumptions.

57. For Christians this claim about the central value of persons springs directly from the content of Christian faith. The relationship in which each person stands with regard to God is the most personal relationship of all. Human beings 'made in the image of God' are inherently valuable by virtue of God's love for them, which has brought them into being. The theme of 'persons in relationship' has in modern times often been seen as having a direct analogue, indeed from the perspective of faith its ultimate source, in the mutuality of persons in the Godhead as expressed in the doctrine of the Trinity. The love of God for each individual is declared on the Cross of Christ, 'who loved me, and gave himself up for me' (Gal. 2.20). And the potential inherent in each individual, the constant possibility of bringing new life out of death, is seen as a direct fruit of the Resurrection. The unity of all human beings in God, and our dependence on one another in a fellowship of love, are declared and signified in the existence of the church. These great theological realities may be very imperfectly expressed and apprehended, and the persons whose value is perceived in terms of them always in fact fall far short of what these realities convey. But the very short-comings, when acknowledged as such, can be a hopeful sign that the value of human beings is not to be judged primarily in terms of their performance. In Christian language, forgiven sinners know themselves and each other to be even more securely held in the love of God.

58. Christian understanding can also illuminate the nature of freedom. There is no true freedom merely in individual self-assertion.

The freedom which springs from, and in turn makes possible, new depths of personal interrelatedness implies a release from self-centredness which lies at the heart of the Christian experience of salvation. Freedom 'from' has to be matched by freedom 'for', and here again a sense of religious perspectives and an awareness of religious tasks, 'the will of God', can expand and intensify concern for others. To say this is no way to claim that such freedom, as expressed most fully in personal giving and receiving, is exclusive to Christians. The Christian faith does, however, provide a mode of access to it and a means of interpreting it, which link it directly with theological insights into the value of persons and, as will become apparent shortly, with a particular understanding of interrelatedness.

59. There is, however, one particular difficulty about this linking of morality essentially to persons. An ethic expressed in terms of persons and personhood does not seem to give value to the natural order in its own right. It is not the purpose of this study to go over the ground recently traversed by the Board for Social Responsibility in *Our Responsibility for the Living Environment* (1986), but it is not hard to see that a 'person' ethic must extend to embrace the whole set of relationships in which human beings stand, including their relationships with their environment, and must respect the rest of God's creatures and creation.

60. This chapter is concerned with the need for moral values, and shared ones, as the stabilising principle for a society, from which deviations can be detected, and judgements made about degrees of tolerance. The notion has been put forward of an 'identikit' approach to the mystery of human nature. Recognition of interrelatedness, freedom and equality before God have been suggested as essential features of personhood. In this cluster of values surrounding persons-in-relationship lies a firm base from which further discussion can be advanced. It is now possible to find confirmation and illumination in a particular conception which Christians have of humanity and society.[1]

---

[1] Parallel to but independent of this present study the Board has published *Not Just For the Poor*: Christian Perspectives on the Welfare State (London, CHP, 1986). It too argues, in a frame and in a language that differs from that used here, that the Christian tradition impels us to be involved with others on an individual and a corporate level. These two studies, separate in membership and different in intention, thus converge in their argument before going on to explore each its own particular conclusions. Readers interested in detailed argument about the welfare state might like to follow it up in *Not Just For the Poor*.

Koinonia

61. The search for basic values has led in the direction of *persons*, understood as interrelated, yet free. A simple word to describe this kind of relationship between persons as we understand them would be useful. It would define for us the direction in which social, economic and political policies ought to drive, in order that human potential might stand the best possible chance of being realised. 'Community' is asked to bear too many meanings already, various and contradictory. 'Communion' might do if it could be rescued from its usual meaning of a particular church service. It is because these shifts in meaning are difficult for many people that for the moment the unfamiliar word *koinonia* is adopted. It is a term very much in favour at the moment in ecumenical discussion as a concept to bridge the long-standing differences between major branches of the churches – Anglican, Roman Catholic and Reformed.

62. This Greek word was used in early Christian writings to signify a relation between persons resulting from their participation in one and the same reality. It is an immensely rich New Testament theme, basically expressing the idea of having something in common, from material possessions at one end of the theological spectrum, to a sharing in the body of Christ and in his Spirit, to participation in the very being of God. The old Latin translation of *koinonia* was *communio*, which shares a root with our words community, communication, commune, common, communism. All these cognate words suggest dimensions of meaning for freedom-in-relationship as it might take shape in normal secular society.

63. *Koinonia* seeks to hold together the two basic values of freedom and capacity for relationship in a dynamic tension of individuals-in-community which does justice to both. It would seem to offer the challenge and the possibility of individuals existing for, and finding their personal fulfilment in relationship with, one another.

64. Interrelatedness can act as a corrective to the sometimes debased common ideas of freedom as self-centred do-as-you-please. It redefines it helpfully by recalling us to that other great truth about personality, that we do not exist other than in relationship with other persons. The classical notion of *koinonia* preserves both the freedom and the interrelationship. The greatest freedom lies in our relations with others (and not in some Crusoe-like solitude) and the best relationships are between those who know that they are free and equal.

65. The concept of *koinonia* and the range of reflections prompted by

it challenge all social agencies – cultural, political and economic – to balance many values together. The weight has to be shifted from time to time between the individual and the community, but never permanently, and always having to answer to the promptings of the larger vision of a society in which all values are held in a just harmony. Without such a vision any society, and its people, will perish. Churches have a duty to society, not just to themselves, to work at this vision and communicate it in word and in deed, and to witness to the common source of all these values in God.

66. But if the sense of *community* is rescued by a proper understanding of what *koinonia* has meant, true interdependence becomes threatened as the scale of society becomes wider. Society is not enriched by the absorption of persons into the mass. It is interesting to watch the two great collective powers, China and the USSR, successively entrenching collectivism, but then searching for ways within the governing philosophy of releasing more of people's energies in the interest of an overall gain both for the society and everyone in it. But our western societies are not immune from the same problems. The complicated checks and balances of the United States' federal constitution shows an imaginative consciousness of this problem, with its extraordinary number of levels of government from the township through the county to the State and the nation. The debate on devolution in Britain in the 1970s was in part an example of conflict between desires for local decision-making and the maintenance of coherence by control from the centre. Note also the tensions between central control and local government in more recent years.

67. This issue is a familiar one for the Roman Catholic Church, which uses the term *subsidiarity* for the notion that in the interest both of individual dignity and of the greatest chance for a sensible outcome decisions should be taken at the lowest level reasonably possible, or at the level nearest to the main point of practical effect. This is because, properly understood, the tenure of power lower down represents not a favour granted by its 'so-called' natural exerciser to another, but rather a retention of it by its natural first-instance holder. Subsidiarity means respecting in any situation those who inhabit it, their perceptions and their skills and subjecting them to higher authority only when absolutely necessary.

68. It would be most valuable to get this concept of *koinonia* into common secular parlance, because words define concepts, and if new concepts are called for, old words with old definitions will not do. Neither 'community' nor 'communion' seems to do what is needed.

CHAPTER THREE

Persons in Community

69. A new touchstone is thus suggested for the value on which British society now and in the future ought to be based – *koinonia*, or persons-in-interrelationship (community, communion). Earlier a brief characterisation was attempted of Britain in a process of change. In this chapter some of the implications of *koinonia* will be explored, particularly with a view to finding out whether some things and some features in society which ought to be held together have been broken apart, whether polarisations have been allowed to develop between views or positions which need to be held in better balance. There is however another way in which apparently contradictory values can be held together. This is commonly expressed in the idea of *polarity*.[1]

70. Polarities, however, are quite different from polarisations. *Polarisations* set up opposition between principles, simplify them down to two, and then demand choice in favour of the one and the abandonment of the other. What is left out does not thereby disappear: it remains to grumble and maybe fester. *Polarities*, in comparison, also set up two or more principles, but then insist that none is discarded, each continuing to be allowed to influence policy-making and strategy. Put crudely, polarisation is where 'if A, then not B'. Polarity is where 'if A, then necessarily B also'. Polarities enable one to explore possible middle ground. Polarisations prevent this. Polarities permit the notion of complementarity. Polarisations do not. Polarisation occurs when one pole of a polarity is let go. The result is neater and clearer but it accommodates less of the truth. The choices open to people are more often to combine and blend values than to suppress them. Reality tends to resist premature simplification. Peace and social justice usually call for the incorporation of as many persons and views as possible.

71. Some of the more important polarities which seem to characterise our society are now discussed.

---

[1] See especially J. P. Wogaman *A Christian Method of Moral Judgement* (London, SCM Press, 1976).

The Individual and Society

72. Two concepts frequently polarised are those of the individual and society. This polarisation may take the form of emphasising the responsibility and the duties of the individual actor as the only one who knows what his or her interests really are. Such responsibilities and duties seem to be threatened by those who exercise power in social or political administration where it is difficult to get beyond generality, and there is a tendency to iron out individual circumstances towards some notional average. People need freedom and self-determination in order to flourish and to act responsibly. If the state takes from people the power of choice and the responsibility for the things that most closely concern them – the education of their children, the provision of health care for themselves and their family, and provision for the future, taking over the money to pay for these and other things – they may come to resent both the apparent inefficiency of the large-scale bureaucracies and the loss of individual freedom involved. They may devote their energies to 'beating the system' in various ways, or they may grow morally slack, take less care over their circumstances than they could, and involve themselves less in charitable and other social activities.

73. The contrary emphasis on social organisation for the common good reflects the importance of the social structures within which human life begins and comes to fulfilment and in which attitudes are formed. It consequently seeks to put up warnings against the familiar temptations of self-interest. If the well-being of others is not given sufficient prominence, division is increased and those people who begin with disadvantages either of genetic endowment or of social or educational stimulation and resource may fall further and further behind the rest. Individual and family skill and judgement are effective within limits, but chance still plays a large part in determining people's fortunes. This view asserts that society should make it a priority to compensate people who have had a bad start in life or who have suffered ill-fortune along the way.

74. To think of people first as persons, rather than as either individuals or performers of particular social functions (voters, workers and so on) ought to help to maintain the necessary tension between the individual and his or her society. The very idea of person necessarily involves recognising both individual uniqueness which other persons need to respect, and also the rich set of relationships which gives meaning to the individual and makes us what we are.

75. Family life frequently illustrates how the individual and the society have to live in harmony, or else each suffers, and how dependent all the individuals are upon each other and upon the models, traditions, laws and economic success of the wider society. Children are obviously dependent, for their happiness and emotional, physical and intellectual development, on the love of their parents, but parents too become very threatened if their children are unhappy or withdrawn.

76. The polarity of the one and the many must be maintained. Human beings are neither isolated individuals nor mere units in a society.

> The destruction of our individuality undermines genuine human society; the undermining of our social nature for the sake of individualism destroys not only society but our individuality as well. A really human society is made up of creative individuals. A real individual is a person fulfilling his or her personhood in community.[1]

The later discussion about majorities and minorites takes up other aspects of this individual/society polarity.

What Kinds of Interrelationships?

77. It is easy to imagine what *koinonia* – community, communion and interrelatedness – might mean in face-to-face relationships. The question is more difficult when the relationships are more distant and tenuous, though no less real. At one level, relationships may be purely about getting something particular done – programmatic, political, goal-oriented.

78. Christians assert a fundamental truth about interrelationship, that we are all bound together not by choice nor by accidents of proximity but rather as part of our being within God's creation. Interrelationship is eternal and universal, stretching back and forward in time, and right round the globe.

79. Such wider relationships are sometimes spoken of in terms of service (one to another) or of solidarity (one with another), and both these terms are hallowed by long secular and religious usage. *Service* is one form of unselfish goodwill, referred to earlier. For Christians it is a familiar New Testament term, focused in the servanthood of Jesus who 'came not to be served but to serve and to give his life as a ransom

---

[1] Wogaman, *Method*, p. 138.

for many'. But it is also common outside Christian circles. Large numbers of people are massively motivated to self-giving of all kinds. However, the idea of service has been criticised as tending to attract to itself notions of superiority and of inequality in resource. 'Service' can produce feelings of self-righteousness in the server, shame in the person served and an odour of paternalism or condescension. Churches as well as all other forms of human association need to be on their guard against manifestations of this warped and debased form of service.

80. *Solidarity* is understood by Christians as a community of being, a shared humanity which is eternal, so that Christians can speak of being 'in Christ' and of being 'members one of another' such that each can recognise in each other a shared fate and a shared destiny. It would be difficult to find a stronger description of solidarity than that which St. Paul described Christ as showing when he wrote, 'him who knew no sin God made to be sin on our behalf; that we might become the righteousness of God in him' (2 Cor. 5.21). In ordinary secular parlance solidarity describes the inspiration which many feel for siding with other fellow human beings in pain or difficulty – perhaps even thousands of miles away. Often, however, there is an exclusive edge to the word, so that 'solidarity' describes relationships within an in-group, against outsiders.

81. 'Solidarity' may thus promote an excessive sense of 'my group right or wrong', while 'service' may encourage an excessive feeling of individualism. The problems can be illustrated from the way that much social and political action is necessarily promoted through 'party solidarity'. Everyday private morality urges one to walk alone with one's truth, while policy-making within a group seems to entail 'following the party line' even in deeply moral issues.

82. All slogans may be misunderstood or misused. For instance even the notion of 'bias to the poor' may accentuate feelings of condescension. A sense of solidarity allied to that of service might prompt those who are not poor to try to perceive the world and life within it in the way that those who are poor have perforce to perceive it.

83. If community and communion is accepted as the basic value for society, then interdependence expressed both in mutual service and in solidarity becomes the kind of relationship between persons to which all should aspire. Some would feel that the longer time goes on and the more the globe shrinks the more obvious it is that such an attitude has to be at the base of all human flourishing.

Roles and Responsibilities

84. Interdependence necessarily makes for complexity, which may be a reason why it is sometimes not readily accepted as one of the principal conditions for human flourishing. In practice, however, life turns on the faithful performance by everyone of particular roles in society, which are limited in scope but vital in importance. Some roles are contracted for, between one party and another; some are statutorily provided; some are discharged by voluntary bodies.

85. The distinction between contractual, statutory and voluntary activities cannot be a hard and fast one since there is much fruitful co-operation. A good example is the hospice movement, usually funded by charitable donations, but employing state-trained staff and benefiting from charity law. Not all expertise is statutory or professional. In many areas it is the voluntary sector which commands the most skills and knowledge, and performs the major role.

86. Voluntary bodies can be large-scale employers, but they also engage the activities of many who have time to give and sufficient means to forgo payment. Others have time to give because no-one wants to buy it. Either way, the fact that they do the work shows that they think that it is needed. Those who support them with charitable gifts agree with them. But why is the need otherwise unrecognised and unmet? The people who experience the need may feel that the means to meet it cannot be bought in any market: for example, relief from loneliness. Alternatively, they may see it as something which the usual embodiment of the non-contractual sector – the statutory services – have not been called upon, or have not taken the initiative, to provide: for example, the Samaritans' service. So needs exist which the forms of interrelatedness among people as organised in the markets and in the public services have left unrecognised and unmet.

87. One of the big advantages that voluntary groups enjoy is that anyone can make a contribution, and the levels of skill necessary may be varied, and broad. A major skill-need of voluntary organisations is for participation, and such bodies in fact provide a training-ground for people to learn participative and leadership and representative skills which they can take with them to other parts of their lives. The disadvantages attaching to voluntary organisations are that they can be rather hit-and-miss, only partially covering a particular need. Even good voluntary organisations may exhibit a tendency towards vested interest. People whose motivation has been strong may be unwilling to

withdraw when the task has been accomplished, or when it has been taken on by the market or by statutory agencies. In this they may not be flexible enough. On the other hand they may be more open to policy or style changes as their personnel change, or they may be subject to inefficiency due to the absence of a strict authority such as a market relationship with a client would involve, or a well-run statutory agency would incorporate. The fine motivation which inheres in voluntary organisations is their strength, but it can render them sometimes unresponsive to the changing needs of their clients. Voluntary organisations, like statutory services, need the feed-back and the self-scrutiny which makes and keeps them responsive and responsible.

88. The role and responsibility of the professional towards the 'lay' person offers another example of the interdependence which complexity brings. Who knows how long ago it was that people learned that specialisation of skill brings benefits for all? In some measure this was known long before the industrial revolution and the divisions of labour that that brought with it. The negative side of professionalisation is its effect on the non-professional, tending to devalue lay people's sense of having useful skills and expertise and encouraging them to become dependent on those possessed or claimed by the professionals. The result overall could even be a diminution in the total skills available to be applied to a problem.

89. The distinction between professional and non-professional is more accurately one between those who know more and those who know less. If the divide is too pronounced the lay person may be ignorant of what is on offer from the specialists, and the professional may find it difficult to identify those areas of the lay public in most need of the skill which he or she has. Such is the consequence of specialisation and role. The demand for professional services is probably endless, but a good deal of it can be met by the laity, if they are given sufficient instruction and back-up. Most of the health-care in society is actually done by relatives and neighbours and much education is done by parents. So effective mobilisation of the laity ought to be a primary task of the professionals. The professionals can then extend their specialisation, to their own, and the public's, greater benefit.

90. To become fixed in a role and too deeply burdened with responsibilities puts a person in danger of losing perspective. A role may be a refuge, and examples of people who have immersed themselves in particular roles and responsibilities in order to escape other problems and issues are not uncommon. There is also danger of a

certain inbreeding of assumptions within specialist roles, so much so that lay criticism or even lay help is resented or excluded. But, conversely, to have a lively sense of responsibility without the skill and opportunity of a profession or a role may leave the problem unsolved and the carer frustrated. More than most other jobs nowadays the professions retain in popular parlance the old and once much more broadly shared character of a 'calling'. If that old vocabulary can be recovered it will serve as a reminder that all work, professional or lay, in statutory, voluntary or contractual undertakings, is a response by persons to a need experienced by other persons within the same community. It is not an individual perquisite to be enjoyed at others' expense, though worthy of its hire. So regarded, all roles and responsibilities are reminders of our mutual interdependence, and are examples of *koinonia*.

The Quality of Interrelationships

91. One of the problems all organisations face, but especially large and complex ones, is that of maintaining a sense of direction, purpose and vitality. This must be particularly true of something as large as a whole society. The question of direction and route to betterment is a real one. There seem to be two main historic strategies for growth and advance, which in popular thought are opposed to each other – competition and co-operation.

92. It would be difficult to maintain that progress is possible without *both* competition *and* co-operation, though at times this does seem to be claimed. 'Compete or die' seems to deny the value of co-operation just as fervently as 'united we stand' argues in the opposite direction. To argue that there is truth and value in both points of view seems to send contradictory signals. The mental picture conjured up by competition is essentially one in which there are more losers than winners. If the truth is more complex than this, maybe the words are at fault, but until new ones are found the discussion must deal with them as they are.

93. Comparison seems to be the way by which we become self-conscious. It is by looking around us and comparing ourselves with others that we discover what we are and what we perhaps could be. In that light, competition may seem a little less potentially destructive, bringing, as it does, a heightened perception of the self alongside others. Competition is maybe an indispensable strategy for living, without being its fundamental basis. It is useful, but it must be kept within some bounds.

94. On the other hand, competition fosters efficiency and en-courages inventiveness. In a world which is for practical and immediate purposes limited these values are virtues, and if competition assists them it becomes an indispensable tool. By competing with each other and offering possible comparisons to be made, people find out what they are relatively good at, and whereabouts in society they can make their best contribution. Advanced societies depend heavily upon specialisation of roles and division of labour, and these call for careful selection of the people who will best do the various jobs. At this point, therefore, competition between rivals is the only reasonable way in which choice of job and choice of personnel can be made.

95. The bounds of competition must lie at the point where the advantages it bestows in terms of efficiency are outweighed by the damage it causes in undermining community. At that point competition has to be restrained. For example, competition may result in one winner destroying for a period all rivals and winning a monopoly position, which cannot be in the long-term general interest. Society may need, in the short term, to put limits round such success in order to promote an increase in competition long-term. The political problem is to identify the point, without causing such confusion that growth, progress and inventiveness cease.

96. Competition can destroy relationship, while talk about 'team-work' emphasises that a prime need in any organisation is co-operation. That is true not merely for activities *within* the organisation, but also for the organisation's encounters with outsiders in the wider community – financiers, suppliers, government departments, sub-contractors. In most projects the harmonious co-operation of several different parties is essential, even though there may have been heavy competition and hard bargaining before the price of such co-operation was established. In personal and sexual relations too, most societies observe and enforce clear limits to competition – it is allowed in courtship, for instance, but not after marriage. Perhaps in essence contracts are two-stage – a competitive one followed by a co-operative one – and what is true of contracts may be true of many other parts of life. Difficulty arises where it is not clear or agreed when it would be appropriate to switch. At least in the case of contracts at law this point is obvious – until an agreement is made, all terms and conditions are up for debate, but once agreement is reached strict and faithful 'co-operative' perform-ance is expected and is usually required through the legal system.

97. How then do people decide when to be competitive and when to be co-operative? This lesson must be among the many learned (or not learned) in childhood. In education throughout this century there has been a move away from using competitiveness as a main tool in formal teaching. Montessori and Froebel both stressed the children's innate desire to learn and to acquire skills and knowledge and said that the educator's task was to assist the 'natural' unfolding of each child's unique programme. These concepts have increasingly qualified an earlier belief that children were resistant to learning and needed the stimulus of rewards, punishment and competition within the peer-group in order to acquire it. Moreover there has been a growing awareness that it is easier for some children than for others to acquire certain skills: learning is not simply a matter of 'hard work' or 'virtue', nor even of innate IQ level. Social factors – such as parental income, breadth of sensory experience acquired in early infancy, degree of affection towards the teacher, personal self-esteem – all affect perform-ance to the extent that scholastic competition on its own can be inherently 'unfair' and may, overall reduce rather than enhance performance. Belief in the value of competition in educational method has been balanced by stress on the effectiveness of collaboration.

98. Within the family too there has been a steady reduction in the value attributed to competition. Every child-care manual now stresses the importance of not comparing children in terms of development, but rather off-sets sibling rivalry, and introduces children to co-operative play with same-age children as soon as they are able to cope. 'Rewards and punishments' are increasingly frowned on, and pressure to perform 'comparatively' is discouraged by the parent. The model of family life held up as the ideal is non-competitive, with the emphasis on 'complementarity'.

99. However, while both educational and psychological theories of childhood have moved towards lowering the value of competition the wider society gives a directly opposite message about competition – and that wider society, through many cultural forms, but perhaps par-ticularly television, penetrates increasingly into the nurturant nest of the child.

100. Children are not immune from this input; whether or not they understand the details, they still glean from it information about human behaviour which says that competition has a very high positive value in the grown-up world; it is both serious and glamorous; it is inevitable and – what is more – desirable.

101. Put somewhat baldly, children are simultaneously nurtured in an atmosphere as competition-free as their 'own' adults are capable of making it; they are taught and expected to channel their feelings of rivalry into mutually supportive enterprises. *And* they are taught – at a great number of levels – that competition is an indispensable instrument for creating political liberty, financial prosperity, recreational pleasure and the survival not just of the nation but of the species itself.

102. The problem for all of us is that both views are 'correct'. In differing circumstances each serves the individual and the society well. Children are thus exposed to value-systems which pull in different directions – unless we really want to say that the values and virtues of public life and private life are somehow different in kind and separable. It seems that some restoration of balance may be necessary in both spheres.

103. The labour market also illustrates the difficulty of finding the right blend of competition and co-operation. A nation like Britain, deeply involved in the world trading system, cannot opt out of economic competition. To do so would mean penury, including the surrender of the social care for elderly, ill or disadvantaged people which economic success alone pays for. In these circumstances businesses have no option but to prefer people with more skill, energy and motivation to those with less. Public authorities must respond to the needs of those who for whatever reason do not fare well in the competition. They have a matching duty, difficult but necessary, to arrange that in meeting these needs they do not undermine the motivation which, given the realities and imperfections of human nature, must be a major engine of the drive for productivity and quality on which national wealth for the benefit of all depends. We simply could not run a society in which the difference between working and not working had no effect on income, even if proposals for a basic citizen's minimum income were acceptable. But equally it would be morally intolerable (quite aside from economically wasteful and in the long run socially destructive) to have a society in which the divergence of income became extreme; or in which excessive concentration on the logic of competition – for example by unrestrained maximising of the rewards reaped by most of those in work – to the exclusion of the logic of co-operation made the number of people on the 'wrong' side of the divide larger than it need be. A balance has to be struck, and to be kept under constant and sensitive review.

104. Comparison with others, and competition in the performing of

tasks, may benefit both society overall and the individuals who make it up, but it has to be kept within the bounds of its usefulness as a tool of efficiency and not be elevated to the status of a basic value either for individuals or for their society. Economic efficiency is not the only 'good'. Without the other values of co-operativeness and interrelationship neither individual nor a society worthy of the name is conceivable. It is interrelationship which constitutes society: competition is no more than a useful and necessary tool for sustaining it.

Valuing Differences

105. The diversities within society are generally enriching – differences of sex, ethnic origin, political ideas and economic roles. What has been said about competition and co-operation, as well as about the person, presupposes that uniformity is not a satisfactory basis for a society, but the question of limits then once again arises. What degree of tolerance for divergent views and practices is desirable for a society of persons in interrelation? Are there some differences which should not be tolerated? How 'pluralist' can society be, without becoming a host to divisions which threaten it with destruction and reduce it to a set of warring camps threatening both interrelationship and personhood? What importance do differences of culture make to the cohesion of a society?

106. Multi-culturalism can mean a number of different things, as Professor John McIntyre has argued.[1] A society might, for example, contain many equal, independent and alternative cultures, existing side-by-side, with their appropriate groups, and expressing themselves in their own art, drama, literature etc. Or, second, one culture may be dominant, and the others subordinate but still independent. An example of this sort would be that of a small ethnic group, in the early years of its arrival in a new country, maintaining the ethos, the imagery, the values of the old country in an alien environment, in a somewhat ghetto-like existence, and economically somewhat dependent. A third hypothetical model might be one culture with a variety of subcultures, all relating to the main one, but taking bizarre forms. Or again, a dominant culture may be challenged by a counter-culture, or collapse spontaneously from within. John McIntyre does not believe that any model other than his second one remotely describes Britain today – a

---

[1] J. McIntyre *Multi-Culture and Multi-Faith Societies: Some Examinable Assumptions* (Oxford, Farmington Institute for Christian Studies Occasional Paper No. 3. n.d.).

dominant culture with subordinate but still independent cultures. This situation imposes quite special responsibilities upon the dominant culture and others upon the subordinate ones. These responsibilities can conveniently be brought under the single heading of tolerance.

107. A pluralist society cannot survive without tolerance. This was the lesson learned in the religious struggles of the sixteenth and seventeenth centuries, and relearned in subsequent centuries as rival political ideologies came into being. But no society can survive unlimited tolerance. At the very least limits have to be set on the intolerant. Nor can a society survive on tolerance alone as its highest value, because it is a value which contains the seeds of its own destruction. If all beliefs and opinions were given equal standing, then no belief would ultimately matter, not even the belief in freedom. Questions about tolerance, like many other questions about values, are thus questions about degree.

108. A tolerant society has to find ways of containing conflicts and making them constructive, without ignoring them, belittling them, misrepresenting them, or allowing them to escalate to the point of irreconcilable division and the breakdown of order. Too tolerant a society offers no purchase for constructive criticism and is thus likely to become deeply and lazily conservative. A society which is afraid of internal conflict may try either to avoid the issues by fudging them, or to suppress the conflict by some act of injustice. The alternatives of compromise and co-existence at least entail the admission that there can be genuine differences which ought to be respected, but fall short of the highest goal of constructive conflict, which would be the creation of some new balance in which both sides have managed to learn from one another.

109. The values which give birth to tolerance or maintain it can thus have a decisive impact on the way it works in practice. A tolerance born out of laziness, weariness with conflict and lack of conviction is not likely to withstand determined attacks on freedom and order. Nor is it likely to make constructive use of differences. But a tolerance based on positive respect for others, on belief in freedom and on a recognition of human limitations can set criteria by which to judge how far it can go. And it is likely to approach differences with enthusiasm and expectation rather than defensively. Indeed the word 'tolerance' becomes unnecessary if there is a strong sense of human dignity, an awed acknowledgement of human possibilities, and a willingness to admit lack of certainty about what finally makes for human flourishing.

110. A test case might be the claim for separate Muslim schools, funded by the State, as there are similar Jewish and Christian schools. This kind of demand is not restricted to religious groups, or to education, but the example may serve for discussion. Within present law, any group can set up any educational system it likes, provided that it meets the Department of Education and Science's standards. If it wanted however to adopt standards which do not enshrine, or are incompatible with, those legally laid down, it would not be permitted to do so. If its purpose is, or if the probable result would be, to create an enclave in society fundamentally at odds with the basic values on which the society rests, for instance by wanting to replace certain features of the law of the land (for instance on marriage) by others based on Islamic teaching, then that could scarcely be tolerated. Such might be what some Muslims want from a distinctive Islamic education, but there might be other, less threatening, motives, towards which the majority in society ought to be more tolerant – respect for food laws, customs, sensitivity about gender difference, and so on. Not everything should be tolerated but some things which some people do not at present tolerate ought to be tolerated. This lesson was learned in modifying, for Sikhs, the law on compulsory wearing of crash-helmets. What minorities may sometimes be seeking is greater tolerance within the present system rather than its overthrow.

111. The strongest basis for a humane and tolerant society lies in the concept of human dignity, freedom and the admission of ignorance. But it has its difficulties. Claims to human dignity and freedom rightly focus on individuals, but, as has already been argued, they can be misused in support of unrestricted individualism by ignoring the extent to which many freedoms can only flourish within the protection afforded by social structures. Every assertion of freedom involves a trade-off between the individual and society, and in a tolerant society the possibility of such a trade-off needs to be accepted. But a tolerant and humane society is not simply one in which individual freedom is maximised. The essential guarantee of freedom is not the absence of constraint, but the possibility of participation in the process by which constraints are agreed and institutionalised.

112. Admission of ignorance in human affairs is an essential basis for tolerance. It sets limits on what can be done by those who think they know what is good for other people. But it too has its difficulties. Too great a confession of ignorance can generate insecurity, and insecurity can provide a breeding-ground for fanaticism and new intolerance. Politicians humble and honest enough to admit the limitations of know-

ledge may be replaced by those who give a greater appearance of confidence. Church leaders who speak too much about the mystery of the Christain faith tend to be less popular than those who can make everything sound clear and seem simple. Periods of unjustified assertion, and the intolerant application of inadequately-based policies, tend to follow periods of vacillation and compromise. There is sometimes a duty to act with much firmness, even though all realise that ideally one would wait for much greater information and analysis. Under this pressure, keeping faith, and telling the truth, can easily become casualties. Some people, disillusioned both by politicians and by the record of the churches, are tempted to place more reliance on the spirit of scientific humility. But it is not obvious that scientific humility is any more widespread or durable than its religious counterpart, or that scientists have proved themselves any wiser than anyone else. Indeed government by 'experts' can become one form of tyranny.

113. The essential balance to be held is that between caution and decisiveness, tolerance and conviction. Both terms in the polarity need each other. Tolerance and caution without decisiveness and conviction can be a recipe for stagnation. Conviction and decisiveness without tolerance and caution can lead to authoritarianism and persecution.

Majorities and Minorities

114. Tolerance, neighbourliness, the willingness to comprehend different views, are values or qualities which make possible the co-existence of a minority culture. These values and concepts do not simply perpetuate themselves; nor are they self-authenticating. They have to be promoted and protected, and it can only be the majority culture which can take the lead in this, not simply for the sake of the subordinate cultures but also in the interest of the survival of its own values. If the majority culture does not work for social cohesion, no-one, in any part of the whole society, can be very much assured about the future.

115. In any society there is conflict. A truly tolerant society is one in which differing values are adequately represented, conflict is contained, and in which neither majority nor any minority feels threatened by others. To get to this point, a society needs to assess accurately how reasonable or unreasonable is fear of what is different, on the part of either majorities or minorities. This in turn requires a willingness to make contacts, and to be contacted. It is unlikely that all differences will shrink into total unimportance, but the areas which the dominant

culture will feel it essential to protect will be clarified, and possibly reduced, and those into which the subordinate culture will be able to expand may be enlarged.

116. Where such a settlement is not achieved, changes in the structures may very well be sought either through the democratic process, or in opposition to it. How, at one and the same time, is it so generally held that democracy is right, and yet also so generally found that minorities are dissatisfied to the point of action outside the law?

117. Democracy is a coveted term because a government whose people allow it to use the word can claim thereby to be governing with their consent. The implication of the adjective 'democratic' is that the politicians and the bureaucracy which does their bidding accept the judgement and the bidding of the majority who are the rest of the electorate. Political liberty involves something more than majority rule, and that is freedom of expression. Only if such freedom exists can alternatives be clearly presented, and without such alternatives a society can stagnate. Of course, freedom of expression by one minority should not infringe the similar freedom which ought to be recognised as the property of any *other* minority. Freedom must be constrained by considerations of justice for others. Perceptions of freedom and justice may be in conflict with one another, but the hard question is how far *koinonia* can be stretched to contain such degrees of conflict. To the degree that that cannot be achieved, seeds of further conflict are inevitably sown.

118. Our immigrant or black communities are a special case of minorities in general, rather than a quite separate category. The things which unite people, the things in which they resemble each other, are more significant than those which divide them, or in which they differ. This can be seen to apply to situations where a minority feels a grievance, and where the consciences of the majority have to be burdened until they are ready to enter deeply into the problem.

> A combination of social disadvantage and cultural isolation could swiftly produce a ghetto mentality on the part of older members of the (incoming) group, and the determination on the part of the younger to shed as soon as possible everything that made them 'different' . . . The members of society of the dominant culture have the responsibility to ensure the assimilation of the newcomers, with a delicacy which does not eliminate the cultural differences from themselves, and with determination to see that no social inequalities are imposed.[1]

---

[1] Wogaman, *Method*, p. 138.

Action is needed on both sides — principally on the part of the majority, but from the minority too.

119. There is a particular need for sensitivity towards people of different colour, because senses of difference are focused irrationally upon merely superficial differences of appearance which are however visible every moment of the day, and are unchangeable. This is why there must be special effort to ensure that black minorities are not disadvantaged. Prejudice, allied to social, economic or political power, makes a formidable combination.

120. The principle of equal access to welfare services and education is an important one. So is the principle of equal opportunity in the labour market. To attempt to ease the sense of grievance by reducing the standard of attainment in education and training properly required for admission to parts of the labour market could well do more harm than good. But the opposite of this – to take great trouble not to discriminate against members of minorities who attain the established requirements of education and training for posts in the labour market and not to set these requirements too narrowly – may be the most relevant form of redress of grievance. Members of the black communities, especially from the second generation onwards, should expect, and be expected, to attain supervisory roles in many forms of employment. This is because they will have established their claim and demonstrated their ability to do so in the same way as do others in our society. The United States encountered the need for this recognition in society earlier than we have done, and by responding positively they seem to have had some recent success in fostering the sense of a more united community.

121. It is possible to give examples showing that when society takes trouble to consider the position of minorities it gains from the experience. In recent years there has been a good illustration of this in the decisive change of opinion towards people with disabilities of body or mind. They used to be categorised, labelled and kept out of sight, individually and collectively. In the space of a few years they have received greater recognition as persons. Unfortunately there has not been as much recognition of the needs of people with mental handicap. The effort to understand the particular situation of particular people, because they form a minority with particular problems, may well improve understanding of how society generally could work better. For example, what makes for more successful policing in Brixton may show how public confidence generally in the police can be improved. To take this kind of example further, if our systems of education and training

40

present such problems to immigrant minorities that they are put at general disadvantage in learning, perhaps what is needed is more attention to the variety of ways in which everyone, with his or her own peculiarities, can learn better. Then our whole society would benefit.

122. The spirit and values of a society are more important than its rules, but rules of procedure provide for all an entry into the process whereby a society decides its actions. A knowledge of the rules enables people to ask hard questions. So the rules by which society makes decisions need to be taught and understood and learned more than they are now. They should include what is involved in winning, and what in losing, an argument. From the victors, what is required is magnanimity. They need to create space for the losing minority and keep developing their notions of justice and human decency so that minorities can sooner or later be brought within the solution arrived at without any sense of exclusion or loss. The losers have to accept, at least for the time being, that they have lost, and stand off from the argument, or risk provoking the winners into bullying tactics. No victory in any case is ever final, because the context is always changing, and history tells of many minorities which fought and lost but won another day.

123. The crux of all this is the notion of distributive justice – the canon by which the rival claims of particular persons or groups of persons within an overall interrelationship are recognised. Justice unfortunately is not the invariable attribute of legislatures, which may be perverse and lag some way behind social reality. Justice needs to be in the hearts of all citizens and not just those of their political representatives. Majority and minority must see themselves as contained within some over-arching sense of citizenship. That, too, has to find expression through some procedure, and the commitment to it will be confirmed through full participation in the decision-making process.

124. A 'human-rights' approach to distributive justice has the advantage that it provides the claimant with protection against the possibility that state officials operate policy unfairly and discriminate between one applicant and another. There is a like protection for the official against allegations of unfairness by clients. A human rights approach, fully worked out, might thus seem to render tolerance redundant over a wide area of human life and bolster it up in the rest. But there is also a 'downside' to the human rights approach. 'Rights' tend to proliferate to the point where anything which is strongly desired is claimed as a right, on the assumption that some universal source, perhaps vaguely described as 'society', has an obligation to satisfy it.

Systems of law based on human rights principles have sometimes tended to encourage extensive, indeed expensive, litigation. Paradoxically, then, a 'human rights' approach, narrowly or rigidly interpreted, does not necessarily reduce social conflict although on balance it has a great potential for doing so.

125. Perhaps the language of polarities and presumptions can provide a method for proceeding. In this way of looking at things law may be *presumed* initially to be just, but it can at the same time be required to submit itself to the test of justice. Justice in turn depends upon the faith held about persons and their interrelationships. Both rules and ends must be contestable in the light of this faith about persons, and subject to revision. Justice is discovered progressively, and is not already 'given' (as the history of law, religion and ideas shows). Religions (for example, Christianity) particularly emphasise the provisionality of all other concepts in the light of some 'final' vision, and discount ideas that everything is merely relative. This provisionality legitimates in principle complaints against all the great institutions in society, including the police and the judges, but the refusal to go all the way towards relativism sets question-marks against private judgements and raises presumptions against law-breaking. Thus, in a society where minorities are given sufficient space and recognition the limits of legitimate expression should not include violence to persons, damage to property or infringing the legitimate freedoms of others, and yet protest groups do not always accept this.

126. It may be that just as individuals in growing up have to establish an independent identity, and feel more secure in their relationship with 'home' when they have done so, equally the same may be true for groups coming in to a society. The 'host' community needs to recognise that. Political and economic *savoir faire* and a sense of security do not necessarily come quickly, and tolerance of risk and change may not be able to grow faster. But the exercise of the virtues of tolerance, 'charity' and neighbourliness, not dissociated from hard conviction, is the precondition of peace in society. The point has much wider relevance. It applies generally to minorities whatever their characteristics. In this sense, everyone of us is involved and may be vulnerable. We all bleed when pricked, as Shylock pointed out.

Ambiguous Attitudes to Authority

127. The persons-in-relationship notion can disintegrate in so many ways. One of them takes the form of ambivalence about legal or social

authority. To be human seems to involve two contradictory urges – to do what one likes when one likes, and to be relieved of all responsibility by simply seeking to rely on someone else to tell one what to do. In the public sphere it is not unknown to find appeals for 'the smack of firm government' accompanied by quite strong resentment of authority. Clergy, particularly bishops, are familiar with the call to 'give a lead' in circumstances where it is quite clear that a lead in only one preferred direction would be welcomed.

128. Ronald Dore's 1984 McCallum Lecture is an illuminating example from industry.[1] Comparing British and Japanese workers' attitudes to management, Dore declares '*machismo* in Britain is largely about the heroic defiance of authority'. In Britain, Dore believes that the legitimacy of authority is always closer to being questioned than it is in Japan. The impulse to defy has so commonly to be reckoned with in Britain that 'leadership' is much talked about while this is rarely the case in Japan. There authority is assumed to reside in occupancy of one's position or office, legitimised through success in strict meritocratic competition in early life. This is irrespective of the charisma or capacity of the particular incumbent. There is not the same automatic confidence, in Britain, in the ability of leaders. The Japanese seem generally to appreciate the need to have a decision-making hierarchy, and the seniority principles on which it operates. Given that, physical and psychological distance between boss and subordinate is not necessary. Hence the managerial overalls and the one-class dining-rooms one finds in Japanese companies. By contrast, British employment relations and authority structures are informed by contractualist assumptions, which are always potentially open for renegotiation.

129. Japanese society, to British eyes, seems very conformist. It has, however, grasped the virtue of co-operation, especially as a tool for competing successfully with the rest of the world. But neither Japan nor Britain has always been as it is now. Studies in patterns of industrial relations in the West have shown that there is no single formula for stability. Companies may thus have some choice over the ethos which they adopt, maybe a different one from the one they inherit from earlier periods. Leaders, whether consciously or unconsciously, express the philosophy of the companies they are leading. If this is done consciously it is difficult to avoid talk about respect for persons and need for interrelationship, values which, in the industrial scene, are only

---

[1] 'Authority and Benevolence: the Confucian Recipe for Industrial Success' in *Government and Opposition* Vol. 20. No. 2. Spring 1985, pp. 196-217.

incidentally likely to appeal to those who work for the company and those who supply it or buy from it. To set out a company philosophy for all to view and criticise is a 'high risk' process that takes on trust that people will not take advantage, and that the result can be defended in public debate and by reference to the company's day-to-day management practice. There is a belief, and plenty of evidence, that such a trusting strategy by a company board does engender trust in return.

130. The problem is that an immense trauma such as shook Japan in 1945 may be needed before people can become convinced that the old ways are not the best ones. Britain is by contrast a very conservative society which has escaped many traumas, though underneath the surface there are signs of deep disturbance, in areas as diverse as race relations, theology, relations between men and women, the creative arts and the economy. In many ways we inhabit a low-performance, low-trust society, rather tired and sometimes fearful. One of the things to be learned from the Japanese is that one is free either to build on one's inheritance or, if one chooses, leave elements of it behind. Change is possible, particularly if goals are shared by enough people in the society to make a difference, but for goals to be shared depends on trust for authority, and trust can only be engendered from above. The attitudes *of* authority are more crucial than attitudes *to* authority, because those in authority, by definition, have more of the initiative.

131. Experience from within the churches can provide examples of both bad and good exercises of, and reactions to, authority. In some parts of the churches the authority ascribed to the clergy, or to elders, is so strong that open criticism of it cannot be entertained. Continual scrutinies of behaviour among the followers are carried out to identify signs of deviation. In other parts of the churches little authority is vouchsafed to anyone, and scrutiny is directed not to signs of revolt but to manifestations of anything remotely resembling ambition or even the milder leadership that is necessary for solving practical problems. A 'happy medium' is to be preferred, where everyone is given the trust and respect needed for the job. Churches, no less than political institutions, have to be worked by ordinary people who are prone to normal human weakness. There are after all no others available. It would be an advance if this lesson could be taken to heart by those who frequent groupings and parties within churches. British churches, and the Church of England, are not exempt from the kind of scapegoating which is found elsewhere in society. Life, church life, seems much sweeter if all that is bad can be located in another branch, far away. Are Christians in Britain *just* like everyone else around them, happy to

thrive by conjuring up bogies, or can they exemplify better than most the virtues of *koinonia* which they profess and from which the whole of society would benefit?

Living with Complexities

132. Many who have followed the argument so far will still be waiting for 'a clear lead' to be given upon one or other of the major dislocations they identify in the balance between individuals and community. Others will have given up in disillusion already. But there is no merit in over-simplifying our descriptions of the world we live in. That way lies tyranny. As a final example of how inaccurate it may be to jump to conclusions, the international trade in armaments may be cited. This hard example has been chosen deliberately because for many people it generates strong feelings and yet accurate information is not widely disseminated.

133. The case that there should be no arms, and therefore no sale of arms, is simple but not widely held, though the pacifist witness continues to be an important element in the life of the churches. However, once it is accepted that armaments are sometimes morally legitimate the questions begin: should every nation always provide its own arms, or should it be able to lend to, or borrow from, a friendly nation? Should one be able to buy from, or sell to, a friend? Readers whose memories go back to the 1939-45 war will be able to supply examples of arms purchases and lend-lease which were welcome. Where arms possession in itself is legitimate, there is no reason why the ordinary concepts of trade should be disallowed or strategic and political motives discounted. But there might also be considerations which rendered the particular transaction difficult to justify, as there are in the cases of trade in items other than armaments. The eager buyer might be a foreign regime to which in general we did not want to give the kind of credence that an open transfer of arms might suggest; or we might disapprove of the particular use it was proposed to make of the arms in question, or we might have qualms about the particular weapons (nuclear, for example) being discussed; or the wider political context or the buyer country's internal economy might suggest that the sale in question was inapt. All these situations raise questions about line-drawing, perceptions of balance, second-guessing the facts at a distance, and other problems. Nor are they hypothetical only. So it is no solution to give it up as too difficult. Small groups of observers, prepared to take time and gather facts, and to build alliances with politicians, can bring quite focused comment to bear. It was such an exercise that led a few years ago to the cancellation of a sale of armoured

cars to a Central American customer. On the other hand, facts may be difficult to gather, even though to those with the requisite skill and application more is discoverable or collectable than we often believe.

134. If there is merit in refusing to oversimplify a situation, and insisting that it may be necessary to consider it as requiring a balance of apparently conflicting policies, then the correct question to ask is not *which* of several possible lines to take (an either/or question) but *how much* of each, *when*, and *in* what circumstances. The answer to the question why Britain is not as successful economically as Japan will be a multiple one. No simple strategy would suffice either to turn Britain into a copy of Japan, or to find some other more satisfactory route than that which either Japan or Britain is currently following. This is not to say that some other new way is inconceivable. Quite the reverse: conceiving new ways is no problem at all. What is inconceivable is that some simple 'philosopher's stone' can be found that will turn all dross situations into gold. The complexity is compounded by the fact that neither the world, nor the Christian's understanding of *koinonia*, ends at the Straits of Dover. In these days of nuclear fall-out and satellite broadcasting the whole world is our neighbour. Britain's general freedom of political and economic manoeuvre is smaller than it was, and is decreasing.

135. The argument of this chapter has been that oversimplification has often left people with an apparently 'straight' choice between two polar positions, when greater sensitivity would suggest that the truth lies at neither extreme, nor even at any clearly definable point in between, but rather in the maintenance of a tension which does justice to each element of the polar pair. In a period of rapid social change there is a need to strengthen the basic moral values on which the possibility of both individual development and social peace depends. These are the notions of *person*, before each of whom the only proper attitude is that of respect amounting to awe, and *community (koinonia)* whose full conditions for flourishing cannot be known or described with final precision. Neither person nor community are notions totally accessible to us, and we should be thankful for light shed on them from many sources including the churches. We must keep examining them, and then ourselves, each other, and our whole community, to deepen our understanding of a commitment to the values they enshrine. Such deepening of our moral base will not remove complexity but it will provide a surer foundation from which to tackle it. The final part of this study considers the means in our society whereby values are in fact chosen and inculcated.

CHAPTER FOUR
Nurturing Values

136. The previous chapters have reviewed some of the interactions between values in contemporary Britain and have emphasised that oversimplification of analysis is easy, but not particularly fruitful and potentially very damaging. The burden of Chapter Two was that the only things which create and hold together societies larger than small face-to-face communities are agreements about some few quite basic beliefs and stances. These agreements need to embrace notions of fairness and justice, honesty and dependability, protection of freedom of belief and speech, care for the elderly, respect for innocent life, for marriage, reputation and possessions, all in the pursuit of what has been called 'human flourishing'. This is a concept which no-one could claim is yet fully enjoyed but it expresses the universal human hope. We construct for ourselves and each other ideas about it which we update and correct in the light of new perceptions. Such human 'flourishing' or 'fulfilment', it has been argued, resides in the combination of freedom and interrelatedness, service and solidarity, and in the set of values which Christians have found within their understanding of *koinonia*, a Greek word for which a better English equivalent than 'community', 'communion' or 'sharing' is still sought. The present concern is to try to suggest how such values can be fostered, and by which social institutions.

137. How far, for example, in a pluralist society, is it the role of education to foster a particular set of values? On what basis can educationalists form clear policy objectives? Is too much expected of institutional education? What is the role of the family? What kinds of families produce what kinds of people? We receive a bewildering variety of sensations via the media, including successive presentations of alternative mythologies about our society. Does the concentration on portraying extreme forms of behaviour shift society's norms? Parties and pressure groups present us with what they assert to be basic values, but does competition here enhance or weaken perception of what is basic when rival bodies are even more likely to explore them apart than together? If there is competition to set values, the importance of democratic and social procedures becomes more apparent, as does the value of participating in voluntary organisations where people can practise and improve social or technical skills. What are the specific contributions which society ought to expect from the churches in the

creation and sustaining of values? We would have liked in addition to have asked questions about the creative arts and leisure activities in general but did not have the time or skill to do so.

138. One member of the group which produced this study has written elsewhere, 'attitudes and opinions typically owe less to individual reflection than to the social processes of upbringing, custom and habituation. Custom and convention are always open to critical analysis but most people, most of the time, take morals as given from their social surroundings'.[1] In a pluralist society, however, increasing awareness of differing social processes existing alongside one another may be changing what was once typically the case, and making for a society in which individuals develop greater autonomy and personal reflectiveness, and custom and convention become subject to a greater degree of critical analysis. The effect of pluralism on social processes is a main motif in this chapter.

Nurturing Values in the Family

139. There will be little argument about the importance of the family as a source of values. Three sets of relationships are universal among all forms of family, however much families vary from culture to culture or epoch to epoch. Each gives rise to a particular and distinguishable set of influences and each has been subject to change. There is the influence which the marriage partners have upon each other (whether or not there are children). Then there is the influence which parents have upon the children and vice versa. Finally there is the influence the children have upon each other.

140. Geographical mobility has thrown more and more emphasis upon the 'nuclear' family of immediate parents and dependent children, and has tended to weaken the influence of the grandparents and the uncles and aunts of the children. In an earlier period these often lived quite close by and interacted frequently with both parents and children. In-laws were then probably a stronger influence upon the married couple than they now are. The increasing size and concentration of economic and administrative organisations, and the greater regularity of work for most people, has meant that employment frequently entails longer journeys to work and more time away from home for the worker, though this may be about to change. Neighbourhood communities are less close than they were, and residence and

---

[1] A. H. Halsey in Abrams et al. *Values*, p. 7.

employment reinforce each others' cultures less strongly than they used to. Employment for so many married women has altered radically the social dynamics of the family in all three of the dimensions described. New sources of strong influence upon family values enter the home through the media. The teenage culture has a much greater influence upon both the teenagers themselves and their parents.

141. Whatever the truth of these generalisations, it is clear that within British society, not to mention the differences between ethnic groups, there is more than one pattern of family relationship, more than one set of values, and more than one mechanism for the transmission of values. Today the responsibility which older and more experienced and stronger and (arguably) wiser people have to protect and educate the others, is still exercised to a greater extent within the family than anywhere else, even counting the school. But where partners are regarded as equally mature and responsible for themselves, respect for each other's interests is another important part of the total value-pattern within the family. This supportive process is of prime significance in those thirty per cent of all households where there are no resident children. In all these educative and supportive relationships there is ample room for the interplay of values. Indeed it is scarcely possible to conceive of family life and relationships which could be value-free. Modern sciences, psychology and sociology, confirm sayings such as 'like mother, like daughter' or 'train up a child in the way he should go and when he is old he will not depart from it'.

142. It is generally acknowledged, of course, that the laying down of value systems is not a straightforward process, and that individual differences and choices and wider social influences make it impossible to be certain what the specific result of any particular family structure will be upon the persons within it. Nonetheless it seems plausible to claim that different family structures produce and nurture different kinds of people. The earliest and deepest experiences of what it is to be a person are mediated by the other persons who constitute the family. Children deprived of appropriate contact do not develop into that normally understood and, in terms of this study, normative person – one who enjoys freedom in *koinonia*.

143. There is evidence, for example, from studies of Israeli kib-butzim that radical changes in the pattern of childrearing have discernible effects on personal development.[1] Children reared col-

---

[1] B. Bettelheim *The Children of the Dream* (London, Thames and Hudson, 1969).

lectively within a single age group and without much sustained parental contact tend, as one might expect, to be more conformist and group orientated, and less able to develop an independent inner life, than those reared in ordinary Western European or North American families. There is also evidence of greater emotional stability in the kibbutz children. Another social experiment, the shift from marriage to cohabitation, has led some observers to see a link between cohabitation, egotism and individualistic attitudes, though it is not clear which is cause and which is effect, nor are cohabiting couples discernibly more selfish than married ones.[1] In another study the typical bourgeois family has been upheld as the best known matrix for producing autonomous yet socialised individuals, who have learned the delicate balance between being themselves and fulfilling a role within a close-knit society.[2] The point being made by all these examples is the simple one that values are nurtured within the family context, not just in response to personal relationships, but also by the way those relationships are socially structured. The picture becomes more complex, however, as the family is set against its broader social background.

144. Anthropologists have suggested that there are four functions fundamental to human life – the educational, the economic, the relational and the reproductive. All these functions have traditionally had their primary locus within the family. In the twentieth century the biologically-long maturing period required by the human infant is extended considerably as a matter of social policy. These primarily family functions have in fact come to be more widely shared by society as a whole – few families are isolated economic units, education after the age of five has been socialised, and relational needs are increasingly satisfied outside the context of the family. Notably, families tend nowadays to accept the sexual mores of their children and do little consciously to control their child's final choice of marital partners. Nevertheless it remains true that the family, ideologically and to as great an extent as it can be managed practically, is the perceived central hinge of this entire process of bringing the new human person from infancy to adulthood and into the wider society with sufficient competence to serve the needs of the wider society.

---

[1] The shift from marriage to co-habitation is illustrated in *Social Trends No. 17,* 1987, page 46, table 2.11.

[2] B. Berger and P. L. Berger *War Over the Family: Capturing the Middle Ground* (Harmondsworth, Penguin Books, 1984).

145. But it is important to stress that what is thus said about the family is said about its *process* in maintaining and socialising the young. The *direction* which such socialising takes is mediated by the family structure, but it is not defined by it; it is initiated by the individual persons who make up the family and by the society in which the family is located, which has itself influenced, though not always intentionally, the structure of the family in the first place. In other words, a family is not a thing by itself, but an integral part of a larger social structure. It is where children are first socialised, but it does not originate the values which it imparts. It is influenced from outside by a wide variety of factors – religion, nation, class, ethnic origin, etc. – and as society changes the family usually transmits the new values which have been determined elsewhere. It is an agent rather than a principal. To realise this may be to liberate the parents from the weight of guilt and the feelings of inadequacy carried by too many of them as they contemplate their difficult task of bringing up children. But the responsibility remains of ordering family life in such a way that love, honesty, reliability and respect are seen to be at the core of human relationships.

146. The danger of treating a family as though it were itself somehow a person, an individual unit to be integrated into the social – a commonly held position in contemporary British politics – is that it tends to obscure the true individuality and personhood of members of the family. The roles of all members of the family are undergoing change, but women are particular victims of this. Their identity has traditionally been defined by their role within the family – and the situation is thus made more serious for them by the 'professionalisation' of child raising. This may threaten to take from the principal carers, usually women, their authority and competence as well as their traditional responsibility in life, without relieving them of the emotional overtones they still feel and which lie close to their sense of identity. It is possible perhaps to be a 'good' teacher or housekeeper because there is a product to measure skill and achievement against; it is more difficult now to be a 'good' mother or wife. Thus within the family – that essential mediator of values – there may be tension between individual well-being and personhood in freedom and the maintenance of the family itself.

147. Each family thus gains its identity and its values from two sources: from the individuals who make it up and from 'outside', from what the individuals in it consume intellectually and reflect on, from the peer groups of both adult and child members, from those other institutions that share – often compulsorily with the individual family

members – their nurturing task (school teachers, health authorities, social service personnel etc.), and, at a further remove, 'elite groups' of politicians, media managers, pressure groups and political parties of all kinds.

148. It is important to focus accurately on these characteristics of the family – as an agent shaped, influenced and constrained by a wider society for the function of mediating value to the young – otherwise more will be expected of child carers than they can achieve, their own personhood will be subsumed into their social function, and they will become loaded with responsibilities which, in fairness, they can never discharge.

149. At the same time the thrust of this whole thesis is that the internal relationships within a family remain highly significant. Human beings have a profound need for stable loving relationships within which their own individuality can be recognised and nurtured. If this is to happen within the family it is vital that the understanding of it as one structure among others which binds the individual into society, which cherishes the fullness of personhood, and which provides a meeting point between freedom and *koinonia,* is not simply politicised and made a purely functional or administrative convenience. The essential internal tasks of the family may well be capable of being performed in structures which do not conform to traditional or to administratively tidy patterns. Experiments in community living, the growing number of one-parent families, the complex relationships between families linked by divorce and remarriage are obvious examples. A changing social order needs to be sympathetic to a wide variety of family styles, within the limits set by the needs of children and the values inherent in *koinonia.*

150. Those who are interested in the nurturing of values cannot neglect the role of the family as the prime locus of learning. But this must not be done simplistically as if all that is needed is more moral and social support for 'the family'. There are values invested in family structures themselves, values mediated through the family by external influences, expectations placed upon the family, some reasonable and some unreasonable, and many unanswered questions about new styles of family life. The New Testament itself has some ambivalent things to say about families, which could be a useful starting-point for further reflection.

Education and the Nurturing of Values

151. Education shares, with all the other social institutions mentioned in this chapter, the problems and possibilities of living in what is now commonly referred to as a pluralist society. In this section attention is focused mainly on school education, although the questions raised and ideas put forward apply to all educational processes. It is sometimes claimed that schools can only reflect the kind of society they serve. If that is true then it is not surprising that, whereas in a more homogeneous society it might have seemed reasonable to expect schools to nurture an agreed set of values, today the validity of that aim is questioned. The educational world finds itself attracting the hopes and expectations of a variety of groups, each reflecting a different cultural, religious or ideological background. It is also at the focal point of political controversy about the aims of education as such, and the degree to which school life should be seen as practical preparation for working life, and how far it should be concerned with socialisation and the development of personal qualities.

152. Questions about *whose* values and *what* cultural heritage should be transmitted, and with what ultimate aim, presuppose larger questions about the kind of society Britain now is, and what it might become in terms of the amount and the variety of cultural pluralism. These questions about social values interact with further questions of particular concern to the teaching profession about what constitutes good education, and in particular what enables each child to value and grow into its own cultural heritage while at the same time developing a readiness to receive new knowledge, to acquire new skills, and to capture a vision of new possibilities. There are also deep differences of opinion about the extent to which schools should be content to serve society as it is, or, rather, how far they should consciously adopt the role of vehicles of social change. Balancing these different objectives is no easy task, and it is not surprising that expectations differ and sometimes conflict in such a complex field.

153. The task is even more complex in a society which experiences a sense of disorientation in the face of rapid change resulting from technological advance, education for all, greater social mobility (both nationally and internationally), and increasing awareness of social divisions. The changes seem to represent for many a multi-faceted attack on the fabric and stability of society. Is it true, however, that stability is the equivalent of unchanging circumstance? If it were, would it not follow that no growth or development was possible? The problem is how to adapt to changing circumstances, accommodate new

insights and respond to new needs whilst retaining sufficient continuity with the past to have its best features constantly available as a resource on which to build. An educational system has to contain explicit or implicit answers to such questions as:

> what priority should be given to the nurture and preservation of our cultural heritage, given that it is still reasonable to think in terms of a dominant culture with subordinate but still independent cultures (para 106);

> what shifts in values are becoming acceptable as signs of increased awareness and understanding within society;

> how can new and old insights into these be related fruitfully to one another, and how can different cultures develop mutual respect and understanding;

> and what would a society be like in which all citizens had the opportunity to lead personally fulfilling and socially valuable lives, and how can education contribute to the realisation of this ideal?

154. Though framed in abstract terms such questions press heavily on all those involved in education who have to face the reality of social change, who are themselves subject to the uncertainty and disorientation it can bring, and who are conscious of working within structures which embody values they may or may not accept. A teacher with a class half of whom, say, are Muslim and half Christian, daily faces searching questions about the kind of cultural environment for which the class is being prepared.

155. Such questions are central to a debate about the nurturing of values. They are being addressed by many in society as well as in the present study and it may be helpful to consider two recent but very different approaches to them. The Swann Report attempted to answer such questions by envisaging members of all ethnic groups living together 'within a framework of commonly accepted values, practices and procedures'.[1] The aim of education would be to enable children both to understand and to respect values distinctive of lifestyles deriving from differing cultural, religious and linguistic backgrounds 'which make up this society and the wider world' and to become aware of the values which are held in common by all groups and upon which the social cohesion of a people depends. Implicit in this answer is the belief that such common values exist, a belief to which this present study lends support. But this still leaves unresolved the problem of how far to give specific attention to the wide variety of beliefs and cultural

---

[1] *Education for All*. Report of the Committee of Inquiry into the Education of Children from Ethnic Minority Groups (London, HMSO, 1985, Cmnd. 9453).

expressions in which common values might be embodied, and to the essential points of difference between different traditions.

156. A common alternative approach is restated by Basil Mitchell.[1] He makes the familiar point that the young do not learn to think for themselves by being presented with a pot-pourri of competing philosophies, but by being introduced to a coherent tradition which they are then encouraged to reflect on critically from within. This process of 'schema and correction', as he calls it, has affinities with Karl Popper's method of 'conjecture and refutation' in which it is claimed first that no-one ever starts with a 'blank sheet' but that all ideas and claims to knowledge have to be tested and subjected to criticism.[2] If this were more generally appreciated it would have the merit of bringing philosophical and religious education into the same general educational framework as the teaching of science. Such similarity of method would surely be a major bonus at a time when the split between science and the humanities is still a strong feature of our culture, and is in danger of being exacerbated by educational policies which place the emphasis on technical expertise as if this could safely be separated from informed critical understanding.

157. Mitchell's approach, though, runs into the same *practical* problems as the Swann Report. The coherent tradition to which he would introduce the young cannot be conveyed in religious education classes, still less be embodied in the whole school curriculum and the ethos of the school itself. If schools are a reflection of society and share its present diversity and confusions, it is already too late to move radically in the direction he recommends. The fact also has to be faced that many teachers are much affected by a climate which is not greatly sympathetic towards religious and reflective studies, let alone towards a particular set of values buttressed by religious authority. And in schools with a large multi-faith population the selection of a single coherent tradition is impractical anyway. However, many of those engaged in education hold strongly, on educational grounds, that their prime task is to draw out strengths latent in their pupils, and thus to transcend and challenge the community they serve. An essential part of this task is to clarify the relationship between 'often conflicting' values, some of

---

[1] 'Being Religiously Educated' in G. Leonard ed. *Faith for the Future* Essays on the Church in Education (London, National Society and Church House Publishing, 1986) pp. 43-52.

[2] K. R. Popper *Conjectures and Refutations: Growth of Scientific Knowledge* (London, Routledge and Kegan Paul, 1969).

which derive from unquestioning commitment to a received tradition and others of which demand the constant and open pursuit of new apprehensions of truth.

158. It is important, though, not to exaggerate the degree of uncertainty and confusion. Many of the strains and stresses are absorbed because educational provision is diversified, and may be more apparent to those who plan overall educational policies than to teachers on the ground. The sharpest and most obvious problems occur in areas where the population contains substantial religious minorities, but these contribute only two to three per cent of the problem. Much more general is the tension between the secular and the religious strands in our culture. Thankfully, the educational system is not monolithic. It is made up of different institutions, some of which exist specifically to transmit a particular set of values. Within the State system there is a wide diversity in educational provision; local schools frequently reflect the values and mores of their particular social background. Church schools and independent schools are further examples of this diversity. Current political controversies over the extent to which education should be centrally controlled by the State need to be seen in this wider context. The points at issue go beyond the standardisation of curricula. They relate to basic questions, which run like a thread through the whole of this study, about the extent to which diversity should be encouraged, even at some cost in social cohesion, and the extent to which a pluralist society needs to be held together by some common core of values, skills and cultural norms.

159. The educational world has its own internal standards and its own implicit value commitments. These do not necessarily coincide with the expectations of the general public, a fact which in times of rapid change can generate misunderstanding, hostility, and the sense of being undervalued. The present low morale of the profession is an ominous sign for the future. 'The great educational debate', once promised in such glowing terms, has been pursued too narrowly. Education as a main purveyor of values needs to be seen within its total context – not simply as one professional activity among others, but as part of the process by which a society reflects on itself, renews its commitment to what is perceived as being of central value, and prepares itself for an unknown future. Within this broad enterprise there is room for disagreement and differences of emphasis, but it is surely in everybody's interest to lift the debate above sterile confrontation.

Values in the Media

160. When the work of people in the media – whether journalists or editors, producers or programme controllers – comes under critical challenge, their standard general response tends to be that they are merely holding up a mirror to ('reflecting') society or reality. That reply tacitly begs two questions: first, whether they are *accurately* reflecting reality, or in fact distorting it; and second, whether and to what extent they are *changing* that reality through the effects they have upon it and through the influence they exert on society.

161. That the role played by the media within society – as purveyors of both factual information and ideas, opinions and values – is an active and not merely a passive one, is the starting assumption of everyone engaged in the advertising industry in western countries as well as of those exercising monopolistic state control of the media in communist and other authoritarian countries. The very fact that, on average, in this country people spend twenty hours every week watching television – a high proportion of their non-working waking hours – provides strong grounds for supposing that, over time, this experience plays a substantial part in shaping both their picture of the nature of the social environment surrounding them and their attitudes and responses to that environment. For many years now, surveys have shown nearly four people in five saying that they rely upon television news, rather than newspapers, as their principal source of information on what is happening in the world. Partly in reaction to this, the popular press has to a considerable extent withdrawn from the business of providing *news*papers and self-consciously become mainly a medium of diversion and entertainment. A further longstanding indication of the reputation of broadcasting as an authoritative medium of communication is that over the past twenty years or so successive surveys of the relative degree of respect accorded to a multiplicity of British institutions show that the BBC has consistently emerged among those most highly-rated.

162. One positive consequence of this move by most people from dependence on the press to dependence on broadcasting as their primary source of news and current affairs is a greater awareness and understanding of social, religious and political attitudes and values other than their own. The impartiality expected of the broadcasting authorities in their coverage of current affairs should expose viewers and listeners to a wider range of opinions and approaches to problems and issues than the newspaper of their choice. The loosening of partisan commitment to one or other of the major political parties by many

people over the last generation is, in part, attributable to this development. In that sense, the emergence of radio and the subsequent dominance of television among the media may have promoted a broadening of horizons and a greater awareness and acceptance of diverse perspectives.

163. In other respects, however, the emergence of a multiplicity of media of communication and the resulting increasingly intense competition between them for public attention has had more negative consequences. One has already been noted: the retreat of the popular press over recent years from serious claim any longer to be primarily *news*papers, and, in their remaining news coverage, the growing emphasis on the trivial and the sensational – the provision of 'circuses' rather than 'bread'. The focusing of attention upon personal stories may be defended as an attempt to humanise the news, but it can have destructive consequences for the persons concerned. They are swept up sometimes into too simplistic a presentation of a story as an opposition of heroes and villains. It can encourage in the viewer or reader an attitude of prurience, and feed the temptation in all of us to 'put people down'. More basic than that is the fact that news – the staple of all forms of large-scale communication – is, almost by definition, concerned with the extraordinary, the exceptional, the out-of-the-way. The journalist, by instinct and by training, tends to develop the attitude that the only good news is bad news and to seek out some basis for getting the most arresting (and often alarming) construction upon events. This ranges from the reporter on a popular newspaper seeking out scandal and discreditable behaviour and motives, to a serious journalist on the 'quality' press analysing the decisions and dilemmas facing politicians and other leaders in unrealistically sharp terms.

164. This tendency has been accentuated over the last ten to fifteen years by a vogue in all the media for 'investigative journalism'. The role played by the American press (since exaggerated by itself) in the unravelling of the Watergate scandal not only increased the resources and effort assigned to journalism of the overtly 'investigative' kind: it also enhanced the existing predisposition of journalists to suspect the statements and motives of public figures and to believe that, if only they dug deeply enough, they would invariably find something disreputable being concealed. This is not to deny that 'investigative journalism' has sometimes performed a useful, indeed vital, function, and one which is all the more necessary where power is concentrated in relatively few hands. Its greater prominence and the spread of the attitudes that underlie it have damaged alike the actors, the journalists and their

audiences. Investigative journalism is from one point of view a logical reaction to the growth, complexity and imperviousness of the state. The fewer the important secrets, the less there is for investigative journalism to thrive upon. A more open society, with readier access to information, would undercut much of this practice.

165. Associated with this over the same time-span has been the loosening by the broadcasting authorities in Britain of the requirement of impartiality within each programme. One consequence of this has been the number of television programmes (or, in some cases, series) in which a 'star' journalist is given independence to present his or her view of contentious issues. Such is the authority of television for many viewers, and so widespread by now the acceptance of the impartiality of the broadcasting authorities themselves, that the view presented in such programmes is not seen by many viewers in its true light. Even a highly 'balanced' programme may produce bias, if it gives equal prominence to all, so that majority views seem to have no greater covering than those of small minorities.

166. The high degree of competition between the media for the public's attention and patronage acts as a powerful force in the same direction. That between the national newspapers has never been so intense as today, nor that between them and the other media. Most of the British popular press is now in the hands of no more than three groups. The national radio networks compete for audiences (as do the BBC and the commercial local radio stations). The two main television channels are locked in a permanent so-called 'ratings battle', as are, if less intensively, BBC2 and Channel 4. The pervasive fact of competition places a premium, for all journalists, editors, producers and network controllers, upon capturing and holding their audience and, if possible, increasing it. Those pressures are increased by two further 'structural' factors. First, such is the amount of space to be filled (for the press), such is the amount of air-time to be filled (for the programme-makers), that they are constantly searching for the novel, the striking, the unusual – whether in the way of subject-matter, or by way of treatment. Second, the audience or the readership is known to have already seen, heard or read so much on subject X, and to have so many alternative magnets of potential attraction and interest available to it on rival media productions, that the pressures in favour of the novel and the out-of-the-way are still further intensified. The media are then as much victims of society as offenders against it.

167. The major question raised by these trends is how far they lead

to a distorted presentation of reality. Two obvious illustrations will serve to make the point. In our big cities it is notorious that many, if not most, people have a seriously exaggerated view of the statistical risks of being violently assaulted. Equally, in 1986 Britain experienced a major reduction in the number of American visitors, thanks in considerable part to a totally misconceived and media-engendered perception of the risks of terrorist attack. Is it the case, more generally, that through the influence of the media, people are led to see the world as a more dangerous, more fearful place than can be justified, with the consequences for their personal values and attitudes that such a perception would tend to promote? Colin Morris has voiced this suspicion.[1] He asserts that the 'base-line' view which we have always hitherto held is that society is really on the whole happy and well-adjusted. It is because this is so that bad events are remarkable, and become 'news'.

168. Related to that is another question: whether the overall effect of media output is to encourage a cynical outlook on life and an attitude to one's fellow human beings characterised by wariness and a limited degree of trust. The amount of space and time devoted to crime and criminal activity, fictional as well as actual; the values embodied by the leading characters portrayed in the most popular soap operas, such as *Dallas* or *Dynasty*, or in many naturalistic television dramas; the assumptions, implicit or explicit, behind so many questions in either 'chat-show' interviews or news and current affairs interviews – all arguably serve to reflect and to promote an attitude that, in order to succeed or even to 'get by' in life, one needs above all to be, in that telling American phrase, 'street-wise'.

169. One further point. In any typical evening's viewing one will find represented, again either implicitly or explicitly, over the range of programmes or even within a single programme (whether drama, 'chat-show', or serious discussion), a wide range of diverse values. While this undoubtedly has its positive aspects, it is arguable that the overall effect is to bewilder many viewers and to induce a relativistic belief that values are a matter of mere subjective preference. There is good evidence that such a belief is gaining an increasing hold, particularly on younger people. Others argue that the media merely reinforce the values which people already hold, and that audience selectivity implies that much of a value nature which comes through the media goes past one without even being registered.

---

[1] 1986 Hibbert Lecture 'What's So Good about the Bad News' (London, *The Listener*, 25th September 1986).

170. Be that as it may, the media are very strong bearers of values in modern society. But are they originators of them? Has the new opinion-forming elite of the television age produced, or rather been produced by, a new form of society? Perhaps the question is once again misconceived: the media form an amplification machine for various value systems. The strong images presented invite the receiver to shorten his or her attention span, and to forget that real-life situations are rarely as simple as they appear to be in the media.

171. The influence of the media should not be exaggerated, however. There is evidence that at the age when they are most engaged in forming an independent existence, with individual views (i.e. in late adolescence), people do not view much television or see all that many newspapers. When they do, they become as skilled as many of the rest of us at letting the images 'wash over' them without making much impact. This unconcern may degenerate into anaesthesis or cynicism but it need not do so. People are reading books more than ever before, and are thus able to supplement, and add detail to, perceptions received via the mass media. These critical approaches to television and the mass newspaper and magazine press are not unhealthy and need encouragement. Many schools are experimenting in this direction, and the long-term prospects for an educated, healthy and critically aware public for the media are by no means poor ones. They would be much enhanced if the media professionals themselves were to accept that their activities have moral consequences, and that their profession, just like others, needs clear and rigorous standards of conduct if the public is to be genuinely served. 'Pervasive Smugness' was the headline given to a report of the 1986 Edinburgh International Television Festival.[1] When the journalist lawyer who had been asked to chair one of the sessions tried to read himself into the question of journalistic ethics in broadcasting, there had been 'nothing to give him'.

Parties and Pressure Groups

172. The search for vehicles of values has run into a number of dead ends. Schools, families, the media all play a role in maintaining human values, but the place where values originate has not yet been clearly identified. In one sense, the question is an idle one, since nurturing is as much about feeding the infant as it is about conceiving it and bringing it to birth. Yet it is important to try to discover the origins of values, lest

---

[1] *The Times* 27th August 1986.

each institution in society should in turn escape responsibility. Maybe it is in political parties and social and political pressure-groups that the origins of values in society are more closely approached.

173. In the popular view, political parties and pressure groups, particularly those in power, are the 'them' whom 'we' resent and distrust. 'They' do things to 'us', not vice versa. This is inaccurate and unjust. The number of mediating institutions linking Deptford or Darlington to Downing Street is very large, but without them Britain could not function. They are not simply 'strangling serpents'. Without them no values of any kind other than purely local ones could be nurtured. When the electorate was small (three per cent of the adult population in 1800 and not reaching double figures until after the 1865 Reform Act) few issues came to Parliament. With the expansion of the suffrage came also improvements in communications, education and social organisation. Without intervening political parties or pressure groups a government would be quite unable to respond to its electorate. It would be in a very poor position to judge the public interest. As it is, governments can feel pressures and then initiate policies which are both necessary and heavily value-laden. They can act with more confidence over a wide range. Democratic choice in national politics presupposes the existence of groups and political parties, each proposing possible answers to a variety of social and political questions, and each incorporating to a greater or lesser degree ranges of values. It is their role to articulate and expound particular policies, and they do this sometimes in response to naked and unanalysed self-interest but sometimes also as a result of the most extensive and careful study and self-examination.

174. Pressure groups can be narrower in their interest than parties; parties, since they seek to be governments, have to address the whole range of Government issues; parties, being broadly based, cohere around a short list of very basic values. But within each party is a host of smaller pressure groups each of which in turn adheres more strongly to an even shorter list. These short (and shorter) lists form the base of a 'ladder' of values that ascends through 'central objectives' to the 'programme'. Political parties exist to put their 'programme' into effect, and pressure groups, lobbies and interests exist to influence the direction or the priority of some particular item of policy. Pragmatism in execution does not belie a strong base of values, sometimes called 'ideology', which can often be read fairly simply from pre-election party manifestoes, and over which very serious internal party battles are fought. A wide variety of other pressure groups compete for public

attention and contribute directly and indirectly to the milieu within which values have to be balanced and political decisions made.

175. In Britain, politics and politicians give rise to endless fascination. They are also frequently the butt of snide remarks. They are low in the rank of callings or professions engendering trust, yet every news bulletin and most newspapers lead with political news, every day and many times a day. This seems to confirm the two contrary views of politics which it has enjoyed throughout history, as on the one hand one of the few callings proper to a gentleman, and on the other a doubtful or even corrupt competition – a 'greasy pole'.

176. Such is the importance, then, of both parties and pressure-groups and of the role of politicians that the degree of self-criticism they need to exercise is a high one. They also deservedly invite a great deal of external criticism, and part of their self-discipline needs to lead them to welcome and invite that. For its part the general public should be more ready to celebrate and give thanks for living in a society which makes concern for all causes including minority ones a possible matter for parties and pressure-groups. Politics is a very important social process, not to be taken flippantly and insincerely by those who profess it, and certainly not to be denigrated by those who merely observe it. Politicians, both local and national, are people we need, and whom we ask to do an essential job for us. Too often, political jostling is treated by the media and its public as some kind of spectator sport. It is actually the most serious of matters, deserving more than lip-service to morality from its practitioners, and greater interest from the rest of us in the principles at stake.

177. Clearly, politics, parties and pressure-groups are powerful selectors and promoters of values, and as such they fully deserve the interest taken in them by any other group concerned about values.

The Role of the Churches

178. The role of the churches as the guardians and purveyors of Christian values seems so obvious to their members as scarcely to need stating. It is not a matter of immediate concern here to ask how effective the churches are in this role. Nor is this the place to question their right to perform it on behalf of a society in which regular churchgoers now form a minority. The point has been made in Chapter 1 that Britain is an old culture, rich in institutions (the churches among them) and with a great deal of cultural and institutional interpenetration. That is our

history, our fate in one sense, and we cannot change it. This is the past on which successive futures are and will be built. It is not possible either for church or society to wish the other away, and it is not permissible for Christians to withdraw from debate about public values and simply leave others unchallenged in their pronouncements.

179. This interpenetration has already been illustrated in the shape of appeals to generally held values, and arguments on rational grounds for moral insights which are not exclusive to the Christian tradition, however much they have grown out of it historically. Most Christians, especially those who are unused to this approach, will want to say more, and to relate what they say more explicitly to Christian faith. But a study of society in its most general aspects cannot limit itself exclusively to Christian foundations and Christian language, if it is to speak to those outside its immediate circle.

180. This final chapter has already indicated the range and complexity of some of the means by which social values are generated and transmitted. The churches are one of these means. For their members they are a key part of the whole process. For those whose Christian allegiance is tenuous, the churches may nevertheless exert a welcome influence, albeit from a distance, by their public witness to unchanging standards of right and wrong. But the churches are also part of the process in the sense of themselves partaking deeply of the character of the society, whether national or international, to which they belong.

181. There is no such thing as a pure undiluted witness to the Gospel, uninfluenced by the context in which it is made, and there never has been, not even in New Testament times. Faith is always received within a particular society and a particular slice of history, and what it is possible to say and do in the name of faith is always to a greater or lesser extent conditioned by this setting. This is why it is foolish to imagine that the churches in Britain could in some sense stand over against the rest of British society, and address it as if they did not share its problems. This study has been written from within the problems. It has sought to approach them with criteria and insights which belong to the best in our society, rather than ones imposed upon it from outside.

182. Such an approach to the issues of our day from within their midst does not however exclude a distinctive Christian witness. In fact it can set the scene for it. A faith based on belief in God entering human life has to take seriously the complexities and ambiguities of this world,

the world in which that life was lived. And in turn implies that the witness, when given, should contain a distinctive element not only in its content but also in its style: definite but not shrill, at times exhorting though without self-righteousness, more often gentle, suggestive, seeking allies. It is not without relevance that Jesus taught in parables as much as in propositions.

183. The Christian tradition also contains strong lines which maintain that the human mind, unaided by special revelation, is at least in principle capable of attaining to the basic principles of a human morality such as are also to be found in the Judaeo-Christian Decalogue. The style appropriate to the churches has been described by Karl Rahner as '. . . morality without moralising. . . We are moralising if we expound norms of behaviour peevishly or pedantically, full of moral indignation at a world without morals, without really tracing them back to that innermost experience of man's nature which is the source of the so-called principles of natural law and which alone gives them binding force.'[1] As one contributor to this study has written, 'the role for the churches is not intensified moral intruction which provides pre-packaged answers, but sustained moral education'.[2]

184. This comment already takes us beyond questions about the style in which the churches should address the rest of society, to the question of what they should be saying to themselves and the style in which this should be said. The frequently repeated criticism that some churches talk only to themselves misses the point that what they say to themselves determines in some measure what they are, and that what they are has consequences for the wider society of which they form a part, whether by action or reaction.

185. There is a place, therefore, even in a study which has tried to avoid the in-language of a Christian group, for some direct statement to the constituency of fellow-Christians. The group which produced this study had no mandate to advise the churches as such, though it did benefit much from ecumenical membership. For that reason what follows is addressed primarily to the Church of England under whose auspices the group met.

---

[1] K. Rahner *The Shape of the Church to Come* (London, SCM Press, 1974) p.66.
[2] J. Mahoney 'Theological and Pastoral Reflections' in Abrams et al. *Values*, p.272.

186. The Church of England has historically been conscious of its involvement in English life and culture. It has been aware of its special responsibility to minister to the whole of that culture, a responsibility which in practical terms it has found increasingly difficult to fulfil in a rapidly changing society. Nevertheless it is still possible for it to witness to the need for the parts to be concerned about the whole. To fail to do so, to turn in on itself and rest content with becoming one minority grouping among others, would be to fail in its particular vocation, to fail in Christian vision, and to contribute to that polarisation and fragmentation of our society which has been highlighted as one of its major ills.

187. It has not been found possible, except in very general terms, to specify the values by which a society should live, still less to list a set of goals for our future society. But the danger of looking for over-simple answers to complex problems can be demonstrated. Narrowness of vision, vested interests, confrontational styles, unreflective polarisation and the distorting effects of the mass media, all these can make disputes, both genuine and artificial, seem irreconcilable, and diminish the chance of mutual enrichment through the recognition of differences. If mere confrontation is to be avoided, differences need to be contained within a moral framework, and it is clear that the quite widely held view that tolerance is all that is needed is dangerously misleading.

188. Tolerance itself needs a moral basis. Indeed the lines from many parts of the argument converge on the assertion that our country needs to rediscover its moral roots. This must entail strengthening the moral values derived from respect for persons and personal life, the enhancement of individual freedom, responsibility and equality, and the recognition that such personal life can only be developed, sustained and fulfilled in the kind of *koinonia* which this study has attempted to describe.

189. The extent to which some individuals lack such freedom in our present society, and some communities fall far short of this ideal, is daily well documented. Since our aim has been general reflection rather than specific recommendation, we have done no more than underline the deep social divisions, and the sense of injustice felt by those who have been marginalised by their lack of skill, lack of work, or simply by living in the wrong place or by suffering from some other general disability. There is no easy way of escaping these problems by seeking to remove from our society the element of competitiveness and its

consequences that some people will become the victims of change. But that makes it all the more important that such casualties are cared for – which is a moral as well as a social problem. Exploration of the notion of solidarity, and an overriding concern with personal dignity and worth, demand that we should think in terms of a society where opportunities of participation, or of finding new roles and ways of contributing, are more widely available than they are.

190. At a time when the demands of a complex society have to be met by increasing degrees of professionalisation, specialisation and bureaucracy, the relation between professional and voluntary organisations, including such major organisations as the churches themselves, is of crucial importance. The development of new styles of co-operation could be a means of diversifying skills and roles, thus enriching the total pattern of social interrelatedness.

191. In all these contexts the Church of England could play a vital part. Any Christian church, and especially a national one, courts particular dangers but it ought also to have special gifts, qualities and insights to bring to the issues this study has considered: breadth of vision, the ability to handle complexity and to live with polarities, moral concern rooted in basic principles rather than detailed prescriptions, wide pastoral contacts and commitments, a recognised place both in the voluntary sector and as an integral part of national life, a sense of responsibility for the whole nation constantly tempered by broader international and religious perspectives, a realistic appraisal of our human capacity to deceive ourselves and serve our own interests, a message of hope in the face of failure, cynicism and despair – all these and more. Insofar as the Church of England fails to do so, then it must address its message to itself at least as urgently as it addresses the nation. The Church should tackle its own problems as an example of how problems can and should be tackled.

192. Above all, the Church can speak with integrity about the unnecessary and destructive polarisations in our present society only if it can itself unite across dogmas and divisions around the person of Jesus. The Church of England's own need to find better ways of handling conflict is obvious. But internal unity is only a beginning. Ecumenism is not for the few and not for Christians only. For the sake of society as a whole all churches have to work at the problem of unity, freedom and community both separately and together. Then the search for human values will be that much more vigorous, and that much more rewarding and rewarded.

Conclusions

193. Britain is an old yet changing society, conscious of deficiencies about basic values. The interplay between different people and the values they hold is a complex one. This study illustrates that fact, time and time again. Unless this complexity is realised by those who call for far-ranging decisions to be taken, and by those who take such decisions, their policies and their actions will be damaging and will fail.

194. As people become more aware of the range of complexity and difference they may become embroiled in fruitless conflict, or else morally paralysed. Some basic core values which transcend surface differences therefore need to be identified and affirmed. The central value is that of 'persons in community' – the widely shared insight that persons are valuable in themselves, but only truly 'become themselves' in relationship with others.

195. The balance between values is often upset – there are many reasons in our society for conflicts to arise. This study looks at a number of such divisions and polarities. The idea of 'persons in community' helps in pinpointing places where the balance has broken down, and in probing more deeply the roots of conflict.

196. Among those who purvey values in our society are parents and children, teachers, media people, politicians and workers in voluntary organisations, and members of the churches. They all need to be constantly challenged. They should challenge themselves and they should expect challenge from others. They need to be made to show whether their actions and policies strengthen rather than weaken the core values on which our society should be based.

197. The churches are among the purveyors of values, so they must accept the same intensity of criticism, and be made to defend any claim that they are living by the values which they purvey. Their claims are higher than most so they need to be more self-critical than most, as agents of both stability and change.

Note of Reservation

by Sara Maitland

Although I worked with the working party for most of its existence I find myself, with regret, unable to put my name to the report. This is not because of specific disagreement with any one item of the content but because I am unable to accept the functionalist view of the Church which underlies the arguments presented here: I do not think that it is the duty of the Church to be 'the heart of a heartless world', to be the social glue of a society, but rather to change, to transform. From this perspective I do not feel happy putting my name to a report which does not, I feel, adequately stress the structural justice issues facing Britain today, both domestically and internationally. In particular this report is, for me, seriously inadequate in its account of class divisions, racism and sexism in our society.

GENERAL THEOLOGICAL SEMINARY NEW YORK

T3-BNI-536

IT TOOK A KILLER

"Are you an accurate shot?" Sebastian Hand asked Drew Claggett.

"I'm the best damned shot that ever lived," the accused killer bragged.

"Are you able to use a rifle and shotgun?"

"Both," Claggett declared.

"Can you also use a knife?"

"I know enough to get by," Claggett said. Then he frowned. "Judge, why are you asking me all this?"

"I want you to teach me how to use every conceivable type of weapon," Hand said. "I intend to kill four men after you finish your instruction. Do you have any problem with that?"

Claggett shook his head, left speechless by the judge's declaration to do murder. . . .

"Sebastian Hand is an exciting addition to frontier fiction. I hope we see more of him."
—George W. Proctor

⊘ SIGNET

(0451)

HOW THE WEST WAS WON

☐ **THE OUTSIDER by Frank Roderus.** Winner of the Spur Award! Leon Moses' life hung on his trigger finger. The odds were against him, but nobody was going to stop Leon from settling his well-earned spread. He was a black man who had to show a lot of folks that courage knew no color—that they'd have to stop his bullets before they stopped him. (156102—$2.95)

☐ **FAST HAND by Karl Lassiter.** Judge Sebastian Hand sentences the Thornberry gang to the gallows for rape. But when they escape and slaughter Hand's kin, the judge trades in his gavel for a gun, and suddenly he's judge, jury, and executioner all in one. (161106—$2.95)

☐ **THE BLOODY SANDS by E.Z. Woods.** Jess McClaren's dad owed his life to Joe Whitley, and now Whitley was at the end of his rope. Jess's dad was dead, and the father's debt was now the son's. So Jess arrived on a range where he could trust no one that wasn't dead to pay a dead man's debt with flaming guns.... (152921—$2.95)

☐ **GAMBLER'S GOLD by Doyle Trent.** J.B. Watts liked no-limit poker and no-nonsense women, and now he was primed for both. He had come across a cache of gold in the New Mexico desert, and he figured his luck had turned. His luck had turned, all right—for the worse. J.B. had bucked a lot of odds, but never odds like these ... with nobody drawing cards ... and everybody drawing guns.... (157206—$2.95)

☐ **GUNFIGHTER JORY by Milton Bass.** Jory draws fast and shoots straight when a crooked lawman stirs up a twister of terror. When Jory took on the job of cleaning up the town of Leesville, he didn't know it was split between a maverick marshal and a bribing banker. Jory was right in the middle— and the only way to lay down the law was to spell it in bullets.... (150538—$2.75)

Prices slightly higher in Canada

Buy them at your local bookstore or use this convenient coupon for ordering.

NEW AMERICAN LIBRARY
P.O. Box 999, Bergenfield, New Jersey 07621

Please send me the books I have checked above. I am enclosing $_____
(please add $1.00 to this order to cover postage and handling). Send check or money order—no cash or C.O.D.'s. Prices and numbers are subject to change without notice.

Name_____

Address_____

City _____ State _____ Zip Code _____

Allow 4-6 weeks for delivery.
This offer, prices and numbers are subject to change without notice.

FAST HAND

Karl Lassiter

A SIGNET BOOK

NEW AMERICAN LIBRARY

PUBLISHED BY
PENGUIN BOOKS CANADA LIMITED

PUBLISHER'S NOTE

This is a work of fiction. Names, characters, places, and incidents either are the product of the author's imagination or are used fictitiously, and any resemblance to actual persons, living or dead, events, or locales is entirely coincidental.

NAL BOOKS ARE AVAILABLE AT QUANTITY DISCOUNTS WHEN USED TO PROMOTE PRODUCTS OR SERVICES. FOR INFORMATION PLEASE WRITE TO PREMIUM MARKETING DIVISION, NEW AMERICAN LIBRARY, 1633 BROADWAY, NEW YORK, NEW YORK 10019.

Copyright © 1989 by Robert E. Vardaman

All rights reserved

First Printing, August, 1989

2 3 4 5 6 7 8 9

SIGNET TRADEMARK REG. U.S. PAT OFF AND FOREIGN COUNTRIES
REGISTERED TRADEMARK — MARCA REGISTRADA
HECHO EN WINNIPEG, CANADA

SIGNET, SIGNET CLASSIC, MENTOR, ONYX, PLUME, MERIDIAN and **NAL BOOKS** are published in Canada by Penguin Books Canada Limited, 2801 John Street, Markham, Ontario, L3R 1B4

PRINTED IN CANADA
COVER PRINTED IN U.S.A.

To my good friends and trail companions
Zach Wyatt and Clay Tanner

1

Sebastian Hand choked as the dust and soot came free in a large brown cloud as he brushed off his jacket. The train rumbled, clanked, and belched fire and black ash as it pulled away from the Ellsworth, Kansas, platform. He bent and picked up the two battered carpetbags holding their belongings.

"The town doesn't look like much, does it?" he asked his wife. From the expression on Laura Hand's pinched, sweating face, he knew she wished she were back in Chicago.

"Your brother said he'd meet us. I don't see Randolph anywhere." She pushed a dirty strand of dark hair back under her calico sunbonnet. Shifting impatiently from foot to foot, Laura peered over the heads of others on the crowded railroad platform as she looked for her brother-in-law.

"You know how it is with Randolph," said Hand. "He'd be late for his own funeral."

"Sebastian, please. Don't even joke about such things. Speak of them often enough and they come to pass. You know that."

Hand sighed. Moving from the genteel society of Chicago to the frontier had made his wife edgy. The railroad trip to St. Louis had been easy enough, but Laura had not withstood the riverboat trip down the Mississippi well and had been sick since boarding the Kansas Pacific Railway passenger car in Kansas City. The dust and soot from the engine had turned them as black as the porter.

"Brother! There you are! Over here!" A boisterous voice boomed and drowned out lesser sounds. Randolph Hand hurried from the stationmaster's office, pushing others aside as he hurried to meet them. "I thought I'd

7

missed you." He caught up Laura in a bear hug that almost cracked the small woman's ribs. She pushed back and smiled weakly at the rotund man.

"You gave us a minute's surprise," Hand said, shaking hands with his brother. "I thought you'd lured us to this lovely city and then abandoned us."

"Ellsworth doesn't look like much," Randolph Hand admitted, "but it will. There's growth in all directions. It needs a judge, Sebastian. It needs *you*."

"It's not every day I'm offered a district judgeship," said Hand. He had worked as a trial lawyer in Chicago for almost two years and had grown tired of it. He felt trapped, at a dead-end in a career that seemed destined to remain forever undistinguished. The money he earned was adequate to support him and Laura, but an intellectual pall had robbed him of any real enjoyment. Worse, he needed a new way to exercise his philosophical leanings.

He wasn't helping anyone. Those he represented were seldom innocent. They were also seldom guilty of more than violating picayune city ordinances. Hand looked along the dusty, narrow street, across the rough-planked boardwalks and rudely lettered signs and down to the muddy bank of the Smoky River. He had truly arrived at the frontier. No rounded edges here. Sharp, vital, dangerous. Problems needed solving here. Problems a judge could decide.

"The editor of the *Reporter* wants to talk with you before too long," Randolph said, linking arms with his brother and sister-in-law. "He's just trying to scoop the Abilene *Chronicle*. Forget about him for now. Let's get on out to my place. Frannie's spent the day cooking. You won't believe the spread she's prepared!"

"Looks as if you've been partaking of that fine home cooking more than you should," said Hand, glancing significantly at his brother's considerable paunch.

Randolph laughed and rested a meaty hand on top of it. "Being a shipping point for all that Texas beef makes meat prices rock-bottom here. Frannie's a right fine cook. The smartest thing I ever did was marrying her. You'll both like her. I'm sure of it." Randolph looked around as they walked to his rig, pointing to the many small cafés. "It's damned near impossible to find a place in town that doesn't serve up prime steaks."

"Other things of a far less palatable nature are served, also, I see," said Laura. She peered curiously at swinging doors leading into a saloon. The smell of stale beer and the sounds of boisterous laughter came from inside.

"That's part of the problem in Ellsworth," Randolph said. "We got a sheriff and an eager police force that wants to keep law and order, but it's just not that easy. The drovers come into town to blow off steam. It gets nasty sometimes."

"That wasn't what got me out here," said Hand. "You mentioned trouble between the homesteaders and the townspeople."

Randolph took their bags and heaved them into the rear of the buckboard. He patted the horse's head and fumbled in a watch pocket for a small lump of sugar. The horse nuzzled him wetly, then took it. A single quick gulp made the sugar vanish. Randolph shook his head to indicate that he had no more. The horse turned away, resigned to pulling three people out of town after having to bring in only one. The pay, a single lump of sugar, didn't seem worth it.

"There's that," Randolph admitted cautiously. "Sometimes it gets violent. Ellsworth has its share of trouble with the Texans, but the folks who live here year 'round are the real source of misery. Nobody'd want to give up the hotels and cafés and prosperity the beefs bring to Ellsworth—nobody except the farmers, who complain that the herds destroy their crops and that the cowboys shoot up their houses."

"Are they unable to restrain their animal instincts?" Laura asked.

"Dear, it's hard on the trail," explained Sebastian. "The drovers don't get paid much. They want to raise a little hell. We just can't allow them to do it at the expense of the homesteaders."

"Well said, brother. Let's hope you get the chance to rule on the herd laws."

"Herd laws?" asked Sebastian. He helped Laura into the buckboard.

She settled down gingerly on the hard seat. Seeing that

dust would be a continual problem on the way to Randolph's house, she daintily held a handkerchief over her nose and mouth.

"It has to do with grazing rights. The homesteaders have been trying to get herd laws enacted requiring fences and control on the beefs. Those wanting to graze across the prairie are opposed to such laws, of course. Along with them are the town merchants. The drovers don't cotton much to the notion, and what they don't like, the merchants don't either."

Sebastian Hand smiled as he studied the buildings slowly going past him. This was the type of place where he could make a difference. Disputes had to be settled peacefully, according to law. A strong judge could turn Ellsworth and its violent ways into a civilized city rivaling Chicago.

He cringed as a saloon door blasted outward. A heavy-set cowboy tumbled into the street, flat on his back. The man shook his head and started to rise from the muddy street. A tall, thin man with a sawed-off shotgun stood in the doorway. Hand grabbed his brother's arm and indicated the deadly tableau.

"Don't let it worry you," Randolph said easily. "That's just old Jake throwing out a rowdy cowhand. He hasn't killed anybody in well nigh a month now." He laughed at his small joke and used the reins to get his horse moving faster.

Hand looked at his wife. She had turned deathly pale behind the handkerchief. He started to comfort her, but she moved away. He settled down on the hard bench seat and tried to ride out the jolts to his backside caused by the rough, pothole-ridden dirt road and the lack of decent springs on the buckboard. Ellsworth wasn't paradise, but it might be one day.

"There's Frannie now!" Randolph Hand urged the horse to work even harder getting up the small incline leading to the simple whitewashed frame house. "She'll have a nice, cool drink waiting for us, you wait and see."

Laura coughed into her handkerchief. She turned cold brown eyes on her husband, accusing him of unspecified crimes. They had been married four years. In that time, he had learned to interpret her subtler signals. There was nothing roundabout her stare now. She openly indicted him for dragging her to this godforsaken wilderness so far from her native Chicago.

Hand stood and stared across the prairie from this vantage. The land was barren, empty and dry this spring of 1876. Kansas has endured drought and even famine before. Recovery had been swift because of the spirit of the people settling here. He admired that, even as he wondered how anyone could live off this dusty plain that stretched level and empty to the horizon.

Randolph!'' exclaimed Laura. ''Why didn't you tell us?''

Hand looked around to see what had brought his wife out of her bad temper. For several seconds he didn't understand. Then he saw the broad grin on his brother's face and the prominent bulge of Frannie Hand's belly.

''Going to be a son, yes, sir,'' Randolph Hand declared. ''He's due about this time next month.''

''Congratulations!'' Sebastian Hand jumped down, helped Laura to the ground, and then pounded his brother on the shoulder. He turned to the pregnant woman and kissed her on the cheek. ''Let's hope it's a girl,'' he said to Frannie. ''Dealing with Randolph is hard enough. Having a miniature version around aping him would be too much.''

''Do come inside. It's hot and getting hotter. By noontime in Kansas it's unbearable. I've made up some of my special lemonade. Don't have any ice, but the lemonade's good anyway.'' Frannie and Laura went inside the clapboard house to find the promised liquid, leaving the men to tend to horse and buckboard.

''Surely am glad you saw fit to take the job, Sebastian,'' said Randolph as he curried the horse. ''Ellsworth needs law brought to it.''

''You said that the nearest judge was over in Abilene. That's not more than sixty miles off. I'm not disputing the need, but paying a judge looks to be a strain for the town.''

Randolph nodded. He led the horse into a stall and fastened a simple rope across the front to keep the horse from straying. "Let's walk a spell and talk. There's plenty of time for you to oh and ah over Frannie's condition."

"You should have told us."

"Wanted it to be a surprise. And I didn't want to think that was what got you out here."

Sebastian Hand stared at his brother and wondered at his real motives for wrangling the judgeship. They had always gotten on well, but it had been more than six years since Hand had seen Randolph. The older brother had taken it into his head that there was a fortune to be made in Kansas. Together with four others, Randolph had started a mercantile store in Kansas City. It had prospered, and Hand had heard of even more opportunity at the western terminus of the Kansas Pacific Railway. Hand was certain that Randolph had flourished here, as well. The house differed from so many of the half-buried sod huts Hand had seen from the train as they came to Ellsworth.

"Tell me about the town," he said. "How's your store doing?"

"Since the railroad finished the link with Denver, we've done respectably well. Nothing like it was in Kansas City, but we're not hurting any." Randolph took a deep breath. "There's more, Sebastian."

"Why draw it out? Tell me."

"I can see that Laura isn't taking kindly to you dragging her to the edge of the world. Chicago society always appealed to her. I always saw that. Can't rightly understand it. Too many stuffed shirts for my taste. But I can appreciate it."

"She knows what it means to me being offered a judgeship. In Chicago there was no hope of it. Politics dictated differently."

Randolph nodded as he stared out across the sunbaked prairie. "It's better out here. Not much at times. The Grange is controlled by the Republicans and no one who isn't approved gets squat."

"Being appointed judge might come from a political decision," said Hand, "but *being* judge can't be."

"Fine words. Just like you, brother. And I'm happy to hear them. Ellsworth is dying out. It doesn't look it now, but it's true. Dodge City, Abilene, the other towns are taking away the Texas drovers. The railroad helps. Fact is, it's about all that's keeping Ellsworth going.''

"The drought is hurting the farmers, isn't it?''

"The Panic of '73 well nigh eliminated most of them. They came back when aid from the East poured in. That didn't set well with many of these proud folks, though.''

"Handouts aren't what they want," agreed Hand.

"They want justice, Sebastian. They want to live good lives without having cattle trampling their fields and eating their silage. They want a town where their families can go without the women being raped and the children accidentally shot in gunfights between drunks. They want freedom from disease brought up from Texas.'' Randolph spat and wiped his mouth before continuing. "We've been real lucky this year. So far, there hasn't been any Texas fever.''

"Splenic fever? From ticks?''

"That's not been showed," Randolph said. "Most of the folks in these parts want a complete quarantine put on the beefs coming in from the south for at least six months to keep their own dairy stock from catching the fever.''

Sebastian Hand's thoughts turned to legal decisions about open range and grazing privileges, contagious diseases, quarantine, and the more general rules of acceptable public behavior. He wondered how many men had been killed in hotheaded, thoughtless brawls in Ellsworth's many saloons and bawdy houses catering to the Texas drovers. Too many, he guessed.

"The ladies are expecting us inside," said Randolph. He hitched up his trousers and started for the house. His brother stared out across the land and saw a curious beauty to it, in spite of the way nature had ravaged it with blistering heat and meager spring thundershowers. Sere grass waved in the hot wind, and in the far distance a few brown specks that might be cows moved, oblivious to the hammer of the sun's burning intensity.

"Sebastian, you coming? I got a passel of boxes for you. I reckon they must be your law books. They arrived days ago.''

"My books!'' The thought of again running his fingers over the finely grained leather bindings confirmed what he already knew. He *wanted* to be judge in this savage land. And by all that was holy, he'd be a good judge.

Sebastian Hand slipped into the coolness of his brother's house and quickly lost himself in acquainting himself with a sister-in-law he'd never met and the prospect of being an uncle.

And judge. Always that, he kept reminding himself proudly. Always that.

2

Sebastian Hand sat upright in the straight-backed, hard wood chair and stared incredulously at the defendant. He couldn't believe he was trying such a case.

He shook his head sadly. Only in Ellsworth, Kansas, could such a dispute turn into bloodshed.

"I tell you, Yer Honor, he's a cold-blooded killer. He done shot up my store, then he tried to kill me."

"Order," Hand said, rapping the gavel. "No one has been killed. This is a civil matter. Did you or did you not pay Mr. Mueller for the boots he made?" Hand stared at the Texas drover.

The man wrung the brim of his battered brown hat in his hands and looked as if he would knead the entire hat like a mound of bread dough. "Your Honor, it ain't like that. He made the boots. See?" The cowboy stuck out his foot. The high-topped, red-bordered boot had a Lone Star emblem set in the side. "They don't fit worth a shit."

"Order," rapped Hand. "There will be decorum in this court. You're saying the boots don't fit and you won't pay. Is that it?"

"Reckon so, Your Honor." The cowboy shuffled around a bit and then added. "I paid that bastard twenty dollars for 'em, too."

"Mr. Mueller, your store, the Sign of the Big Boot, has been in business for several years."

"I have, Judge Hand, and I'm proud of our reputation. We make more boots for drovers than any other store in Ellsworth."

"Is it possible you gave this gentleman the wrong pair?" Hand stared hard at Mueller. The hardheaded German started to protest, then subsided.

"There might have been other boots that looked like

15

those.'' Mueller's admission came grudgingly. He might be obstinate, but he wasn't stupid. Hand had provided a way for everyone to settle the dispute honorably.

"Then it is decided. You will give this gentleman another pair of boots that fit to his satisfaction.'' The drover smiled from ear to ear. The smile faded when Hand added, "And you, sir, will pay Mr. Mueller an additional fifteen dollars for damage done to his store. *And* court costs of two dollars.''

"But—''

Hand rapped his gavel smartly and cut off the cowboy's protests. "Court adjourned.''

He rose and left before an argument could break out. Hand felt weary to the bone. He had been on the Ellsworth bench for almost a week and had heard nothing but trivial cases—cases not much different from those he had represented back in Chicago. In a way, he knew he should be thankful. Violence erupted routinely in Abilene and Wichita courts when unpopular decisions were issued. Hand glanced over his shoulder at the sleepy-eyed bailiff and knew any such outburst in his court would go unchecked.

"Sebastian, have time for lunch?''

"Hello, Randolph. Cheated any cowboys today?'' He shook hands with his brother.

"Haven't seen any in to rob them blind. Send a few my way. I heard how you stood up for John Mueller. Nobody's got a gripe coming to them the way you handled it.''

Hand brushed it off. "I don't want the Texans getting riled. They may be the lifeblood of commerce for this town, but they're also a stick of dynamite with its fuse lit.''

"You're going to have to do something about the police,'' said Randolph. "Happy Jack is harassing the Texans again. It's not going to be long before one of them shoots him in the back.'' Randolph snorted and then spat into the dusty street. "If something's not done about Morco, *I* may shoot the son of a bitch in the back.''

"I've spoken with Sheriff Whitney,'' said Hand, "and he can't or won't keep Happy Jack on a leash. The man's a house afire when it comes to patrolling the streets. I'll give him that. But you're right, Randolph. The man doesn't have a lick of sense when it comes to dealing with the drovers."

"He well nigh ran one out of my store the other day. Claimed he saw the Texan spit on the sidewalk." Randolph spat again. "Hell, spitting adds to the water in the air. We need it this year."

"How's business, other than this?"

"Can't complain. We're on our way to doing another hundred-thousand-dollar year in supplies for the drovers and groceries for the homesteaders. All I have to do is keep them separated when they're in the store at the same time, and I can sell to both."

Sebastian Hand walked along, thinking hard. Happy Jack Morco had been hired on as a policeman when James Miller defeated the incumbent Jim Gore for mayor. The proprietor of the Drovers Cottage Hotel had been inclined to look the other way when his clients got into trouble. Miller took a more forceful stand and insisted on keeping the high spirits of the cowboys in check. To that end, he had hired four extra policemen to aid Sheriff Whitney. John "Happy Jack" Morco was the most vicious of the anti-Texas element in Ellsworth. At every turn he arrested drovers on trifling violations of the city ordinances.

Ellsworth was only a third-class town by Kansas law. That meant it could put a police force out to keep order, and it could deputize any able-bodied man between eighteen and fifty if a posse was needed. Hand saw this as an improvement over the lynch law that had reigned supreme before 1869.

It also polarized the power groups in town. As more homesteaders settled around Fort Harker to the south along the Smoky River, they insisted on keeping the Texas longhorns out of their fields and the cowboys out of the places of business they patronized. Although the homesteaders provided 'round-the-year business, the summer months, when the drives ended and the beefs were penned and waiting for shipment to St. Louis and Chicago, brought hundreds of thousands of dollars of much-needed cash into the town.

Not only did the cowboys spend money in stores such

as Randolph Hand's General Store and Godsoll's Fancy and Staple Goods of All Kinds store, they bought boots from John Mueller and stayed in Drovers Cottage and the other three hotels along South Main Street—and they drank like fish. Hand heaved a deep sigh. If he could moderate the cowboys' intake of intoxicating beverages at the ten saloons, he could cut Ellsworth's crime by three-quarters.

If he could get rid of Happy Jack, he might be able to stop the other quarter. The man incited more than he cured in the way of crime.

"I'll have to talk to the sheriff again. He might be able to assign Morco to some other beat."

"Don't hold your breath, brother," said Randolph. "We've been after Whitney for months to do just that. He won't listen. I think he's afraid of his own deputy."

Sebastian Hand nodded. He could believe it. There was a wildness in Morco's eye that he associated with madness. When the man had introduced himself to Laura, Hand had wanted to interpose himself and protect her.

"The Central Café has a special on stew," said Randolph. "I surely do recommend it. Miz Parsons has been making it since I got to town, and it's better than anything I ever got in Chicago."

"That's going some. But from the look of your belly hanging out, you know good food. Doesn't Frannie feed you enough that you have to go looking for other folks' cooking?"

"She's a good wife," Randolph said soberly. "Becoming a father is about the best thing that's happened to me. When are you and Laura planning on starting a family? You've been married a goodly time now."

"We've been trying," said Hand. "We've just not been blessed yet. But we will."

"All things come in time," said Randolph.

They sat down at a table near the window. From his vantage point, Hand saw the railroad depot and the edge of the wooden awning of Jerome Beebe's Mercantile House. Everything in Ellsworth revolved around the cattle trade. Without it, the homesteaders surrounding the town could never keep Ellsworth alive. The weather had taken a bad turn for two years and worried rumors of

Rocky Mountain locusts swirling down from the mountains to the west worried everyone, town merchant and farmer alike.

But it was the longhorn that kept Ellsworth thriving. The real threat of the locust wasn't in destroying crops. If the insects devoured the sere grass, the cattle penned for fattening before shipment back East would go hungry. That meant everyone went hungry.

"It hasn't been like I thought here," said Sebastian Hand. "I feel as if I'm sitting on the lid of a big cast-iron pot and someone's lit the fire under the pot."

"Getting too hot for you?" asked his brother. Plates of savory stew and hard black bread were placed in front of them. Randolph dived into the meal with a startling gusto. It looked as if he hadn't eaten in weeks.

"It's not hot enough," said Hand. He tried to put his chaotic thoughts into words. "I want to get things right here. I want to solve Ellsworth's problems. Heaven alone knows there are issues aplenty to litigate. But no one's brought them forward. Things are going to erupt."

"Nobody wants that," agreed Randolph. "Fact is, people are still used to settling disputes without recourse to the law. Look at them. Chances are neither will ever call for the sheriff. They'd rather shoot it out."

When he saw what his brother meant, Sebastian Hand shot to his feet and raced from the restaurant. Two cowboys stood in the street, hands on their six-shooters and ready to draw. They had reached the point of shouting insults at each other. In another few seconds one would run out of indignities to heap on the other and would pull his pistol.

"Stop!" yelled Hand. "I'm the judge in Ellsworth and I won't have you gunning each other down in the streets of this town."

"What?" roared one, a man with a wilted handlebar mustache and a deep, pulsing pink scar over his left eye. "Who'n the bloody hell do you think you are taking his side?"

"I'm not taking anyone's side," said Hand, walking up to the Texas drover. He smelled the liquor on the man's heavy breath. The cowboy took a half-step back and curled his fingers around his gun butt, ready to draw on Hand.

"I'm unarmed," Hand said, pulling away the tails of his coat to show he didn't wear a holster. "You'll hang if you gun me down."

"You really the judge in these parts?" the man asked, his voice slurred. He wobbled now, the cheap whiskey he'd drunk finally taking a full toll on him.

"I am." Hand glanced at the other cowboy. This one showed more sense—and sobriety. He held his hands in front of his chest and backed off, not wanting trouble. When he figured he was out of range, he turned and ran.

"Never shot a judge before," the drunken drover said.

"You're not going to now, either," Hand said, advancing slowly.

"For Christ's sake, Sebastian, be careful. That's Ben Thornberry. He'd as soon shoot you as look at you."

Sebastian Hand ignored his brother. He had faced down vicious dogs in his day. To show any fear, to be distracted for even an instant, would spell death.

"Give me your pistol. I'll give it to the sheriff. You can get it there later."

"You're not funnin' me, are you, Judge?" Ben Thornberry wobbled even more. "You mean it when you say you'd give it back?"

"Sheriff Whitney will have it." Hand reached out and closed his fingers around the other man's wrist. He tightened his grip just enough to throw Thornberry off balance. As the cowboy staggered, Hand plucked the six-shooter from his grasp.

"Sebastian!" cried his brother. "That was a damned-fool thing to do. The Thornberrys got a reputation."

"There's a deputy. Give him this. Have the sheriff keep the six-shooter until Mr. Thornberry is sober and able to account for his behavior. Now, Randolph, let's get back to lunch. I have to hear another case this afternoon."

Hand went in and collapsed into the chair, realizing what he had just done. His legs suddenly turned to damp string. Trying to pick up his fork and finish his stew, he found that his hand shook too hard. He had never thought of himself as a physically brave man. The close brush with death had been unintentional on his part. He hadn't considered the consequences; he had simply acted to preserve the law.

Randolph entered the restaurant and sat across from his brother. "I gave Thornberry's pistol to the deputy. That coward was standing in the doorway of Zachariah's Funeral Parlor watching the whole thing. He didn't once make a move to help you. I ought to cut his ears off!"

"Someone has to keep the peace in Ellsworth," Hand said, his voice strong. His racing heart slowed and the impact of what he'd done passed. He looked sharply at his brother. "Don't go telling Laura about this. She has no need to know."

Randolph shook his head, eyes wide as if seeing a new side to his brother.

"You're going to need more grit than that, Hand," came a gruff voice. "You *are* hearing the Connelly case?"

Hand turned and stared at the tall, weather-beaten man standing beside his table. The wide stance, the squared shoulders, and the set jaw showed more belligerence than was called for.

"You have the advantage, sir. You know my name. Who might you be?" Hand looked up at the man and wondered if this simple question would cause him to strike out. He had finished with Thornberry and wanted only a chance to finish his meal and try to ease some of the tension still knotting his shoulders.

"I'm George Hindes." The mans jaw jutted out and pulled the already dry, taut skin even tighter. It reminded Hand of a leather drumhead. The walnut hue to the sun-tanned face showed that the cowboy had spent a great deal of time outdoors. From his clothing Hand knew he was a drover—and one who was well-off. Silver ornaments dotted his belt and hat band and the ornately hand-tooled gun belt had cost more than most cowboys would earn over a three-month drive.

"You own a herd?"

"The best damned herd what ever came out of Texas," Hindes said. "And that sodbusting jackass Connelly ain't going to tell me my beefs are sick. Spanish fever, my sainted aunt!" Hindes' voice rose to a pitch that drew everyone's attention. "Those longhorns are clean. Not a sick cow in the whole damned herd, and you're going to tell these fools that. I can just as easy take my herd over to Wichita and ship from there."

"They won't take sick cows, either, Hindes," came a new voice. Hand leaned back in his chair and peered past the cattleman. "You don't rule the roost like you used to. The Texas fever scares too many of us. We don't want it getting to our dairy cows."

"You, you're the sniveling pantywaist who's trying to pen up my cows for six months!" Hindes spun on the portly newcomer and reached out to throttle the man, who had to be Connelly.

Hand started to intervene but didn't have to. Sheriff Whitney entered the restaurant and drew his six-shooter. The sound of the pistol cocking caused a silence to fall over the room.

"That's more like it, gents," said Whitney. "You got disputes, you take 'em up before Judge Hand—in court. You don't prejudice your case while he's eating his lunch. Now, the pair of you get the hell out or I'll run you both in for disturbing the peace."

"We're not disturbing the peace, Sheriff," protested the portly Connelly.

"You're disturbin' *my* peace. In Ellsworth that's reason enough to run you in for twenty-four hours."

Both Hindes and Connelly grumbled but left.

"Thank you, Sheriff," said Randolph. "That was getting out of control quickly." He took out a handkerchief and wiped the sweat from his forehead.

The sheriff ignored Randolph. He faced the judge and said in a menacing tone, "You don't go doin' my job, Judge. Never. I gave Thornberry back his six-shooter since you didn't have any cause to take it from him."

"Sheriff Whitney, the man was drunk and disorderly in public. He threatened another man. I performed my duty as a citizen. Your deputy stood by and watched."

"Judge, you're not listenin' too hard. Don't go gettin' in my way. I don't like it—and you won't, neither, if you keep doing this." The lawman spun and stalked from the restaurant.

"Inhospitable cuss, isn't he?" muttered Randolph.

"I'm beginning to understand the problems facing Ellsworth," said Sebastian Hand. He turned back to his cold stew, his appetite gone. What was he going to tell Laura?

3

"It's what I came to Ellsworth for, Laura. I feel . . . great!" Hand couldn't put into words the thrill he had experienced as he heard the opening arguments in the Connelly-Hindes case. He leaned forward, arms on the table. His intensity made Laura stiffen slightly.

"You're happy to be hearing a case about some hideous cattle disease?" Her tone carried both shock and surprise. Seldom had she seen her husband this animated. It lay beyond her understanding to determine the true cause. In Chicago he had been listless much of the time and dissatisfied with his law practice. She could understand that. She failed to grasp the importance of a civil lawsuit having to do with tick-spawned splenic fever.

"I am!"

"Why, Sebastian? It doesn't make any sense to me."

"This is the heart of the problem with Ellsworth and other cow towns like it. The farmers and drovers are always at one another's throats. They should learn to work together. Ellsworth can't exist without the influx of cattle money. Randolph said he makes more than a hundred thousand dollars a year off the Texans. He uses some of the profit to sell more cheaply to the homesteaders. In a way, the homesteaders are profiting from the cattle trade."

"They might be profiting, but all you're doing is stepping in front of drink-crazed cowboys."

"Where did you hear that?"

"Sebastian, nothing is secret in this town. There are only about six hundred people here, and gossip travels fast. Why did you try to face down a drunken cowboy?"

He looked sheepish, almost like a small boy caught doing a forbidden act.

"It just happened. I never even thought about what might happen if he drew and fired. I just walked over to him and ordered him to give me his pistol. He did."

"You could have been killed," she accused.

"It didn't seem likely at the time. I just never thought about it. Afterward, I was frightened. Isn't that strange? Facing the man, I was as calm as if I was sitting in my own home and reading. When it was all over, I shook like an elm leaf."

"Promise me you'll let the sheriff handle such disagreeable men in the future. It is his job, not yours." Laura stared at her husband and saw that he was genuinely perplexed at his own behavior. This was another quirk in her husband's deportment that had come out since they'd moved to Kansas. And she didn't like it, either.

Laura looked around the small house and shuddered. It was so different from the modest house they'd enjoyed after their marriage in Chicago. They had not been rich, but they had survived.

"I don't like living with your brother and sister-in-law," she said suddenly.

"What? Oh, that's nothing to worry over, Laura. We're having a house built at the edge of town. I'm making more money than the sheriff. We can afford it."

"That's not the point, Sebastian." She looked at him, her brown eyes boring into him. "How much *are* you making? What is it worth to listen to odious details of sick cows all day?"

"Sheriff Whitney is paid a hundred fifty a month. I'm getting two twenty-five. I know that doesn't sound like a princely sum, but it's more than I made in Chicago."

"And you're a judge."

"I can make a difference, Laura. *That's* what makes this so good."

She shook her head. Nothing made coming to the frontier good. The weather had remained unrelentingly hot and dry. She and Frannie had to haul water from a tributary to the Smoky River because the rain-fed cisterns were dry. Carrying the heavy jugs up the steep hill from the creek wore her down. She wasn't a frail hothouse flower, but there ought to be a better way to fetch water. There was so much else that had to be done.

And with Frannie pregnant, much of the heavier work fell on Laura's shoulders.

"You're not going to make a difference to any of them," she said, trying to keep back the bitterness she felt. She saw the shock on her husband's face and knew she'd failed.

"I can," he said softly.

"This Texan will never come back to Ellsworth if you decide against him. And we have to live with Mr. Connelly the year 'round. His farm isn't two miles down the road from here. What are we going to do if you decide in the drover's favor?"

"I'll be fair. These are the important decisions. The herd law has never been enforced, but I might be able to strike a fair compromise with the cattlemen because I don't think the local fear of Texas fever is justified."

"You are already biased in favor of the townspeople," Laura accused. "You're calling it Texas fever, just like they do. The drovers call it Spanish fever. And neither of those is the proper name."

"Splenic fever," Hand corrected himself. "You know what I'm getting at. They waste time and money arguing. I can settle those arguments. Connelly isn't really afraid of the fever. He wants Hindes to keep his cattle from destroying his fields."

"There's going to be little enough for anyone because of this drought." Laura wiped at the sweat beading her forehead. She heaved a deep sigh. "I'm glad you're happy here, Sebastian."

He stared at her for a moment before saying, "You're not? You want to return to Chicago?"

"No, Sebastian, I want to be with you. You're more important than where we are. But I do so wish the heat would break. Living in an oven is enough to wear down a body."

He went around the table and hugged his wife. She turned her lips upward to him. He kissed her soundly.

"I knew there was a reason I married you," he said.

"You're more compassionate and possess more wisdom than I'll ever have. You ought to be the judge."

Laura pushed away and laughed. "Don't be ridiculous, Sebastian. A woman could never be a judge. No one would ever listen. I've got to get back to work."

He grabbed her arm and kept her from leaving. Solemnly, he said, "It'll get better. The weather is unusual this year, and we won't be staying with Randolph much longer. You'll like the new house. I'll take you by to see it this evening when it's cooler."

"I'd like that, Sebastian." She pressed her face against his chest, then broke away. "It's *so* hot."

He had to agree. The sun beat down outside with relentless fury. Inside his courtroom it would get even hotter when Connelly and Hindes started arguing.

Sebastian Hand wiped the sweat from his face with a large blue-and-white bandanna. He looked around to see if anyone noticed this awkward, undignified gesture. It hardly seemed fitting for a black-robed judge to be so discomfited by the heat, but he was.

No one noticed. The others in the courtroom were sweating, too. Hand heaved a sigh of relief and looked at the notes in front of him. A few droplets of sweat had fallen to wrinkle the paper. He worked through the smudged ink stains under the perspiration. His mouth had turned to cotton. He motioned to his bailiff.

"Before we get down to the case, can I get a drink of water?"

"Not much water around, Judge," the portly bailiff said. "Reckon I can get over to Murgatroyd's Saloon and find a pint of whiskey."

"No!" Hand exclaimed. Those assembled in the courtroom stared at him for his outburst. He took a deep breath and then said quietly, "There will be no liquor in this court. It befouls the brain and robs everyone of good judgment."

"If'n you say so, Judge," the bailiff allowed. "Water's mighty scarce right now. It's easier to find whiskey in Ellsworth than a good drink of water."

"Try," urged Hand. He turned back to the documents in front of him. Both sides had lawyers, but it wasn't obvious from the poor grammar and the faulty logic in both briefs. Hand looked up and gestured. The attorneys came to the bench.

"Before we start," Hand said, "do either of you want more time to rework your case?" He looked expectantly from one man to the other. Connelly's lawyer was dressed as if he was as down on his luck as most of the homesteaders. Hindes' lawyer was decked out like a strutting peacock Mississippi riverboat gambler, complete with velvet tabs on the collar of his bright-green coat and a threadbare brocade vest that still showed signs of what he had eaten for lunch.

"I'm ready to present my client's case, Your Honor," said Hindes' lawyer. "The only objection there can possibly be to bringing those beefs into Ellsworth lies in Mr. Connelly not getting the feed-lot fees for them. Greed, Your Honor, it is greed and nothing more that lies behind this case."

"I protest," shouted the other man. His eyes widened and he balled his fists.

Hand rapped smartly with his gavel. This was going to be a difficult afternoon—and it had nothing to do with the merits of the case. The contentious lawyers depended solely on loud voices to make their point. Neither had bothered to cite a single relevant precedent for Hand to rule on.

"Gentlemen, please. Let's get going. It's too hot to draw this out all afternoon."

But the case did last through the day. Hand's bailiff found a pitcher of water and brought it for the thirsty judge. An hour's diatribe by Connelly's lawyer saw the pitcher emptied—and Hand felt even more drained. By the time the drover's lawyer had finished poor-mouthing both Connelly and his legal representation, the sun was setting.

"There's no reason to continue this tomorrow," said Hand, rapping his gavel to quiet the court. They had drowsed through the heat of the afternoon. Many had left. A few had returned to hear his verdict in the case.

"You gonna keep those damned diseased cows off my land, Judge Hand?" asked Connelly. "I'll kill them if I catch 'em eating my crops and giving Texas fever to any of my dairy stock.''

Hand wondered if Connelly meant the cattle or the drovers. It didn't matter. Hindes' lawyer shot to his feet to respond.

"There's no Spanish fever among the cattle. Examine them. You'll find every damned one of the longhorns free of disease, Judge. It's only men like Connelly who are afraid of progress that prevent the beefs from being brought into Ellsworth and shipped to the East.''

Hand rapped his gavel for the final time, he hoped. "I have the facts in this case. We're all tired, but it is obvious to me that no veterinarian has been able to give good reason to quarantine the longhorns.''

Hindes and his lawyer slapped each other on the back. Connelly's face clouded with harsh anger.

"However, there is no reason not to enforce the herd laws that have been passed.''

Hand's pronouncement caused a silence to descend over the room.

"What's that mean, Your Honor?'' asked Connelly's lawyer.

"It means that Mr. Hindes can bring his cattle into Ellsworth for shipment on the Kansas Pacific Railway, but he may not cross Mr. Connelly's land without permission.''

"I won't give it,'' shouted the homesteader. "Those cows of his are sick!''

"There is no indication that the cows carry splenic fever.''

"You mean to tell me I got to swing way south of town, out past Fort Harker, and ford the river before I can get my cattle to the railhead across that damned street?'' asked Hindes. "That'll take an extra day of travel. More! The cows will be starving to death. And my trail hands won't take kindly to the delay getting into town, neither.''

"There are commercial feed lots available for your beefs, sir, if you think they need fattening before shipment,'' said Hand. "I commend you to any number of them in Ellsworth. The Reverend Essick operates such a service, as does Mr. King and one or two others. All are reputable.''

''They'll rob me of any profit I might have made off this drive,'' grumbled Hindes. ''This is theft. You Ellsworthites are all in cahoots. You mean to rob us blind. You won't get away with this! There are other towns. Dodge City wants us. We don't have to take this from you!''

''Mr. Hindes, I'll ignore your outburst—this time. As to moving your herd to Dodge City, go on.''

Hand saw his brother in the rear of the courtroom shaking his head and gesturing. He knew what bothered Randolph about his words. Ellsworth—and Randolph Hand—needed the flood of money offered by the Texas cattlemen. Telling them to take their herds to rival cattle towns such as the upstart Dodge City didn't set well with any of the local merchants.

''I will. I'll do that very thing, Judge,'' declared Hindes. The drover stood defiantly for a moment as his lawyer tugged at his sleeve and whispered urgently.

Hand tried not to smile. He knew what was passing between the men. If Hindes took the cattle to another town, it meant added days on the trail—and the trail was already littered with the carcasses of dead cows. There wasn't enough grass to support a full-sized herd of longhorns, not with the weather as dry as it was. Even more difficult to find would be water. The sixty miles to Abilene lacked water except for homesteaders' stock ponds.

Getting to Dodge City would be even more difficult. Hindes would lose most of his herd. When he lost that many, he imperiled his lawyer's fee.

''Uh, Judge Hand, could we approach the bench for a moment?'' asked the lawyer. ''We got to smooth out some of this misunderstanding before it gets everyone into a stew.''

''I'm already stewing,'' said Hand. Impatiently, he motioned all parties to approach the bench.

''We can't afford to lose any more of the 'horns,'' said Hindes, almost pleading. He had changed his tone drastically. ''If we agree to your terms, can we still bring them into Ellsworth?''

''You are most welcome to.'' Hand turned to Connelly

and said, "There's a quarter section of your land between Mr. Hindes herd and the railhead."

"The Texas fever," muttered Connelly. "Don't want it infecting my dairy stock."

"There is no danger, Mr. Connelly," Hand assured him. "Ticks cause the fever."

"Never been proved," the homesteader grumbled.

"If Mr. Hindes paid you for portage across your land—and guaranteed to replace any of your stock lost to splenic fever—would you consent to allow him to use your land?"

"He'd have to pay for any of my milk cows that died from the fever?" Connelly peered at the drover, his eyes narrowed. "He'd be long gone before the cows died."

"Mr. Connelly has four head of cattle," Hand said. "Mr. Hindes, will you place the sum of one hundred dollars in escrow in the Ellsworth National Bank for the term of one year?"

"You mean I can't get my money for a full year?"

"When you return to Ellsworth with your herd next year, the money will be yours—unless Mr. Connelly's cattle need to be replaced."

"There's no fever among my cattle."

"Then you'll get your escrow back in one year."

"Ahem," cut in Hindes' lawyer, clearing his throat loudly. "Allow me to offer another suggestion. Release the money after six months, and I will wire it my client."

Hand saw that this was satisfactory to the cattleman. He got a night's grazing on Connelly's land, Connelly got paid for it, and the bank held insurance money against an outbreak of splenic fever. Hand ordered the two lawyers to draw up papers according to the terms he had outlined. A small smile crossed his lips when he saw the two men—homesteader and drover—shake hands before they left the courtroom.

He had averted violence between the two factions—and more. He had brought them into agreement where each thought he had the best of the deal.

Sebastian Hand went back to his brother's house with the feeling that he had done a good day's work.

4

"It's coming right along, Laura. We'll be able to move in within the week." Sebastian Hand stood back and stared with pride at the house that would soon be theirs. The walls had gone up and the rafters stuck out, needing the finishing touch of a real roof. Getting the wood for the house had been costly, but the town of Ellsworth had insisted on it. Hand was glad now that he had not pressed the matter and demanded less elegant quarters.

Sod huts dug halfway into the ground might be cool in the summer and warm in the winter, but the dirt floors, the walls, and the ceiling were depressing. His wife had recoiled in horror the first time she had seen one. He thought she would have boarded the first train for Chicago if they'd been forced to live in one.

"It's as good as Randolph's," she said hesitantly.

"It'll be better, once we get settled. Randolph has said we can order furniture from back East. He knows several good carpenters around Ellsworth who might be able to make what we need, too."

"There's no lumber here," Laura said without inflection. "I miss the trees. I miss the water. Looking out over Lake Michigan always soothed me."

"You said it frightened you. The storms that came across the lake were always the worst of the winter," Hand reminded her. Even as the words left his lips, he knew logic wasn't what Laura wanted. She pined for Chicago and the home she had known all her life. It was difficult for him to communicate to her the excitement he got from sitting on the Ellsworth bench and being a presiding judge.

He tried to put it all straight in his own mind and found that he couldn't. "Excitement" wasn't the exact word he sought to describe the feelings of contentment, of satisfaction, of belonging to a community. The whole time they had lived in Chicago he had never considered himself part of that society. He had been an outsider looking in. Ellsworth had opened its collective arms and welcomed him.

He was saddened that Laura did not think of the town as her home, too. It was as if he had left a city that had grown too large and come to a home he had never suspected to exist. How could he share this with her?

"I'm feeling faint, Sebastian. May we go home—back to Randolph's? Frannie needs help preparing dinner. I promised to fetch some water for her bath, also. She's very close to term and is incapable of doing much for herself."

"I noticed she's as big as a whale," said Hand. "Is the doctor satisfied with her health?"

"The town doctor is a drunkard and a gambler," Laura said primly. "I am able to act as midwife. I would not want your Dr. Gutherie within a mile of Frannie when it's her time."

"I hadn't noticed the doctor spending that much time in the saloon," said Hand. He wondered if this were simply a way for Laura to feel in control. Kenneth Gutherie wasn't the best doctor in Kansas, but he was far from the worst. He had actually gone to medical school in Boston, unlike many of the frontier doctors who depended on crude experience and fast amputation.

When Laura didn't answer, Hand said, "I'll get the water. How much do you need?"

They trudged up the small rise to Randolph's house. Laura pointed to a large washtub. He silently nodded and started for the river. He had to make three trips before the tub was filled. Wiping sweat from his forehead, he sank down and stared at the setting sun. The huge orange wafer flickered and wobbled as it slipped below the horizon. He had hoped for a respite from the ever-present heat. If anything, he sweated even more. How it could be this humid when there was so little rainfall had become a mystery second to none for him.

The only consolation in the heated wind he felt drying the skin on his face was that he need not heat the water in the washtub. It would be warm enough without applying fire to it first.

Hand found peace within himself, even though he knew his wife did not like Kansas. She would. The stark territory would grow on her and she would come to appreciate the people and the legal and cultural issues that made it so important for him to be here. He stood to his almost six foot height and stretched mightily. Carrying the water had strained muscles he was unused to using. After they got into their own house, he would have to do more of the chores. It wasn't fair leaving them all for Laura.

He started into the house when he heard Randolph calling to him. His brother waved from the bottom of the small rise as he hurried. Hand frowned. His brother seldom ran when he could walk, and he never walked if a horse and carriage was nearby.

"Sebastian, don't go inside yet. I need a word with you in private."

"What's the trouble?" Hand asked. From Randolph's tone, the trouble brewing might have already boiled over. He remembered their earlier talk about the Ellsworth police force. Chauncey Whitney let his deputies run the town as they saw fit. Happy Jack Morco ran out of control in his hatred of the Texas drovers. With George Hindes' herd of longhorns on the outskirts of town, that meant a passel of cowboys were ready to flood the saloons and whorehouses.

"There's going to be big trouble tonight, Sebastian. I know it."

"Tell me about it." Hand settled down and put his back against the wall of the house for support. He still ached from carrying the water from the stream.

"The sheriff is out serving process."

"I gave him a stack of papers right after court let out this afternoon," said Hand. "I didn't think he'd leave immediately. There were enough summonses to keep him on the trail for a week."

"He ought to have sent a deputy, but he didn't. He wanted the money himself."

Hand sighed when he heard this. It was unfortunate that the Ellsworth police force was paid by the small jobs they did. Serving process netted the sheriff five dollars. Arresting a drunk only paid two dollars and fifty cents. Whitney would rather serve process than arrest troublemakers, both from the ease of the work and because of the amount of money he received.

"He left Morco in charge? Is that the problem?" asked Hand. This was unfortunate but not unexpected—and it wasn't the crisis his brother made it out to be.

"Happy Jack is in charge," Randolph admitted, "and you know what he thinks of the drovers. He's already locked up four of them."

"We knew there would be trouble when they got to town," said Hand. "They've been on the trail three months, and their pay is burning a hole in their pockets. Some of them might have as much as a hundred dollars to spend."

"I know that," Randolph said in disgust. "Where do you think I make most of my money? They replace damaged gear and buy supplies to get back to Texas."

"Then you're not telling me anything I didn't know. What is eating at you?"

"The town is going to blow apart when Morco puts enough of the trail hands into the jail. He has been riding several of the cowboys especially hard." Randolph stared directly into his brother's green eyes. "You remember Thornberry. He and his brothers are Morco's target for tonight."

"Thornberry? The one I took the pistol from?"

"His brother Jake is George Hindes' right-hand man. His trail boss. I've heard rumors of what Jake Thornberry has done in other cattle towns at the end of a long drive. It isn't pretty. The man is completely without morals."

Hand laughed. He had seen a never-ending stream of amoral men pass through the courts in Chicago. He had defended many of them and seen that they received a fair trial. Many had been acquitted, in spite of their guilt. A few he hadn't minded seeing sent to prison for a well-deserved sentence. But they seldom created the ruckus his brother expected from Jake Thornberry and Happy Jack Morco.

"Laugh if you will, Sebastian. This is serious. Morco is preparing white affidavits."

"What are you talking about? What are white affidavits?"

"You weren't here during the vigilante days. Morco gives the affidavit to whomever he wants to leave town. If they don't, they're fair game. He can gun them down."

"That's illegal. That's a violation of due process and—"

"I know, Sebastian, I know! But that's the way things were done before you arrived. Anyone being served had to leave or face the law—and maybe a band of vigilantes. If they've been given warning, they're liable. That's the way it works."

"Not in *my* Ellsworth. They should be arrested only if they've committed a crime. And then they aren't judged for it anywhere but in *my* court."

"You need not worry about that," Randolph said grimly. "If half of what I've heard about Thornberry and his two brothers is right, they'll commit some crime just to challenge Morco."

The judge closed his eyes and let out a deep sigh. That played into Morco's hands, if true. He wanted the cowboys to goad him into gunning them down. Ellsworth would be ablaze with renewed cries to form a vigilance committee if anyone died. Serving the white affidavits on the Thornberry brothers would surely cause the bloodshed.

"Let's go talk with Morco and try to knock some sense into his hard head. We might be able to convince him his job is on the line if he stirs up any trouble."

"Him being Happy Jack is enough to start trouble," Randolph said grimly. "I've seen the way he talks to the drovers. No self-respecting man can take that tone and his cutting words without wanting to draw down on him."

Sebastian Hand had no truck with anyone unable to control their anger. Still, he understood what his brother said. The cowboys might have had several quick drinks and be on the lookout for a woman to bed. Morco getting in their way would only create trouble for everyone. The saloon and whorehouse keepers paid hefty fees to Ellsworth's city fathers to run their businesses. They expected the lawmen to keep order, not create a predicament damaging to their customers.

"Sebastian, where are you going? Randolph? You're both not going into town, are you? What's wrong?" Laura stood outlined in the doorway by the dim light within the house.

"Nothing, Laura. We'll be back shortly."

Hand's wife stared at them from the door, her concern and vexation apparent by the set of her shoulders. Before Hand reached the bottom of the rise, she had turned and vanished into the house.

"She's got a burr under her saddle, Sebastian. You're going to have to talk with her."

He nodded absently. His mind raced ahead to what he would tell Morco. If he put it to the deputy wrong, Morco might ignore the law entirely and simply gun down the Texas drovers he disliked so. What he needed to do was instill a sense of duty in Happy Jack Morco, to fire him with the need to keep the peace and put his personal feelings second. As judge, Hand knew he had little control over the law-enforcement personnel. With Sheriff Whitney out of town, he had almost no influence, but he could try.

He and Randolph had started down the boardwalk toward the sheriff's office when they heard the screams. Sebastian Hand looked at his brother, then both ran hell bent for leather toward the alley, where the screams had turned to whimpers. Before either got to the alley, gunshots rang out and the whimpers vanished.

Hand rounded the corner of Goldsoll's store and stared into the blackness of the narrow alley. He saw nothing moving. He hesitated for a moment before entering.

"Wait." Randolph's shaking grip on his shoulder stopped him from going to investigate. "This is what Morco gets paid for."

"What's going on?" came a gruff voice. The men turned to see Happy Jack Morco striding up, a shotgun riding in the crook of his left arm. "I heard a gunshot."

"In there," said Sebastian Hand. "We heard someone crying out and came to see what happened. There was a shot before we even got to the corner."

Morco pushed past the judge and cautiously poked at

the debris littering the alley. He stopped halfway down the alley. A muffled, "Goddamn" came echoing back to the Hand brothers.

Sebastian Hand hurried down to stand beside the deputy. He stared down at the body. The blood rushed from his head and made him suddenly faint. Never in his life had he passed out. He wanted to now. Gorge rising and burning in his throat, he turned to vomit.

Randolph stood beside his brother and made small trapped-animal noises in his throat. "Never seen anything like it," he muttered.

"You two see who done it?"

"We just heard the shot. We didn't see who did it," Randolph said. He put his arm around his brother's shoulders.

Sebastian Hand tried to keep his eyes off the dead woman and couldn't. Her skirts had been ripped off and she had been raped. Blood pooled under her where knives had been used to flay her flesh. A single shot between her eyes had mercifully put her out of her misery.

"Who is it?" he managed to ask.

"Looks to be Mary Fitzwater. There's gonna be hell to pay for this," grumbled Morco. The deputy struck a lucifer. In its sudden flare he peered at the dry dust in the alley. "More'n one of the bastards did this. See this track? Boot heels cut for spurs with a Spanish rowel. Just like them Texas bastards wear."

"Don't go railroading them, Morco," warned Sebastian Hand. "I'll try whoever you bring in, but you've got to prove it in court. Don't go arresting the first Texas drover you find."

"I got my suspicions from all that's been said tonight, Judge. I got to find the other deputies. This is more'n I can handle. You watch over the body while I get Doc Gutherie. He was over at Murgatroyd's Saloon last I saw him." Happy Jack Morco went off, whistling tunelessly between his broken teeth.

"How could anyone *ever* do this, Randolph?" Hand stared in gut-twisting horror at the woman's tortured, raped corpse. "They must have been animals. Worse!"

"Better keep those opinions to yourself," said his brother. "You're going to hear the case when it comes up. And it will. Somebody's got to pay for this. Everyone in Ellsworth liked Mrs. Fitzwater. Her husband's a councilman and about the only politician in these parts who's respected by everyone. And Patrick Fitzwater's going to have blood in his eye. Count on it.''

"Animals," murmured Sebastian Hand, still staring at the woman's lifeless body. He began to worry about Laura's safety. She and Frannie were alone—and Ellsworth, Kansas, was not dignified, civilized Chicago.

5

Sebastian Hand stared at the four defendants. He recognized Ben Thornberry as the man he had outfaced in the street. How long ago had it been? Hand couldn't remember. It might have been days or it might have been decades. It had only been two days since he and Randolph had heard the shot that killed Mary Fitzwater.

Happy Jack Morco had gotten the three other deputies and had tracked the men down in the Sun Dog Saloon. In spite of Morco's predilection toward violence, he had performed his job as well as anyone could have. He circled the four men at the bar, then asked where they had been. Hand refused to listen to the wild stories circulating in Ellsworth about the capture, but his brother had given him some idea what had happened then.

The three Thornberrys, Jake, Matt, and Smelly Ben had laughed when confronted. Their cousin, Marsh Aylesworth, had tried to run. One deputy cold-cocked Aylesworth with the butt of his pistol. The others had kept their scatterguns leveled on the Thornberry brothers. The arrest went as smooth as silk, much to Morco's chagrin. He had hoped to cut down the Texans where they stood when they went for their weapons.

Sebastian Hand forced himself to look away from the four men. They sat defiantly, their lawyer talking quietly with George Hindes. All four men worked for the Texas cattleman—and Hand had seen the lawyer before in the Connelly case. He still wore the tattered vest and looked like a down-on-his-luck Mississippi gambler.

For the sake of a fair trial, Hand hoped the lawyer's luck was good. The prosecuting attorney had a strong case from all Randolph had relayed to his brother.

"Let's begin," Hand announced, smartly rapping his gavel.

In the rear of the courtroom, Patrick Fitzwater growled, "Hang the bastards. Even that's too good for 'em after what they done to poor Mary."

Others in the room echoed the man's call for immediate lynching. Hand rapped his gavel again for silence. He wanted no disturbance in this case. It was too important. Ellsworth had to have law, not a lynch mob.

"Your Honor," began the defendants' lawyer, "I don't reckon it's possible for my clients to get any kind of fair trial in this town. Everyone's riled up over Mr. Hindes' herd having Spanish fever. They just want to see someone's heels kicking in the air, and they picked on these four gentlemen."

"It has been decided that Mr. Hindes' longhorns are free of any splenic fever. I heard that case. That part is irrelevant." Hand glanced at the jury box, where twelve Ellsworth citizens sat stony-faced and silent. "As to the other part of your motion, these men don't appear to have any personal animosity toward your clients. Change of venue is therefore denied."

The city attorney rose and began his case immediately by calling Randolph Hand. A motion to strike his testimony was overruled. Hand further struck down the motion for him to disqualify himself since he was an eyewitness.

"From my brother's testimony, he did not see who fired the bullet, nor who raped Mrs. Fitzwater. Neither did I."

The Thornberrys' attorney grumbled over this but subsided. The testimony from Happy Jack Morco was more damning. He detailed how he had tracked the four men to the Sun Dog Saloon and how they had been arrested.

"That one, Marshall Aylesworth, tried to hightail it out when we came in," testified Morco. "That's a sure sign of guilt."

"Order," rapped Hand. "Deputy Morco, you are not to draw conclusions like that. Leave the verdict to the jury."

"That's fine with me, Judge, as long as they know the bastards gang-raped and killed poor Mrs. Fitzwater."

Pandemonium in the courtroom drowned out Hand's

attempts to silence any further outbursts from the deputy. It took the bailiff five minutes to settle everyone down.

The prosecuting attorney called the doctor who had examined the body to the stand. Hand closed his eyes, took a long drink of water to steady himself, and tried to force the image of the woman's half-nude, bloodied body from his mind.

"Nasty doings," declared Dr. Gutherie. "Seen worse in my day, but nothing done by a white man. The Cheyenne can do terrible things with a knife, worse than this. But not even the Sioux match what I found done to Mrs. Fitzwater."

As the doctor described the nature of the wounds inflicted during the rape and how a single bullet had ended her life, her husband broke down and cried.

"Pantywaist," called out Jake Thornberry. "Only a damned lily-livered coward cries—"

The bailiff smashed Thornberry in the mouth, knocking him backward onto the courtroom floor.

"Say that again and I'll bust your damned-fool neck," the bailiff growled.

"Enough," ordered Hand. He felt control slipping away. He admonished the bailiff for his attack, then continued the trial the best he could.

Patrick Fitzwater had to leave, two friends accompanying him. Hand signaled to Morco to watch over the man and make sure he didn't do anything foolish. Happy Jack shrugged and left the room after seeing that the other deputies were on guard.

"There will be no more outbursts, or I'll have the defendant gagged."

"Go on and try it, you—" Jake Thornberry got no farther. His attorney pulled him down and spoke urgently to him. The cowboy sat and glared at Hand with hate-filled eyes.

Dr. Gutherie finished his testimony.

Hand drank another glass of water. It settled to his belly and pooled there in a hard lump. He sweated more than usual, even though the day was somewhat cooler, with the heavy banks of clouds moving in from the west with their leaden promise of rain. "Any more witnesses?" he asked the prosecutor.

The small man bobbed his head nervously. "Got one more," the city attorney said. "The barkeep at the Sun Dog Saloon."

"Objection!" cried the defense lawyer. "What can he know?"

"Let's find out," said Hand, still uncomfortable under the combined stares of the four defendants.

The bartender sat down and immediately launched into his tale. "They came in all liquored up. I don't know where they been, but they were as smug as if they're foxes in the henhouse. I heard that one, Marsh Aylesworth, say he ain't never had it so good. Then the other one, Smelly Ben Thornberry, allowed as to how he'd had better before killing her down Texas-way. They all laughed at that."

Hand listened with half an ear to the man's testimony. He studied the defendants' reaction to being overheard. Sullen expressions and intense hatred were uniform among them. If he had held any slight suspicion that Happy Jack Morco had railroaded these men, it vanished as they glowered at the bartender. They knew he told the truth—and it hurt their case.

George Hindes spoke rapidly with his lawyer. The attorney shook his head. He let the testimony stand unchallenged. Hand sighed when he saw that. The case for the prosecution had just been won. Gutherie's testimony meant nothing. Randolph Hand's certainly hadn't. Morco's might carry some weight since his skill as a tracker was known locally, but no one had seen the crime being committed. The four bragging about what they'd just done as they walked into the Sun Dog Saloon damned them to hell.

The defense tried to show how upstanding the four men were. The prosecutor tore apart these arguments with two arrest warrants on Matt Thornberry and the suspicion of a murder committed in Texas by his younger brother, Smelly Ben.

"That's all I have, Your Honor," the prosecutor finished.

The closing argument for the defense was too weak to sway the sentiments of the twelve men on the jury. It took only seven minutes for the jury to file back in and the foreman to declare, "The four sons of bitches are guilty as sin, Your Honor. They done all those horrible things to Mary Fitzwater, then they upped and kilt her to keep her from identifying them. That's the way we find. Guilty!"

Hand went weak inside. He was glad he was sitting down. Otherwise his knees might have buckled under him. This was the only possible verdict that could have been returned honestly. That didn't lessen its impact.

This was the first trial he had presided over where men's lives hung in the balance. He had ruled on affairs affecting livelihoods, but never lives. And now he had to pass sentence.

"Your Honor," said Hindes' lawyer, "we hope you'll show mercy. This is the first trouble any of these fine gentlemen have been involved in since coming to Ellsworth. Take that into account."

Hand was taken aback by the plea. He shook off his shock and said, "You're asking for clemency because they haven't raped and killed anyone else? That's absurd!"

"Hang 'em!" someone at the rear of the courtroom cried. "That's only fair after what they done to poor Mary!"

Hand restored order. "I don't know who spoke in the rear of the room and I don't care. I am judge and I decide the sentence. Rise for sentencing."

The bailiff forced the Thornberry brothers and their cousin to their feet.

"You have been tried and found guilty of the most heinous crime imaginable," Hand said. His mouth was drier than Death Valley, and his entire body shook like a leaf in a high wind. It had taken him only a split second to come to his decision.

"I sentence you, Jake, Matthew, and Benjamin Thornberry, and you, Marshall Aylesworth, each and every one, to be hanged by the neck until you are dead. Such sentence will be carried out at noon on the day after tomorrow."

"That'll give us time to get a gallows built," shouted Happy Jack Morco from outside the courtroom. "Those bastards will swing good!"

Hand rose and stared at the four men. If anything, the

hatred in their eyes had intensified—and he was the focus for it. He turned and walked steadily from the courtroom. Only after he reached his small office did he stumble and almost fall. He pried open the sticky center drawer in the desk and pulled out a flask of whiskey he had taken from his bailiff. Two quick pulls on it almost emptied the small bottle. Even the burning liquor in his belly didn't quell the shaking and the emptiness inside him.

He had sentenced four men to death. He didn't know if that bothered him the worst, or that they deserved it for their brutal, senseless crime.

6

Laura Hand stared at her husband in horror. She had never seen him so pale and drawn. She cleared her throat to speak, but he shot her a wild, almost crazed look that kept her silent. She and Frannie went about getting dinner ready. Laura wished that Randolph would return from the store and speak with Sebastian. He had refused to even mention the Texans' trial, though she had heard the verdict.

"We're going ahead and eat without Randolph," she said finally. "Frannie says he might be longer than usual at the store tonight. He's taking inventory before getting the new shipment in from St. Louis."

Hand did not answer. He stared ahead at a bare wall, as if it fascinated him.

"Dear," Laura said, sitting beside him, "what is it? I've never seen you like this." He tried to pull away. She didn't allow it. She gripped his arm and kept him close to her.

"I just killed four men," he said. "With the rap of a gavel, I sentenced four men to death."

"They aren't men," she said in a low, intense voice. "I've heard what they did to Mary Fitzwater. That poor woman. They don't deserve any mercy."

"I didn't give them any, but I'm not sure I gave them justice, either. There wasn't anyone in Ellsworth not convinced of their guilt. Even I thought they had done it."

"There's nothing wrong with that—if they did commit the crime. You don't believe they are innocent, do you?"

Hand closed his green eyes and shuddered. The memory of the Thornberry brothers and their cousin in court drowned any doubt he might have. They were guilty.

They had raped and butchered a young woman for the sick thrill it brought them.

"They did it," he said. "Is it right for me to kill them?"

"You're protecting others from them," Laura said. "In a way, you're protecting me. And Frannie and every other woman in Ellsworth. I heard that one had arrest warrants out for him."

"For murder," he acknowledged.

"See? If the Texas authorities had caught them, they wouldn't have come here and committed murder again. They'll never do it again."

"I know," Hand said, staring into his wife's deep brown eyes and finding compassion there. "It doesn't make it any easier. I never thought I'd feel this way. Passing judgment is harder than I thought it would be."

"You've done the right thing. They'll never harm another soul. Think of the innocent lives you've saved by sentencing them to hang."

Sebastian Hand did—but the inner pain he felt over the decision did not abate.

"That son of a bitch," muttered Jake Thornberry. "We shoulda kilt him when we rode into town. We coulda just rode up and gunned him down. I told Hindes he wasn't no good."

"What judge is?" asked Marsh Aylesworth, fingers laced behind his head. He lay flat on the floor, staring at the iron bars overhead. The cell was hardly large enough for two men. It held all four of the convicted killers. "These homesteaders only want to keep us from having fun."

"It's always that way, like Marsh says," cut in Smelly Ben. He sat to one side of the cell, his back against the outer wall. He lived up to his appellation. Bathwater, soap, and Benjamin Thornberry were distant acquaintances, and had been for months.

"When we gettin' out of here?" asked Matt Thornberry. He clung to the bars and tried to see into the sheriff's office, where Happy Jack Morco and another deputy played cards. He caught occasional flashes of cardboard dropping onto the table and heard the deputy complaining about Morco's luck.

"George Hindes is a good man to work for. He won't let us rot in here."

"We ain't got time to rot, Jake," pointed out Matt. "We're getting our necks stretched come day after tomorrow. Hell and damnation, I hear the carpenters working overtime getting the gallows built." He tipped his head to the side and strained. The distant sound of hammers echoed through the still night. Matt Thornberry stood up to his full five-foot-eight height and ran his thick fingers nervously through bushy red hair. "I don't want to die in this two-horse town."

"You worry too much, Matt," his brother said. Jake Thornberry sat on the edge of the single bed with its straw mattress and thin blanket doubled under him. His rear end hurt him something fierce; he wanted nothing more than to sit in a tub of hot water and ease the pain stabbing into him. His gray, almost colorless eyes followed the narrow corridor out to the office, where the deputy finally gave up and refused to play further with Morco.

George Hindes would get them out. He had before. He understood the pressure of the drive, how the cowboys worked hard for little money and how they needed to vent some steam when they got to town. What did a few homesteaders matter, anyway? His brothers and cousin worked better than any dozen other drovers. Hindes wouldn't turn his back on them.

"What if he can't come, Jake? What, then? What if the town sheriff has George all holed up and won't let him out?" Smelly Ben had taken up Matt's worry. This irritated Jake.

"You two will be the death of me yet. George Hindes is an honorable man. He ain't like these Ellsworth faggots. You think they can keep him buttoned up if he don't want it? He'll get us out. You got to trust him."

"I want out of here, Jake. I don't want to die with a rope around my neck." Matt Thornberry refused to be consoled.

Jake duplicated his brother's nervous gesture and ran his hands through his own thinning red hair. Finding lit-

tle under his fingers, he moved to tug on his beard as he
thought the situation over. What they said might be true.
The judge had been a hard-ass about the sentencing, and
none of the others in town looked on them favorably
enough to protest. The thought occurred to Jake that they
might have picked the wrong woman to have fun with.
They should have used a whore. None of the holier-than-
thou Ellsworthites would have so much as raised a finger
against them then.

"What do you think, Marsh? Think we ought to wait
for George to come get us out?"

"I think Hindes is halfway back to Texas," his cousin
said, not taking his eyes off the bars above them. "He
saw that the town wanted our blood. He's not riskin' his
own damn neck for us. Not this time. We might have
gone too far."

"Dammit, no," shouted Jake Thornberry. "We got a
right. The only damned problem we got is with that
judge."

"I want a piece of him," said Smelly Ben. "I want it
bad."

"We all do," said Jake. "He's gonna pay for what he's
tryin' to do to us."

"Won't none of us care much if we don't get free,"
Matt said. "There's something mighty forgiving about a
corpse. We won't think nothin' of what he's done to us
after they plant us six feet under in their potter's field."

"We deserve a better funeral than that," grumbled
Smelly Ben. "I want to be buried in Texas with the rest
of the family. It's only fittin'."

"They tell us what's fitting—as long as we're in this
cage." Jake Thornberry rattled the bars so hard his teeth
clacked together. He controlled his rage against the law
and Sebastian Hand long enough to realize they had to
get themselves out of this. His brothers were right.
George Hindes wasn't likely to crawl out on a limb for
them this time. He still had beefs to sell and transport to
Chicago slaughterhouses. Risking a profitable market for
the Thornberrys and their cousin wasn't in his greedy
makeup.

Jake studied the cell and saw no way for them to pry
loose the welded iron bars. In spite of the usual humidity,

not a speck of rust showed. The bars were impervious to anything they might do. Jake paced the tiny floor, stepping over his cousin a dozen times before coming to the conclusion that the back wall of the prison cell was too thick to break through. If they had a week to excavate, they might make progress on the floor. He doubted they'd have more than a few minutes at a stretch to dig, though. Getting rid of the dirt would be a problem. If they threw it out the window, someone would see it in jig time.

They didn't have weeks. They had days. Two days. The sound of the hammers driving nails on the gallows came to Jake Thornberry and drove him crazy. He rattled the bars again.

"Calm down," urged Marsh. "Gettin' out of here is going to take more than shaking the whole damned cell."

"The deputy. The dumb one. He's how we get out."

"You got a plan, Jake?" Matt Thornberry jumped up and stood close to his oldest brother. "What do we do?"

"I want to cut that judge's throat for what he done to us," declared Smelly Ben, already assuming they had escaped. "Nobody cages me like an animal. I don't like it at all."

"Shut up," Jake ordered. "It's dark in here. With that oil lamp blown out, it'd be even darker. Hard to see. Get the blanket off the bed. Put the straw mattress up into the bars on the window to cut out all the light."

Jake Thornberry watched as Matt and Smelly Ben did as he ordered. He took the blanket and rolled it up into a thin rope. He made a few tentative snaps with it and assured himself he could snuff out the flame. He silently pointed to the bars overhead. Both Marsh and Smelly Ben climbed up and hung from the bars like giant tree sloths. Although partially hidden in shadow, they were still noticeable.

They vanished when Jake Thornberry flipped the blanket out and deftly knocked off the lamp chimney and put out the flame. The tinkle of breaking glass brought the deputy on the run.

"What's going on in here?"

"Run, Marsh, run, Ben," Jake yelled.

In the darkness it looked as if the bars over the window had been ripped free. With both Jake and Matt urging their brothers to run, the deputy jumped to the wrong conclusion.

"Jailbreak," he roared. "Get the hell against the wall. Damn your eyes!"

He fumbled open the cell door and motioned for Jake and Matt to leave the cell. They did, hands held high over their heads. He put them in the other cell and secured the door before going to the window. It took the deputy a second to realize that the bars were in place. The straw mattress stuffed into the opening only gave the appearance of black night time sky.

He never got the chance to cry out. Marsh Aylesworth dropped from the darkness above and crashed down on the deputy with both feet. Air knocked from his lungs, the lawman was easy pickings for Smelly Ben. The burly, stinking man swung his meaty fist and broke the deputy's nose. His second punch found the side of the man's head. The temple crushed like a hen's egg.

"Get his pistol," Matt urged. "And get us the hell out of here before the other one sticks his head in!"

Marsh grabbed the dead deputy's six-shooter and hastened to free his cousins. Jake yanked the pistol from Marsh's hand and went to the office door. He peered out cautiously, then laughed.

"We got it made, gents. The other cocksucker's left, probably to get liquored up."

"Let's not wait for him," said Matt. "I want to blow this town. Now!"

"We got unfinished business," Jake said. "We got to settle the score with that judge. No Kansas judge is good enough to sentence Texans to swing."

"Kill the bastard," Smelly Ben said.

"I want to get the hell out of town," Matt Thornberry complained. "They'll be looking for us real soon. We done kilt another of their townsfolk." He gestured with his thumb, indicating the dead deputy.

"So they catch us and try us for killing him. So what?" demanded Jake. "They can only hang us once. I say we go and get even with the judge. He owes us."

"Kill the judge," agreed Marsh. "It's his due for what he done to us. We didn't mean no harm. Who was that woman, anyway? Nobody special."

"Kill 'im," Smelly Ben chimed in.

Matt swallowed hard, then nodded vigorously. It wouldn't matter much if they took a few extra minutes getting even with Sebastian Hand. It might even help. It'd show these sodbusters they shouldn't fool with Texas cowboys.

"You sure this is the place?" asked Marsh Aylesworth. "It looks like there's three people inside. Nobody said nothing about the judge having a family."

"I heard mention of a wife," said Matt. "Might be more."

"That makes our revenge all the sweeter," said Jake. He had taken a double-barreled shotgun from the sheriff's office. His brothers had six-shooters, and Marsh carried both a Winchester rifle and a Colt Army taken from the lawmen's arsenal. They had enough firepower to take on a dozen judges.

"You thinkin' on killin' his kids?" Smelly Ben asked. "I don't cotton to that. Women don't matter, but a man's son is something else."

"If'n it's a little girl, you can have her, Ben," Jake said.

This made his reeking brother think hard. "All right. It's a deal, Jake."

They dismounted from their stolen horses and circled Randolph Hand's house. Jake peered in a glass window, marveling at the wealth it took to put glass-pane windows into a house. Most of the homesteaders in these parts built sod houses and used waxed paper for windows, when they even bothered with windows. Plate glass was a luxury on the prairie. It only made Jake more inclined to take revenge. Judges shouldn't enjoy such extravagance.

"There's two women inside, Jake. And a man. He looks something like the judge, but it ain't him. We got the wrong place."

"The hell we do. That must be his wife. You say the man looks like him? Might be family."

"Could be a brother. The family resemblance is there, even if this one's a mite on the fat side."

Jake patted his brother on the shoulder. Smelly Ben

smiled. He liked it when he won Jake's approval for a job well done. Jake motioned for him to circle the house and guard the back way. He didn't want anyone escaping when they made their grand entrance.

Jake had his cousin at his right side with the Winchester leveled and Matt on the left when he kicked in the door.

Laura screamed when she saw the men and their weapons. Randolph froze, then dived toward the rifle rack mounted on the wall. Jake shot him in the legs as he moved. Randolph fell heavily, fingers just missing the wooden rack as he crashed to the floor.

"Don't none of you ladies go gettin' any fancy ideas," Jake said. The smoking shotgun in his hand emphasized his words.

"Who are you?" asked Frannie. She cradled her protruding belly and backed toward the rear door. She shrieked when Smelly Ben came up behind her.

Laura moved to her brother-in-law. His right leg had been partially severed. His left had taken two of the heavy 00 buckshot pellets. He bled profusely. He tried to speak, but he had turned pale and cold.

"He needs help. Get a doctor. He's bleeding to death."

"Now, ain't that a pity?" asked Jake, moving so he could look down on Randolph. "He's gettin' blood all over that fancy-ass carpet of yours."

"The doctor," Laura pleaded. "He's dying!"

"Nope, don't look that way to me," said Jake. "Does it look that way to you, Matt?"

"He looks deader'n a doornail to me," said his brother. "From the mess, you must have cut an artery in his leg. Don't take long to bleed to death, does it?"

Laura almost fainted when she realized the outlaw spoke the truth. Randolph had died without making a sound. The huge pool of blood under him soaked the rug thoroughly and seeped between the floorboards. She lowered his head gently and sat beside him, shocked into silence.

"This one's got a bun cookin' in the oven," joked Smelly Ben, swinging Frannie around and trying to kiss her. The woman slapped him. He took scant notice.

"She's yours, Ben. I promised."

"She's pregnant," protested Laura, coming out of her shock at Randolph's sudden death. "You can't—

"We can do anything we want, lady. What's your name? You wouldn't be the judge's mizzus, now, would you?"

"Don't go foolin' with her, Jake," Matt protested. "We came for the judge. Where'n the bloody hell is he?"

"Out," blurted Laura. "He wasn't feeling good. He went for a walk."

Jake smiled crookedly. "Won't be back for a while, is that it, Miz Judge? Then my brothers and me, we got to do something to while away the time. Smelly Ben's already got himself a woman. I reckon the rest of us get to take turns with you."

Laura Hand fought. It did her no more good than it had Mary Fitzwater.

An hour later, Smelly Ben asked, "What we gonna do with them, Jake? They both sorta upped and died on us."

"What's the difference?" asked Jake. "We're waiting for the judge. I reckon he's got to come back sometime."

"I don't like this," Matt said. "We ought to get out of here. Somebody's gonna find us if we stay too long. When they find the deputy, all hell's going to be out for lunch."

"You worry too much, Matt. And I don't like you puttin' evil thoughts in Smelly Ben's head, neither. We got nothing to do but wait for the judge. I want him, Matt. I want him so bad I can taste it. No judge sentences me to hang and gets by with it."

"Jake," cried Marsh Aylesworth. "We got big trouble. That deputy, the one what tracked us before. I see him down the hill. He's got a dozen men with him and they look like they're on our trail."

"Damn, the man must be part bloodhound." Jake looked at the dead women and Randolph Hand's blood-drained body. It had been a good night. But he wanted Sebastian Hand.

"Let's get out while the gettin's good," Jake said. "We can come back for the judge after we get rid of that posse."

The fugitives ducked out the back door and got to their

horses. By the time Deputy Morco found the slaughtered Hand family, the Thornberrys and their cousin were a mile down the road. Before Happy Jack got his men in the saddle again, the Texans were five miles distant and riding hard.

But they'd return. Jake Thornberry still yearned for real revenge on Sebastian Hand.

7

Sebastian Hand paced for more than an hour before growing as tired in body as he was in spirit. Sentencing men to death had been more difficult than he had ever anticipated. The recurring thought came clearly: he had done the right thing. The Thornberry brothers and their cousin deserved their punishment. Hand fought with his personal demon, though, over it. Intellectually, he knew he was right. Emotionally, he still considered himself a killer. They had slain one woman. By his act he had killed four.

"No," he said to himself. The night wind blew through his lank black hair and tried to wipe the perspiration from his forehead. "I did nothing. The law did it. What I did lay within the legal system. I only carry out the law. I don't write it. I did my job and nothing more."

Again the intellectual answer was less than fully satisfying, but it helped more than anything else had. He turned back to his brother's house and Laura. He had been curt with her, and this bothered him. She had only wanted to comfort him and help him come to grips with his problem. He would make it up to her.

At the creek where he had drawn the water for Frannie's bath, he paused. A dozen horses were tethered around Randolph's home. Hand paused, wondering what was happening. He started up the steep rise. Halfway to the front door a cry went up that startled Hand. Happy Jack Morco came out. Behind him stood Sheriff Whitney.

"We wondered where you'd got off to, Judge," said Morco. "You all right?"

"What's wrong? Why are you men here?" Hand looked past the deputy to the sheriff.

56

Chauncey Whitney stood outlined by the light from inside. The set of his body showed dejection.

"I reckon you'd best talk to the sheriff about that," Morco said. "It ain't too pretty."

Hand rushed forward. Sheriff Whitney grabbed him and swung him about. Hand slammed into the wall, almost knocking the wind from his lungs.

"Don't go in. Not yet, Judge," said the sheriff. "Where you been for the last hour or so?"

"Walking. I . . . I had things to work out. Walking helps sort them out." Hand pushed free of the sheriff and spun to look into the house. He saw his brother lying in the pool of dried blood. Unlike finding Mary Fitzwater, he didn't vomit. A strange, numbing coldness started at his heart and spread rapidly throughout his body.

"Your brother's been murdered," Whitney said. "The Thornberry boys got out of jail. Killed Pete and came right over here. Used a shotgun on Randolph, from the look of it."

"Laura," he cried. This time both Whitney and Morco grabbed him.

"Don't go blamin' yourself none, Judge," Morco said. "They're killers. You done right sentencing them the way you did. If you'd been here, they'd've killed you, too."

"Laura?"

"She's dead, Judge," Whitney said in a mournful tone. "They did bad things to her and Frannie."

"Frannie's dead, too? You're wrong. This can't be true. You're making a mistake."

"No mistake. Can't be none." Whitney tried to stop him from pushing into the house and failed. The sheriff shrugged and followed. Morco left. Hand heard the sound of horses' hooves but paid little attention. He couldn't take his eyes off his wife's body. The Thornberrys had done to her what they had done to Mary Fitzwater. He couldn't bear to look at his sister-in-law. The blood soaked the floor and stained the walls higher than waist level.

"They're savages, worse than any Injun," said Sheriff Whitney. "Morco might not be the best deputy I ever had, but he's hell on tracking. He wants them, too. We'll get them back, Judge. They'll pay for this. We'll get them hung all right and proper, wait and see.''

"They escaped?" Hand's mind refused to comprehend the ugly scene. "How could you let them? Why weren't you there? You let them escape the jail?''

"Judge Hand, we didn't let them do anything. They're dangerous criminals. They killed the deputy. He was a friend of mine. They came over here, probably to even the score, as they saw it.''

"They killed my family. My wife, Randolph, Frannie." Hand sagged and sat in a chair. Even as he touched the chair, he shot bolt upright and ran from the house into the night.

The night swallowed him as he ran, trying to flee his misery.

"We outrun those fools an hour ago," Smelly Ben complained. "Why do we have to keep ridin' so hard, Jake?''

"We're laying a false trail," he told his youngest brother. "We ride until they think we'll never stray from the road and will end up in the Rockies. Then we'll circle back.''

"That's not too smart," complained Matt. "They'll be watching for us. They aren't gonna let us prance on back into their damned town without knotting up a new hangman's rope for us.''

"You worry too much, Matt," Jake said. "We started on revenge, but we got a ways to go. I want that judge. We got to show 'em they can't treat us like dirt.''

Matt Thornberry shook his head. He kept looking over his shoulder, certain that the posse would overtake them at any instant. Jake had odd notions at times. This was one of those times. They had put the fear of God and the Thornberrys into that judge. There wasn't any need to return to Ellsworth.

"Matt's right for a change," spoke up their cousin. "They're madder'n a stepped-on rattler back there. They might not even wait for the hangman. Shoot us on sight is my guess.''

"Then don't guess, damn your eyes," flared Jake. "Let me do the planning, like I always do. If it wasn't for me, you yahoos would still be trying to grow cotton down on the Brazos.''

"I never liked breakin' my back for nothing," said Marsh, "but this time we're in deep trouble."

Jake Thornberry seethed as he rode. He couldn't get the picture of the hanging judge out of his mind. The expression on Hand's face as he pronounced sentence rankled. Jake was going to erase that memory and replace it with a new one; he wanted to see Judge Sebastian Hand begging for his life. He wanted to hear him cry when they told him what they'd done to his wife. He wanted Hand to plead for mercy.

And then they'd kill him. Jake rubbed his hand up and down the barrel of his shotgun. It had been over too quick with the judge's brother. The single blast had cut off his legs. He wanted Hand to suffer—and know who was responsible.

"We cross the river and head back," Jake decided. "We've been out here long enough."

The sun rose behind them and cast long shadows in front of their horses. The dumb animals jerked and started at the movement of their own silhouettes. Jake wanted to put the shadows behind them and get on with his vengeance.

"I'm gettin' hungry, Jake. I want some food," complained Smelly Ben. "We can't go on forever like this. My horse is gettin' tired, too."

Jake nodded brusquely. He pulled in and motioned for them to head for a stand of cottonwoods. He needed a rest himself. His butt had stopped aching and now burned like a hill of ants had crawled into his flesh. Someone had told him about a French general with the same problem. Jake didn't know or care about any foreigner. He just needed to get out of the saddle for a spell to ease the pain.

"There's a stream. We can water the horses and get some for ourselves," said Matt. He was the first off and into the shallow water and dunk his head.

Jake approached more carefully, slipping to the muddy bank and then twisting about to get his rear end into the water. The relief of the water flowing sluggishly past made him shiver. The only thing that would feel better would be killing Judge Sebastian Hand.

"We'll hole up for the day," he decided. "We can relax and give the horses plenty of time to rest. We're gonna be riding them hard after we get Hand."

"What's so goldanged important about this judge?" Matt asked. "He's been taught a lesson. His woman and brother are dead. Ain't that enough to give him the message not to fool with us?"

Jake said nothing. It wasn't enough. Not by half. Hand had sentenced them to death. Jake Thornberry would return the favor—and he'd do it right. Hand would pay with his life.

Sebastian Hand sat on the porch and stared as he had all night. He couldn't bring himself to enter the house again. All he could do was stare across the prairie at the thunderhead forming in the west. It might bring much-needed rain. He hardly noticed it. His thoughts kept spinning like a wheel, coming back to seeing his wife dead on the floor.

The sound of a horse's hooves drumming on the dry ground caused him to look up. Sheriff Whitney sat astride his horse some distance away. When he was sure Hand recognized him, he urged his horse forward.

" 'Evening, Judge. I wanted to tell you that Happy Jack is still on their trail. I came back to keep order in Ellsworth while he's out. They won't get away scot-free. We'll find them and hang the lot."

Hand had no answer. He knew the Thornberrys might be halfway to Texas by now. They'd be fools to stay where Morco could find them. They knew the deputy hated Texans and would rise in everyone's estimation if he caught them.

"I wanted to stop by and see if you needed anything." Whitney stared at the judge for a few seconds and got no answer. "You have a gun you can use?"

"What?" Hand looked up, startled out of his reverie. "Randolph had a rifle."

"Here, take this." Sheriff Whitney fumbled in his saddlebags and pulled out a heavy object. He held it for Hand.

"A six-shooter?"

"Remington. All loaded and ready to fire. You do know how to use a pistol?"

"You aim and pull the trigger. There's not much to it."

"This is a heavy thumb-buster, Judge. You got to treat it with care. And don't believe it's as easy as aiming and firing. You got to do it . . . Hell, never mind. Keep the damned thing with you if they take it into their heads to come back."

"They're gone. They may be crazy killers but they're not stupid. They know what'll happen to them if they show their faces in Ellsworth again."

"Even their boss has disowned them," Whitney said. "Hindes says he's putting out a fifty-dollar reward on each of their flea-ridden heads."

"He had nothing to do with it. He was only their boss." Hand spoke to convince himself the Texas drover was innocent, that his cowboys were the true culprits. Many in town didn't agree. Hand had spoken with several to soothe their ire.

"You going to be the proprietor of your brother's store?"

"I hadn't thought about it. I'm the only family left," he said, a catch forming in his throat. He swallowed hard and fought back the welling tears at the corners of his eyes. "I've never had the mind for business. That was my brother's bailiwick."

"If you're going to sell the store, Mayer Goldsoll said he'd quote a price. You'd better act quick, though. He's only here during the summer months to cater to the drovers. He goes back to St. Louis for the winter."

"I'll consider selling. I have no desire to be a businessman."

"Don't blame you. We've each got our niche in the world. I wouldn't have taken this job and given up my business if it wasn't for the way Happy Jack irritated the drovers. The mayor wanted a more moderate sheriff, and I got myself appointed." Whitney spat in disgust. "The stupidest move I ever made."

"Is there anything else you need, Sheriff?" Hand held the heavy Remington and wondered what he would do with it. He had never fired a pistol before. When he was a child, his father had taken him and Randolph hunting. Only ten, he had bagged a rabbit using a small-bore rifle, but he knew it had been more luck than skill. Weapons had never interested him.

Especially now they repelled him. Laura had been shot repeatedly. Frannie had been cut down with a single bullet to the back of her head. And Randolph had a leg wellnigh blown off with a shotgun. Hand refrained from throwing the six-shooter the sheriff had given him into the darkness.

''Just making my rounds. You get some sleep now, you hear?'' With that Sheriff Whitney wheeled his horse about and trotted toward town. In a minute even the echo of his horse's hooves had been swallowed by the impenetrable night.

Hand sat back down, the heavy pistol resting on his lap. Sleep eluded him. He couldn't get the picture of Laura lying dead on the floor out of his mind.

He heaved a deep sigh when he heard Whitney returning. He stood and peered down the rise trying to locate the sheriff. He frowned when the horse stopped—and yet it didn't. It took him seconds to realize that more than one rider approached.

''Who's there?'' he called. The Remington became a comfort to him. He pulled back the heavy hammer and readied the weapon. ''Answer me. Who's out there?''

''Who would you like it to be, Judge?'' came Jake Thornberry's mocking voice. ''You want us to tell you how good your woman was—before we killed her?''

Hand fired blindly into the night. The Remington bucked hard and almost broke his wrist with its unexpected recoil. He shouted incoherently. He had fired at the voice. He had no idea where Jake Thornberry really was.

''You missed by a country mile, Judge. Want to try again?''

Jake's voice cut at his very soul.

Hand fired again, with no better results.

''You purt near winged my horse. Be more careful,'' came Marsh Aylesworth's voice from his right.

Hand spun and fired.

"He's not got a clue where we are, Jake. Let's take him now and get this over with."

Hand recognized the other brother. Matt Thornberry had seemed the least of the four. What had he done to Laura? Simply standing by and watching was crime enough for Sebastian Hand. He fired and fired and fired a final time. The hammer fell on a spent cylinder.

"He's out of rounds," came Smelly Ben's disembodied voice from near the porch. Hand threw the gun toward the sound. Smelly Ben laughed.

Hand roared and charged. His fists worked like hammers as they strove to find a target. Smelly Ben grunted when a wild blow grazed his cheek. That was the last time Hand connected. He was soon swinging wildly, much to the killers' amusement.

"Let him spin around a few more times," cried Smelly Ben, enjoying Hand's predicament.

"I'll kill you. I should have had them string you up on the spot. As God is my witness, you'll pay for what you did to Laura, Frannie, and Randolph!"

"Look at who's talking," said Marsh. "You're the one what done us wrong. We was only havin' fun with the woman. We didn't mean to hurt her none. You should have let us go. We was only blowing off steam."

"Yeah. It gets mighty lonely on the trail," said Jake. "But you've riled me plenty. Like Marsh here said, you shoulda let us go."

A pistol barrel struck Hand on the side of the head. Stars spun in crazy circles around his head. He stumbled but didn't fall until an outstretched leg tripped him. As he rose, the twin barrels of a shotgun pressed into the back of his neck. The cold metal felt like the gates to hell.

"I could blow your damned head off," Jake said. "But that'd be over too quick. I made that mistake with your brother. One shot and he upped and died on us. He wasn't any fun at all."

"Make it fun for us, Jake. Go on. You know how," Smelly Ben urged.

"I know how," Jake agreed in a low, menacing voice.

Hand scuttled along like a beetle as he tried to tackle Jake. A hard barrel crashed into the side of his head. He wasn't even sure who had swung the weapon. He dropped facedown into the dust, panting and trying to calm himself. If he panicked, he died. But how could he fight four killers, all armed and with their weapons trained on him?

A soft whistling noise caused him to come to his knees. Hemp rope fell around his body, pinning his arms to his sides. Hand struggled to no avail. When the horse took off, it jerked him over hard. He crashed into the ground and was dragged along behind.

"This is fun, Jake. You know how to have fun," the dim-witted Smelly Ben crowed. "Can we drag him around some more?"

"No, Ben, this is a judge. We got to treat him with respect."

"Respect?" Marsh spat in disgust. "He's a murdering son of a bitch."

"I noticed that," Jake said, playing along. "Or did I? What did he do to us?"

"He sentenced us to die," Matt grumbled. "Let's kill the bastard and hightail it. That sheriff's going to be back. I can feel it in my bones."

"Shut up, Matt," Jake Thornberry snapped. "You're spoiling this for Ben and me."

Marsh spoke up. "He wanted to hang us. That's what he tried to do to us."

"Give him a taste of his own medicine," Smelly Ben said. "String him up!"

Hand looked up and saw the cottonwood towering above the ground. Any of the bottom limbs was high enough to hang a man.

"You got the horse from the barn?" asked Jake.

"Here it is," Matt said. "Now, can we get on with it?"

"Knot the rope. Make sure he sees every turn. There's thirteen of them, Judge. One for every mother's son at the Last Supper. When Matt's done with it, we're going to put it around your scrawny neck."

Hand fought down the panic. He was going to die. His family was gone. What did he have to live for?

Even as the thought flashed through his mind, a core of iron resolve formed. He wasn't going to let these savages break him. Die he might, but it would be with dignity. He struggled to his feet.

"Get him on his horse," Jake ordered.

"I'll climb up," Hand said. Even with his arms pinned at his sides by the rope, he was able to slip over the horse's back and push himself upright.

"He's cooperating, Jake. Why's he doing that?" asked Smelly Ben.

"Shut up. It's a trick. He's trying to escape. But he won't. We won't let him." Jake jerked the rope from his brother and tossed it over the lowest limb a good five feet over Hand's head. He fumbled as he fitted the noose to the judge's neck.

"Keep it just a tad on the loose side. That way when he falls off the horse, his neck'll snap quick," Marsh suggested.

Hand fought to stay upright on the horse after Jake backed off. The horse shifted position slightly and munched contentedly at a clump of dry grass. A single blow to the horse's rump would send it racing across the prairie—and leave him dangling by his neck.

"Do it, Jake. Do it," cried Smelly Ben.

"Not yet. Let the judge think about what he tried to do to us. The Thornberry clan don't take kindly to being sentenced to die, Judge Hand." Jake walked around to where his victim could see him. "Your horse getting a mite antsy? Think it might look for a new clump of grass?"

"Why are you doing this, Thornberry?"

"You just sit there and think on it, Judge. You think real hard. Sooner or later, the horse is going to move. A bug might bite it. The water sounds mighty appealing, especially to a thirsty horse. Or, like I said, it might get the notion to find more grass a bit farther afield. When it moves, you die."

Hand wanted to shout obscenities, to call Thornberry every insulting name he could think of. His silence angered the man more than any verbal attack.

"Leave him," Jake ordered. "This might take all night. I want to be long gone when they find him."

Hand fought to keep his horse steady when the animal stirred.

Jake Thornberry rode up beside him and whispered, "Good riddance, you son of a bitch!"

Those were the last words Hand heard. The three brothers and their cousin rode into the night. Hand's legs ached as he steadied his horse with his knees. He tried to wiggle and get free of the rope binding his arms to his side. He dared not move much, or the horse would bolt.

The rope around his neck cut deeper with every passing second.

8

Time passed in odd spurts. For a few seconds Sebastian Hand was afraid he would die. Then for an eternity he was afraid he wouldn't. The horse moved restlessly under him, cropping at grass and stretching its neck to reach a juicier patch inches farther away.

Hand shrugged his shoulders in a vain attempt to get free of the rope the Thornberry brothers had draped around him. He stopped when he realized that further effort would only cause the horse to bolt. The noose cut deeply into his neck.

He wanted to die—and he didn't.

With Laura gone, what did he have to live for? His brother and sister-in-law were cruelly slain also, making his litany of tragedy even longer. Even with this idea sprouting within his brain, a hard core rebelled against dying. He would live. He would live and find Jake, Matt, and Ben Thornberry. He would find their good-for-nothing cousin Marshall Aylesworth.

And he would kill them.

Hand blinked sweat from his eyes and tried to see. The darkness of the night was impenetrable. Or did his vision dim from the blood being cut off to his head? The chafing around his neck kept him aware of his continued life. He still lived.

The horse took a full step forward. Hand held back a cry of alarm. He used his knees to squeeze on the horse's shoulders to keep it in place. He began choking as the rope tightened even more around his throat, but Hand fought back. He gritted his teeth and concentrated on maneuvering the horse. The animal swung around in a tight circle, guided by its unwilling rider's legs. The pressure eased on his neck—for the moment.

Hand considered shouting for help. He was afraid it might spook the horse. He realized time was draining away. The horse wouldn't stand stock-still forever.

"Judge Hand, you around? Me and the mizzus came over to see how you are. Where are you, Judge?"

The voice from uphill around the house caused the horse to stir nervously. Hand tried to call out. The horse moved enough to choke him again. Only strangled noises came out of his mouth. The vision of dangling by the end of the rope and choking to death filled him with dread.

He fought harder against blacking out or panicking. Either spelled his death.

He wiggled farther back on the horse's haunches and loosened the rope a mite. He gurgled rather than shouted, "Help! Down by the creek. Help me!"

"What's that sound, dear?" came a woman's voice. "Do you think the judge is fetching water? It's not far. Let's see if we can help him."

Hand heard rather than saw Connelly and his wife coming downhil. He gurgled and hissed and tried to warn them to advance carefully.

The horse raised its head as the Connellys approached, then let out an aggrieved neigh and sped off. For a brief instant, Hand hung in midair, as if defying gravity. Then he fell, the rope tightening around his neck.

He felt the harsh hemp strands cutting through his flesh, stopping blood and air rather than snapping his neck. He was dying and knew it. Night closed around him like a shroud.

Then he was lying on the ground, staring up into his neighbor's face. Connelly held a smoking shotgun in his hand. It took Hand several seconds to get his wits about him and realize what had happened. Connelly hadn't cut him down—he'd used the shotgun to blast through the rope. His quick reaction had saved Hand's life.

"Let me get it free, Cecil." Mrs. Connelly worked on freeing the rope.

Blessed air gushed into Hand's lungs. He coughed and rolled onto his side. The circle around his throat where the noose had been burned like fire. He held down his rising gorge and tried not to choke anew.

"Get the damned ropes off him," Connelly grumbled.

Harsher hands rolled him back. The snick of a knife told of the parting ropes around his arms. For the first time in hours—in an eternity!—he was free of pain and the threat of death.

"Thank you," he gasped out.

"Who did this to you, Judge? What animals would . . ." Connelly's voice trailed off. "Son of a bitch! It was them Thornberry boys, wasn't it?"

Hand nodded, not trusting himself to speak yet. He rubbed the burned area on his neck and finally sat up. He took several more seconds before he heaved himself to his feet. The weakness in his legs didn't surprise him; the strength filling him did.

Resolve hardened in him. The Thornberrys and their cousin would have to die. If Sheriff Whitney and his deputies couldn't stop them, Sebastian Hand would.

"Let me help you back to the house, Judge," offered Connelly. "Me and the mizzus just came by to pay our respects. You've done wonders for Ellsworth and we appreciate it."

"What Cecil is trying to say," Mrs. Connelly cut in, "is that we want to offer our condolences and try to share your grief however we can. We didn't know your wife too well, but we all knew and respected Randolph and Frannie."

"Randolph'd give us supplies on credit when the others wouldn't. He saved more than one of the homesteaders around here during the past few bad years." Connelly cleared his throat.

Hand wasn't listening. His eyes were focused on the darkness, as if he could ferret out the Thornberrys.

"What can we do for you, Judge Hand?" asked the woman.

"Nothing. Wait," he said suddenly. "Do you know how to use a pistol?"

"Well, I reckon I do somewhat," allowed Connelly. "I'm not much of a marksman, but I can shoot with the best of them in Ellsworth."

"It's around here somewhere," Hand said, searching the dirt for the discarded Remington. He found it ten feet past where he'd thought it would have landed when he'd thrown it at one of his attackers. Their assault blurred in his mind, and the three brothers and their cousin melted into one evil giant.

"That's a real thumb-buster," said Connelly. "It looks the world like one Sheriff Whitney has."

"I got it from him. He came by earlier to tell me that Morco was on the trail and that I didn't have anything to worry about." Hand's bitterness cut and slashed.

Mrs. Connelly took a step back and stared at him as if he'd grown cloven hooves.

"Sheriff Whitney never had a lick of sense when it came to choosing firearms," said Connelly. "Let me look it over." He took the heavy pistol and studied it. "Cap and ball. You have to load each cylinder individually. The new Colt Peacemaker with its cartridge is a better choice."

"Show me how to load it." Hand sweated rivers. His face burned with fever and his entire body shook. He hardly noticed. With an intensity unlike anything he had ever experienced, he watched as Connelly showed how to load the almost-four-pound pistol.

"It'll break your arm if you don't grip it hard," Connelly said. "It's got a heavy frame for a reason. It takes up some of the recoil."

"Cecil, please," the woman pleaded. "This is neither the time nor the place for such things. We should inform Sheriff Whitney of what has happened. He'll want to go after those awful men."

"She's right. We're wasting time."

"No!" protested Hand. "I need to know how to defend myself. I want to stop them."

He spoke too loudly. It frightened both the man and his wife.

"Look, we'll get the sheriff. You stay here, Judge. They won't get far. We'll form a posse and hunt them down like the animals they are."

Hand held the Remington and knew he wouldn't waste ammunition again. He would kill the Thornberrys and then rob Marsh Aylesworth of his life, too. They had done terrible things to him, things no man should endure. Killing Laura had been awful. Killing Randolph and Frannie had added to it. But they had gone too far. They had frightened him, humiliated him, made him feel less than a man.

For that he could never forgive the Thornberrys.

He looked around the house for the cap and ball needed to load the Remington. Failing to find it, he thrust the heavy six-shooter into his belt and stormed out, going into town on foot. He heard music playing in a saloon. Men laughed and sang and women made lewd suggestions. He ignored them all as he made a beeline straight for his brother's store. He had never paid much mind to the ammunition and weapons Randolph sold. Now he damned himself for that oversight.

He needed ammunition. He needed the means to kill the Thornberrys.

He got to the front door of the general store and found he had neglected to bring along the keys. Knocking out a window, he gained entry and trashed around in the stock like a bull in a china shop. After several minutes of searching, he found the locked storage box where Randolph kept the ammunition.

Connnely had told him how to load the Remington. He had thought he understood. Hand rapidly discovered he had missed several salient points.

The ball kept rolling out of the Remington's cylinder. He tried tamping it down hard with a rod hooked to the underside of the barrel, but this didn't work. Cursing, he went wild with rage. Thoughts of Laura and what the convicted killers had done to her calmed him enough to succeed in loading the pistol.

Hand left the store and went hunting for the Thornberrys.

He kicked open the doors to the first saloon he came to and drew the Remington, ready for a fight. The piano player stopped and stared. The noise in the saloon dropped and silence became suffocating.

"Get you a drink, Judge Hand?" came a trembling voice. The barkeep hunkered down behind the bar and peered over the top. Only the top of his head could be seen.

"Where's Jake Thornberry?" Hand bellowed. "I want him. I want him!"

He waved the Remington around. The unfamiliar heavy

weight threw him off-balance. He staggered. His finger curled around the trigger and he fired. The cylinder had been loaded with too much powder. The explosion almost deafened him. Splinters blew back into his face where the .44-caliber ball smashed through the saloon's wooden floor. Worst of all, the recoil almost broke his thumb.

Using both hands, he cocked the heavy pistol again. The loud protests that had risen again turned to frozen silence. Hand waved the pistol about and sent men diving under tables.

"Thornberry," he cried, "where is he?"

"Judge," came a quiet voice from behind. "You're making a passel of trouble for yourself. None of us want that, now, do we?"

Hand spun. Sheriff Whitney stood in the doorway. He held a Henry revolving rifle, and it was aimed directly at Hand's midsection.

"The Connellys told me what those boys upped and done to you. That's a damned shame. You put down that hog-leg and we'll talk about how to get them back in jail where they belong."

"I want them!"

"You're upset, Judge," the sheriff said soothingly. He approached the distraught man slowly, the rifle never wavering. "Why don't you and me go find Doc Gutherie and see if he can't give you something to calm your nerves?"

Whitney glanced at the bar. The bartender shoved a bottle of whiskey across and then ducked back behind the bar.

"Reckon we don't need the doctor's medicine. Old Petey fixed us both up good. Have a snort, Judge." Whitney gestured toward the bottle with the muzzle of his rifle.

"I want them, Whitney. I want them!"

"You're lookin' powerful thirsty. Have a drink. It's all right. I'm payin' for it. Go on, Judge."

Hand grabbed the bottle and upended it, taking a stiff shot from it. The bitter taste made him gag. He started to take another, but the sounds in the saloon started to fade. Hand looked around. The saloon collapsed into a tunnel. He saw a decreasing circle of light that the sheriff completely filled. Then his green eyes stopped focusing. He sighed, slumped, and dropped heavily to the floor.

The barkeep's bottle laced with knockout drops had worked better than anything the Ellsworth doctor could have given him.

9

"He's gone plumb crazy, I tell you," the man sitting in front of Goldsoll's store said. He spat a large brown gob, then returned to his domino game. "There'll be hell to pay if somebody don't get him under control real soon."

"You don't know what you're saying," said the other. "He's the best thing that's happened to Ellsworth. Crime's dropping something fierce. Nobody wants to go before Judge Hand. They know they'll end up in prison if they do."

"He's worse than Judge Parker over in Fort Smith. And they call him the Hangin' Judge. Hand's sentencing men to prison for what don't amount to a hill of beans."

"Detroit's got plenty of room for these scalawags." A domino fell and the game ended. "I say good riddance to 'em. They do the crime, they should pay for it."

Hand stopped at the end of the boardwalk and listened for a few seconds more to the two men. They were so intent on their domino game that neither saw him as he passed by. Hand took no pleasure in their idle talk. In the three months since Laura had been killed, he had taken a grim pleasure in getting the riffraff off the streets of Ellsworth. Many were Texas drovers; in Happy Jack Morco he found an unlikely ally.

Sheriff Whitney chastised his deputy for his overzealous execution of all the town's laws, but more often than not, Judge Hand fined or sentenced the arrested miscreant to time in jail. The rumblings among the drovers grew, but none openly contested the strict enforcement. They knew what lay behind Hand's one-man crusade to clean up the streets of Ellsworth.

There wasn't a one of the cowboys who wouldn't have

traded the Thornberrys and their cousin for a single night of carousing without interference by the law.

The one punishment Sebastian Hand had yet to mete out again was hanging. The threat of strict lawmen and a stricter judge kept the gunplay in town to a minimum. No one had been murdered after Hand's family had died. He wondered what he would do if such a case came before him.

His jaw tensed and his fingers curled into fists so tight that his fingernails cut into his palms. He knew what he would do. Death by hanging. He'd swing the bastards until the buzzards wouldn't touch their putrid flesh.

"Judge, you got a minute?" called Chauncey Whitney. The sheriff waved to him from across the street.

Hand took a deep breath and let it out slowly. He didn't want to speak with the lawman. Whitney had been slacking off since . . . that night. "What is it, Sheriff? I've got to be in court in five minutes. My docket is full again."

"They're just now bringin' the prisoners over from the lockup. The deputies won't be in court on time, so's we can talk." Whitney spat into the dusty road and looked up and down Ellsworth's main street. "Sure is peaceful today."

"I mean to keep it that way."

"That's what I want to talk to you about. It isn't your place to keep it quiet. That's my job. Yours is to pass judgment after we catch the crooks."

"I do my duty, you do yours—after a fashion."

Whitney bristled at the insult. "It's not my fault we couldn't run down the Thornberrys. They're trailwise and had a heap of reasons to keep on riding when they left you."

Hand said nothing. He started for the courthouse.

The sheriff hurried to catch up with him. "I don't want you giving direct orders to my deputies. They're starting to ignore me and sass me because you're telling them to do other things."

"I'm telling them to enforce the laws of this town. We are a third-class township, and I mean to keep the streets safe for the people who live here. I want none of the drovers shooting up the saloons or endangering lives."

"That's something else I been meaning to talk to you about, Judge," said Whitney. "You've been orderin' the deputies to close down the whorehouses."

"They are illegal."

"They pay a fee to stay open."

"They are illegal," Hand said coldly.

"This is crazy, Judge." The sheriff wrung his hands together and then shook his head as if he didn't understand what was going on. "You cut off that source of entertainment for the cowboys and they get mean. The men runnin' the cribs get even meaner."

"It is illegal. I will not abide by anyone breaking the law in Ellsworth."

"Turning the cow town into a powder keg and then playing with fire isn't the way to keep the peace, Judge Hand. I'm warning you up front and proper; don't send Happy Jack out to dog the drovers. They don't like it, and I sure as hell don't."

Hand coldly said, "Maintain discipline in your own ranks, sir. I have business to attend to now—legal business."

He started into the courtroom when he saw a small boy of eight or nine sitting forlornly on a hard wood bench. He went over and asked, "Where are your parents?"

"Pa's dead," the boy answered. "My ma is around somewhere. She said for me to wait here."

Hand took out his pocket watch and checked the time. Sheriff Whitney had said the prisoners due for sentencing would be a few minutes late. He had time to spend. He sat down beside the boy.

"How did your father die?"

The towheaded boy stared up at him, blue eyes wide and innocent. "He got killed by robbers on the way here from St. Loo. Ma was real broke up over it. Still is."

"And you? How do you feel about it?"

The boy shrugged. "I miss him." For all the indifference in his voice, the slight boy couldn't hide the tears welling up at the corners of his eyes.

"It's never easy losing someone close," Hand said. His voice echoed in his ears, sounding hollow and distant. It might have been another man speaking. "How long ago did he die?"

"Almost a month back now. We had to stop and find a place to bury him. Then Ma decided to come on to Ellsworth. We was supposed to settle down south, out by Fort Harker."

"Your mother can't own the land," Hand said. "Only an adult male can."

"She knows. She thought she'd see firsthand. I reckon we might be heading back to St. Loo. Ma's got family there, but I don't much like them. Cousins and stuff like that. They're dull. And none of them like me much."

"Did the law ever catch the men who killed your father?"

"Don't reckon the marshal in the nearest town was even told. Ma said it wouldn't do much good. Who's going to go chasing across the prairie to find a bunch of robbers? It's been mighty hot these past few weeks. Is it always this hot in Kansas?"

Hand put his arm around the boy's shoulders to comfort him. Tears flowed freely now. He tried to find the words to convince the child that everything would be all right. They caught in his throat and refused to come. As much as anything else, he realized this was his problem. He couldn't put his own grief into words.

He couldn't even be satisfied with revenge. Sheriff Whitney had failed to track down the men who had killed Laura and Randolph and Frannie, with her unborn child.

"Judge, you got a minute?" came a husky voice from the direction of the courtroom. "We got to talk. It's real important."

The boy looked up and wiped his tears. "Are you the judge?"

"I am, son," said Hand. "You wait here for your mother. She'll be along soon enough, I reckon. If she isn't, you come and ask for me. Promise?"

"Yes, sir," the young child said, still in awe of talking with a real live judge.

Hand wished that the position meant more. He wanted to soothe the child, find the men who had robbed and killed his father, and bring them to justice. They'd hang. He'd trip the lever that would send them to perdition, if only the law could find the murderers.

But the law wouldn't find them. It couldn't. There was

too much crime and too few lawmen. Kansas was rapidly becoming settled, but the influx of the Texas drovers created tension. Where there was tension, there was gunfire and killing.

"Judge, please. We got to talk."

"All right, Mr. Hammerschmidt. What can I do for you?"

"We been talking, me and some of the other businessmen, and we think you're overreacting. You've been a holy terror since the, well, since your misfortune."

"Since the Thornberrys brutally killed my wife and brother," Hand said coldly.

"Since that, yes, sir, since that and the other unpleasantness."

"And subsequent to them trying to hang me," Hand finished for the struggling man. "What's your point, Mr. Hammerschmidt?"

"Me and some of the other merchants in Ellsworth think you're being too harsh with the Texans. They bring a considerable amount of money into this town. Your brother knew that. He made a pretty penny off outfitting them."

"Randolph's store is for sale. Are you making an offer for it? Mayer Goldsoll is interested also."

"I'm a saloon owner, not a tradesman."

"You are also a whoremonger and a caterer to drunk and disorderly drovers."

"We pay for the right. Sheriff Whitney takes five hundred dollars a year for our license."

"That is a license to serve liquor, not to rent whores."

"They go together, Judge. Look, I ain't sayin' you'd want to partake of some of my ladies, but it must get lonesome out there on the hill all by yourself. Stop by my saloon and—"

Hammerschmidt stopped in midsentence when he saw the dark, deadly thunderclouds of anger forming on the judge's face. He took a quick step away.

Hand relaxed a mite, his fists unclenching. The set of his body told he still wanted to take Hammerschmidt apart limb by limb. "You disgust me, sir."

"I don't mean nothing by it, Judge. All I was sayin' was for you to ease up. No need to get your dander up.

We need to make a profit so's we can keep the town running after the cowboys go back to Texas. Is that asking so much?''

Hand pushed past the saloon owner and went directly to the bench. He donned his robes and motioned to the bailiff to fetch him some water. He was going to get thirsty this afternoon. He had a lot of sentencing to do.

He'd barely settled himself and put his papers in order when Sheriff Whitney came into the room with his string of manacled prisoners. Hand glanced at the docket and remembered the details of each and every crime.

The first one, a drunk-and-disorderly, received a fifty-dollar fine or fifty days in jail. Hand's frustration mounted when the cowboy passed across the tattered, beaten greenbacks for his fine. The next wasn't as lucky. Hand ordered the sheriff to lock him up for thirty days for disturbing the peace.

"Your Honor, can I say my piece?" asked Chauncey Whitney. Hand motioned for him to proceed. "We don't have room for any more prisoners. There's six in each cell now. They have to sleep in shifts 'cause there's not enough room for more than two at a time to stretch out on the floor. We had to take out the single bunks. You give us any more to lock up and I don't know where we'll put them.''

"That's not my problem, Sheriff," Hand said icily. "They break the law, they pay the price society has set on them.''

"This town's gonna have to build a bigger jail. And it's going to have to be a whale of a lot bigger. We're not going to be able to squeeze more into my two cells without using a crowbar.''

"Bailiff," Hand said, "find the sheriff a crowbar. Make it a long one. Next case.''

Whitney grunted and left the courtroom.

Hand watched him leave, then returned to this work. There were a half-dozen more cases to be heard—and criminals to be taken off the street.

What Chauncey Whitney said worried a mite at Hand. Might the sheriff be right about him being too harsh? When Hand looked up and saw the small boy with his mother at the rear of the room, he knew he wasn't wrong.

The robbers, the murderers, the lawbreakers in Kansas had gotten away with their crimes for too long. He might not be able to get his revenge on the Thornberrys, but he would make sure others didn't commit the same crimes.

He straightened on the bench and pushed the memory of his dead wife and brother to a corner of his mind. Sheriff Whitney had six more felons to jail before the end of Sebastian Hand's afternoon court session.

10

"That don't make no never-mind to me, Judge," said Sheriff Whitney. The man shifted slightly in pain, adjusting his injured left arm in its sling. "Me being soft on crime isn't why they winged me."

"Morco got the man who shot you," said Hand. "In a way, it's a pity Morco killed him. I'd've liked to send him to prison as an example to others."

"The streets are quiet now, Judge," Whitney said, "but that's only because the new wave of drovers hasn't come in yet. The season is drawing to a close for them to get their beefs to market. I'm afraid you may have chased off the stragglers. It's just as easy for them to go to Wichita or Abilene or even Dodge City."

"Let the lawless go elsewhere. Ellsworth welcomes any law-abiding drover."

Whitney snorted. He fumbled in his pocket and got out a plug of Sweet Mist chewing tobacco. Owing to his injury, he clumsily bit off a half inch and took longer than usual getting it back into its metal-foil wrapper.

"You're living in a dream, Judge. Get too tough on those hombres and they go somewhere else to hoot and holler. Can't rightly say I blame them, either."

"You were almost killed last night and yet you're defending them?" Hand shook his head in disbelief. "Why, Sheriff? Why not admit that the town is more peaceable now than it was six months ago when I came."

"It's more peaceable because there's nothing quite as tranquil as a corpse. You've let Happy Jack go crazy with his hatred of the Texans."

"He enforces the law," Hand said coldly. He remembered how Randolph had argued that Happy Jack Morco was a mad-dog killer intent on nothing more than rousting Texans. Randolph would approve of the deputy's behavior now. Anything that avenged Frannie's death, even in part, was worthwhile.

Hand still found the memory of Laura too painful to bear, even after all the months. Instinctively, his fingers found the scar around his own neck where the Thornberrys' rope had cut deeper than the flesh. It had blighted his soul and strangled a part of him that had once been human and humane.

"I'd get rid of the son of bitch except you would make a federal case out of it," admitted Whitney.

"How's your arm, Sheriff?" Hand asked nastily. "Feeling any better now that Doc Gutherie cut out the slug?"

"You're a man filled with hate, Judge. I don't like seeing that in anyone, especially a man who's supposed to have the community's best interests at heart."

"I do," Hand snapped. "I'm upholding the law. I didn't make the law, but by damn, I will enforce it to the letter!"

A gunshot caused them both to spin around. It took Hand several seconds to realize it came from across the street, over by the cattle-feeding pens owned by the Reverend Essick. The Presbyterian minister had a small cattle-fattening business to supplement his sparse income from his church.

"Somebody's rustlin' the cattle," Whitney cried. He drew his six-shooter and raced down the street, grunting in pain as he ran.

Hand followed more slowly, not wanting to be unarmed and in the middle of a gunfight.

"Get him! Stop the thief," cried the youth tending the cattle in the fattening pens. "He's makin' off with a dozen of the best we got. Stop him!"

Whitney jumped agilely onto the rail of the corral and sighted over the top, using the fence post as a rest for his heavy pistol. He cocked the hammer with his good thumb and aimed carefully.

"I got you square in my sights, mister. Give it up now or I'll drill you!"

Hand stopped at the far corner of the corral and saw decisions being made by both men. Sheriff Whitney considered squeezing off a shot and taking out the rustler. His arm had to be hurting him something fierce; the memory of how he had let the cowboy get the drop on him the night before had to rankle.

The rustler sat astride his horse, a lariat in his left hand and his right resting on the butt of a six-shooter stuck into his belt. The scarred face scowled. He had not expected to be caught this easily. Shooting it out with a lawman who already had the drop on him was risky. The sheriff might not be able to shoot straight. His pistol might send its slug off-target. He might be able to duck low and get on out of town before a posse could form.

Hand watched all this flash across the rustler's face. A decision was made. The rustler took his hand off his pistol and raised it. The hand with the lariat rose to join the right.

"Don't go makin' any mistakes we'll both regret," the rustler called out. "This ain't what you think it is."

"I know what I'm seeing," Chauncey Whitney declared. "I see a damned owlhoot caught in the middle of a crime. Get on down, off that horse and come on over here. Try to touch that pistol and you're buzzard bait."

"Wouldn't think of it, Sheriff," the rustler said, seeing the glint of sunlight off the man's star. "I was just out here lookin' over the stock. I intend to buy a few and start myself a ranch not ten miles out of Ellsworth."

"You lyin' son of a bitch." Whitney motioned the rustler to turn around. As Hand approached, the sheriff said, "Get his gun, Judge. I'd do it except I've got this broken wing."

"How'd that happen, Sheriff? A tragedy, I'm sure," said the rustler.

"If'n you don't shut up. I'll shut you up good and proper."

The scar-faced man looked over his shoulder. "Are you really the judge in this here town? I heard you was a hangin' judge. You don't string up simple businessmen inspecting stock, do you?"

"If they deserve it," Hand said in his emotionless voice.

"Get moving," urged Whitney, pushing the rustler toward the overcrowded jail.

"I got to—" The rustler spun suddenly.

A shot echoed down the street. The rustler fell back against the corral rail, a startled expression on his face.

Hand stared down at the rustler's pistol. He hadn't fired. Sheriff Whitney hadn't fired. He looked up and saw Happy Jack Morco with a smoking six-shooter. A second and killing shot would have followed the first except that Hand had moved into the line of fire. From the evil fire in Morco's eye, Hand wondered why this had deterred the deputy.

"I wasn't doing anything," the would-be rustler said. "I wanted to show you a bill of sale for the cattle. I bought them."

Hand saw that the man hadn't been injured seriously. The leaden slug from Morco's pistol had grazed the side of his arm. A thin trickle of blood welled up and then oozed sluggishly to soak into his denim shirt.

"Let me look at it." Hand reached into the man's pocket and pulled out a wadded-up sheaf of papers. He opened the top one and saw what looked like a bill of sale. It was faded and a good year out of date.

"This isn't a bill of sale, Sheriff," Hand said. "He was trying to con us."

"And he tried to kill me," protested the rustler. "You keep him away from me—or give me back my pistol and let me defend myself!"

"Get on over to the jail. Nobody's going to kill you, unless you try something else." Whitney got the rustler to his feet and moving.

Hand frowned and turned away, going to the deputy. "Why did you shoot? He was only reaching for a sheaf of papers." Hand held up the thick wad for Morco to see.

"I couldn't tell. Better to be safe than sorry. Look what happened to the sheriff."

"I've been wondering what really happened last night," Hand said. "The cowboy drew down on the sheriff and you shot him?"

The suddenly shifty expression on Happy Jack's face

put Hand on guard. He had seen men prepare to lie before. The deputy had that look about him.

"The cowboy was going to kill the sheriff, so I shot first."

"I heard different," Hand lied. "I heard you cut the Texan down in cold blood."

"That wouldn't bother you none, now, would it, Judge Hand?" asked the deputy. "It did happen that way. I shot at the drover and missed. The sheriff don't know that it was my bullet that winged him. When he fell, I got a clean shot at the cowboy. He was going for his pistol by then. I had to kill him."

Hand nodded, turned, and walked off without a word. He hadn't created the monster that was Happy Jack Morco, but he had given him new life in his feud with the cattlemen. Hand wasn't sure what bothered him the most: having the deputy killing twisted in his guts; having him do it because he thought the town judge approved was even worse.

"Thank you," Hand told the young man who had been tending the Reverend Essick's feed pen when Drew Claggett had tried to ride out with the ten head of cattle. "You can leave the stand now. Any more witnesses?" he asked the city attorney prosecuting the case.

"That's it for the prosecution, Your Honor."

"Mr. Claggett, are you sure you don't want a lawyer to defend you?"

The scar-faced man rose and presented a curiously noble picture. "Judge, I been shot at for no good reason by Deputy Morco, I been stuffed into a cell with nine other men so's we all had to stand, and I listened to testimony from what ought to be an honest youngster. The boy is mistaken, the others in the cell weren't there because they wanted to be, and the deputy's a murdering son of a bitch."

Hand rapped his gavel when Morco blasted to his feet to protest. "Go on and make your point," he told Claggett.

"Your Honor, the boy's mistaken. I had the right to check out those cows."

"Reverend Essick is in Kansas City on business and

cannot be reached,'' pointed out Hand. ''Your receipt is old and looks to be a forgery in any case.''

''Judge, having a lawyer's not going to change the verdict in my case. The boy's honest but mistaken. The deputy is hell-bent to kill anybody from out of town he can get in his sights. And you've got one hell of a reputation for railroading anyone brought before you. Do what you will.''

Hand sat for a moment and stared at Drew Claggett. The man was impetuous and impudent. He begged for the worst sentence that could be meted out. He had been caught red-handed rustling cattle. Hand straightened the other tattered, sweat-stained papers that had been in Claggett's pocket with the forged receipt. Two were arrest warrants charging Claggett with bank robbery and murder. Hand scanned the murder poster and saw that the scar-faced man was accused of gunning down a man in a saloon brawl.

He looked from the posters to Claggett. The man stood quietly, concern on his face but with no trace of fear. More to Hand's liking, there was no arrogance.

Not like that he had seen in Happy Jack Morco's expression. Not like that he remembered in Jake Thornberry or Marsh Aylesworth.

''I've considered this case from several different viewpoints,'' said Hand, ''and I find the defendant not guilty. Sheriff Whitney, release your prisoner. Mr. Claggett, you are free to go.''

Pandemonium broke out in the courtroom. The crowds had come to see their fearsome judge sentence still another criminal to prison. They had witnessed nothing less than an abrupt change in him. Drew Claggett had been caught by the sheriff in a crude attempt to rustle cattle belonging to the reverend—and Judge Hand, the most relentless judge in Ellsworth's short history, let him go scot-free.

''Mr. Claggett, approach the bench. I want a word with you.'' Hand looked up and saw Morco frowning. The deputy touched the butt of his six-shooter, then left the courtroom. Hand didn't doubt he went to find another victim.

Drew Claggett stopped just a few inches away from

the desk Hand used for his judicial duties. "I don't rightly know what got into you, Judge, but I want to thank you. You don't have to tell me. I'll be gone before sundown."

Hand turned the wanted posters around and showed them to Claggett. The man's eyes widened.

"I know about these," Hand said. "This one I need more details on, though." He tapped the poster naming Drew Claggett a murderer and offering a one-hundred-dollar reward.

"He tried to gun me down. He missed with his first two shots. He didn't get a third."

"He fired first?"

"There's no way for you to know that, Judge, except me telling you that's what happened."

Hand studied the spider webbing of white scars on Claggett's face. The man had seen his share of misery. He also was either the best damned liar Hand had ever heard or he told the truth. Hand believed the latter.

"I'm not running you out of town. I want your help."

"Mine?" Claggett looked over his shoulder. Sheriff Whitney stared at him as if he carried the plague. Happy Jack Morco had not returned. Others stood and talked in small knots, trying to decide what had happened to their "hanging judge."

"From your own account, you are an accurate shot. Can you also draw?"

"I'm the best damned shot that ever lived," Claggett bragged. "As to being fast with a pistol, I'm about average. I don't get into fights because I'd lose."

"Are you able to use a rifle and shotgun?"

"Both," Claggett said, brow wrinkling in confusion.

"Can you also use a knife?"

Claggett's hand unconsciously went to his cheek. "The Mescalero Apache did this to me with a blunt knife. I don't cotton much to using knives, but I know enough to get by." He frowned even more, making the scars stand out in bold relief on his weathered face. "Judge, why are you asking me all this?"

Hand took a deep breath. He had come to his decision. He was not going to back out now. "I want you to teach me how to use every conceivable type of weapon. I intend to kill four men after you finish your instruction. Do you have any problem with that?''

Drew Claggett shook his head, left speechless by the judge's bold declaration to do murder.

11

"Don't go tryin' that, Judge," said Drew, sounding aggrieved at the way Hand attempted the quick draw. Claggett shook his head in exasperation. "You'll be drawin' flies on some stinkin' barroom floor if you get the hammer of your six-shooter tangled up in your vest."

Hand took a deep breath and tried to compose himself. Claggett refused to let him use a holster. The soft leather slowed the gun as it slipped out, the gunman claimed. Getting the barrel tangled up caused the first shot to go awry. Having the pistol stuck into his belt at his left side hardly seemed better to Hand.

"Cross draw is better," maintained Claggett. "You can get to your pistol when you're on horseback. Nothing says you only need your six-shooter when you've got both feet planted on the ground." He settled down on stump and worked at a plug of Old Mail Bag. Drew spat and moved the tobacco to the other side of his mouth. "You ain't never going to be good at a quick draw, Judge."

"I have to be."

"You've got some half-assed ideas about facing down these men, don't you?" Claggett shook his head. A flash of pity crossed his face before he spoke. "Don't. That's a word of wisdom I know you ain't likely to take. You're not a killer."

Hand stared at the line of bottles and tin cans he had set up on a fence rail. Each one turned into the face of a man who had ruined his life. Marsh Aylesworth. Jake Thornberry. Ben Thornberry. Matt Thornberry. He lifted the pistol he had taken from Randolph's store and fired one slow shot after another. Every time he fired, a can flew into the air or a bottle burst apart with an echoing snap.

89

"Good, Judge. You're gettin' to be a durn fine shot, but there's a difference when you're standing face to face with another man. You got to kill then. If you don't, you're the one who's going to end up in some potter's field."

"I can learn," Hand said resolutely.

"You're doing good. Better'n I'd've thought when you asked me to teach you how to use a gun." His keen dark eyes looked at the six holes in the line of cans and bottles that Hand had just created. "You'll never be a gunman."

"I won't shoot them in the back."

"You want the satisfaction of watching their faces as they die, is that it?"

"No!" Hand's reflexive denial took him by surprise. He felt his face flushing. Claggett had come closer to the truth than he wanted to admit to himself.

"Most men killed out in these parts get shot in the back. Look at Bat Masterson. Quite a reputation for such a puny little dude. Don't think he's ever kilt anybody while he's been a sheriff. I know of one he shot in the back 'fore he got the job over in Dodge City. Reckon he's done the same to the others, but his reputation is such that nobody tangles with him. Rumors have a way of ragin' out of control like a prairie fire."

"You want me to stop? Is that it? You want me to let those murdering bastards go free?"

"I don't care what you do, Judge. You let me off when another man would have stretched my neck. I'm beholden to you for that. I am." Drew eyed him, dark eyes boring into Hand's soul. "Maybe too much. I'm givin' advice you won't take, but I feel obligated nonetheless. Let the Thornberrys go their way. Someday they'll end up six feet under. I've seen their kind. They never live long."

"I've got to do . . . what I must," Hand finished lamely. The sight of Laura, his brother, his pregnant sister-in-law all rose to haunt him. His left hand strayed to the rope burns on his neck, a permanent reminder of his own brush with cruel death.

"All right," Claggett said, heaving himself to his feet. "You got to do what you got to do. At least try to stay alive while you're after them. And you'll do it by not wearing a holster. They're damned uncomfortable and flop around when you least want them to. I suggest you get yourself a seamstress to put leather pockets in that long coat of yours."

"Leather pockets?"

"You'd be surprised how fast you can reach into a pocket and get a six-shooter out. The leather lining keeps the hammer from hanging up on a loop of thread or cloth fold when you go to pull it out and get it into action. More'n one marshal of my acquaintance carries his piece that way. Down El Paso way, Dallas Stoudenmire's kilt more men than you can shake a stick at."

"He keeps his pistols in his coat pockets?"

Drew nodded solemnly. "You might have to file off the front sights to keep the barrel moving out smoothlike, and you may want to saw off an inch or two to keep it from getting tangled up, but it works."

"I don't want to turn this into a belly gun." Hand stared at the long-barreled Remington Army.

"That's a good pistol," allowed Claggett. "Not the one you want, though. Hard to reload, 'less you have another pocket full of loaded cylinders. You got to knock out one cylinder, then replace it with another if you're in a long fight."

"I don't intend to get into day-long fights."

"Smart," said Claggett.

Hand glared at him, wondering if the man was being sarcastic. He couldn't tell. "What do you suggest?"

"I got this six-shooter down in New Orleans. One of them Frog gunsmiths worked on it for me." Claggett drew his own pistol and held it up for Hand to admire. The barrel gleamed blue and cold. The dark sweat-stained wood grips had seen much use. A scar on the butt showed where Claggett had removed a lanyard pin. "They call it a Lefaucheux 1870. It's got a solid frame so you don't need to worry about wear and tear knocking the barrel out of alignment and having the pistol blow up in your hand."

Hand studied the pistol. "Is it a double-action?"

"No need to use it that way, but it beats hell out of thumb-cocking a Peacemaker," said Claggett. "I can get off a couple shots in the time it takes another man to get his single-action cocked. And it's accurate. The French navy uses these. See? If you get into a hand-to-hand fight, it's damned near impossible to knock it out of your hand because of the checkered wood grips. Good grasp on it. And it fires a .44 bullet. None of them pansy calibers the Frogs usually use. A man gets hit with a slug from this and he stays down.''

Drew passed over the Lefaucheux. Hand took it and studied it carefully. His long fingers rested easily on the double-action trigger; a man with a smaller hand would have trouble with it. For Hand it felt as if he had been born for this weapon.

"Solid frame," Claggett went on. "See how the loading gate is hinged to swing upward? Makes loading easy. I can put in six cartridges in the time it takes you to break open that Remington Army of yours and replace the cylinder.''

"You could carry the equivalent weight in extra ammunition,'' said Hand, seeing the possibilities.

"Fifty rounds about equals the weight of a couple spare cylinders,'' Claggett said. "Try it. See how it fires.''

Hand sighted along the rear sight notch carved into the barrel lug and lined up the front sight. The Lefaucheux fit him perfectly. The six-shooter sent its heavy .44 slug flying with uncanny accuracy. Hand had practiced enough to be a good shot. His marksmanship improved again using Claggett's pistol.

All six shots struck dead-center. Six cans with the Thornberrys' faces on them died.

"Reload. Here. Do it fast,'' urged Claggett.

Hand fumbled at first, then fell into a rhythm of using the ejector rod and loading the cartridges. He closed the get and fired six more times. Six additional cans and bottles popped off the rail as if dynamite had exploded under them.

"You're accurate enough—as long as nobody's shootin' back at you,'' observed Drew. Before Hand could protest, Claggett pointed to a pair of rifles leaning against a rock. One was an old Henry with a revolving cylinder and the other was a more modern Winchester. "I'll match you. Take your pick.''

Hand slid the Lefaucheux into his coat pocket and rested it in the bottom so that he could draw it out quickly.

He picked up the Winchester and levered a cartridge into the firing chamber.

"I put a few bottles up on that rise. See it?" Claggett pointed fifty yards away. "You start on the ones to the right. I'll take the ones on the left. Whoever finishes off his targets and the one in the middle wins."

Claggett pulled the Henry to his shoulder and began a methodical, measured firing. One bottle after another exploded into sunlit fragments. Hand hesitated a moment at such accuracy, then began to work on his own targets.

Claggett shot the center bottle a split second before it came into Hand's sights.

"Judge, you're doing as good as any man can. I don't reckon there's much more I can teach you."

"But you beat me!"

"Not by enough. There's not more'n three or four men west of the Mississippi who can match shooting like we just done. Most of the gun slicks rely on fear. They ain't half as good as their reputations. The ones that are fast can't hit shit. The ones that can shoot . . . don't." His dark eyes bored into Hand once more. The message was clear: don't go after the Thornberrys.

Hand couldn't take that well-meaning advice. The demon driving him was more potent than life. He stared at the shattered targets Claggett had set up for them to blow apart. He was shattered just like them. He lived on borrowed time. Jack Thornberry might kill him. Any of them might. But he had to stop them, to get even for what they had done.

"It's better'n you might think," Claggett said.

"What?" The man's words confused him and caught him off-guard.

"The law. Those Texas boys might have slipped free of Kansas law, but they'll run afoul somewhere else. They'll be brought up on charges and won't get away."

"You're a fine one to talk about the law," Hand scoffed.

"I told you what happened in that saloon brawl. The other fellow shot first—and second. Some of the problems after that have been my own doing, and I damn well know I'll run out of luck one day. But you're wrong. The law is the way to stop men like the Thornberrys and their cousin.''

"I thought that was true once," Hand said. "I'm not so sure now.'' He reached into his pocket and gingerly pulled out the Lefaucheux to return to Claggett.

"Keep it. And get yourself a spare. That Frenchie gunsmith down in New Orleans does himself a land-office business. That's a finer weapon than any Colt that was ever made." Claggett spat out the last of his chewing tobacco a greasy puddle on the dry ground and said, "A hideout gun might just save your life, if you're intent on pursuin' those drovers.''

"Thanks," Hand said. That single word covered the marksmanship training, the pistol, and the advice Drew Claggett had given. "I've got to get into town for the afternoon session.''

"You make it sound final.''

Hand shrugged. He had learned all Claggett could teach him. It was time to put his newly honed skills to the test.

He had four men to kill.

12

Sebastian Hand stretched and tried to work the kinks out of his cramped back. His shoulders were tense and his back felt as if someone had beaten him constantly with a chain for the past twelve days. He had decided to buy a horse and ride rather than taking the Kansas Pacific Railway to Denver. The notion that he might need a horse to chase the Thornberrys when he found them rattled about in his head like a stone in an empty tin can. Right about now, he wasn't so sure about the wisdom of riding to Denver.

The railroad would have gotten him here quicker and in some comfort. A few cinders in the eyes and burned holes in his clothing would have been a relief compared to the way his butt ached from the long days in the saddle.

Still, in spite of the long hours on the trail, he was not disappointed that he had chosen this way to travel. More than learning valuable trail skills, he had been alone and able to think about all Drew Claggett had said. For a gunman, the scar-faced man was a strangely reluctant teacher. He had insisted that revenge wasn't going to be enough for Hand.

Claggett was wrong. Every instant Hand lived, he felt more hatred for the Thornberrys and their cousin. Life without his beautiful, loving Laura was unbearable and grew worse the more he dwelled on her memory. He had thought sitting on the Ellsworth bench and presiding over intellectual points of law would fulfill him. It had cost him all he treasured in the world.

His brother, his wife, his idealism. All had been crushed under the Texans' boot heels. Passing judgment on others had been a job he had taken seriously. Killing the Thornberrys was a duty he was taking even more to heart.

His hand brushed across the inner pocket in his coat. Arrest warrants rode easily there, warrants he had signed minutes before he resigned from the Ellsworth judgeship and had set out on the Thornberrys' trail. There had been vocal protests among many of the business leaders in the town about quitting his post. A few had liked the notion of him leaving the town for good.

It would always be like that, he knew. Not all his decisions in Ellsworth had been applauded. He hoped they would be remembered as fair, if they were remembered at all.

The arrest warrants crinkled in his inside pocket. He reached to the side and touched the outer pocket of his jacket. He had paid thirty cents to a woman in Ellsworth to line it with leather. The past twelve days he had practiced reaching into the pocket, finding the Lefaucheux resting there, and drawing and firing. In this respect Drew had been right.

He could draw and fire faster this way than he ever could with a side holster—and it didn't matter if he was on horseback or afoot. The sturdy double-action French pistol came to his grip easily, quickly, and it fired with deadly accuracy. With any luck, the second Lefaucheux would be in Denver waiting for him. He had contacted the New Orleans gunsmith and ordered the backup pistol, as Claggett had suggested.

With it, Hand would feel balanced. His left pocket had been similarly lined and only awaited the comforting weight of the .44-caliber Lefaucheux 1870.

He stretched again and yawned, wondering if he should rest or press on into Denver. A brief stop in Limon and use of their telegraph office had given him hope of finding the Thornberry brothers in Denver. A bank robbery committed by four men answering to their descriptions had prompted him to come here.

Hand wasn't sure how he could track them down when the Denver marshal hadn't been able to. A coldness settled in his guts. To the local lawman, they were only bank robbers. To him they were more—much, much more. The scar around his throat would never go away. Those on his soul cut even deeper.

He came to his decision quickly. He would get into Denver. There he could rest, if he needed it. The way he felt, he could ride for the next ten years if he had any hope of catching his prey. He turned north and started up an insignificant valley running parallel to the Rocky Mountains. The dust and soot rising from Denver alerted him to the city long before he could see it.

The city sat in a shallow bowl at the eastern edge of the mountains. Railroads ran into the city from all directions. The soot and ash from the locomotives' exhaust stacks filled the air. Dust churned from the commerce in the city's streets in spite of the brick paving. Hand felt a quickening of his pulse. It had been days since he'd seen a real city. In Limon he had spoken only with the telegraph clerk.

But Denver! This was a city. In its way, it reminded him of his hometown of Chicago. With that memory came others he'd as soon have not endured. Laura. They had met at a social. Their romance. The wedding. The years spent in law school and working as a lawyer. Their plans for a family that had never happened. He had wanted so much for them.

No more. It was all dust.

Hand rode resolutely into Denver, seeking a suitable hotel. He asked several people, got conflicting answers, and finally went to the railroad yards. There he asked one of the workers where the dignitaries stayed when they came to town.

"Mister, there's only one place in this city," came the answer. "You want to stay at the Palmer House. The General himself stays there. It's that good." The yard worker spat, wiped his hands on a greasy rag, and added, "If'n I had the money and good sense, that's where I'd stay."

Hand thanked the man. It was the work of only a few minutes to find the hotel built by the railroad magnate. He stood and stared at the three-story structure, thinking how much Laura would have approved of such a fine building.

A lump formed in his throat. Denver looked a great

deal like the Chicago Laura loved so much. The brick streets carried a few trolleys, a sure sign of civilization. Down the street loomed the opera house and more than one fine restaurant proudly advertised its cuisine. Laura would have liked Denver a great deal.

Hand took a deep breath and strode into the lobby of the Palmer House. To the far left a half-dozen clerks and bellhops worked. He went to the desk to register.

The clerk's gimlet-eyed inspection found Hand wanting. The man had been on the trail too long to care about a menial's opinion. He had more money riding in his pocket than most who came into this hotel, perhaps even the railroad magnates. Randolph's store had been worth more than he had thought. A large mercantile firm from St. Louis had offered him two hundred thousand dollars for it. Hand would have sold for a fraction of that price to be free of the memories it brought him.

Still, the money would prove useful. It gave him a base to pursue the Thornberrys; in that sense, they had wrought their own destruction. He could follow them forever and never worry about money.

"This is an exclusive hostelry, sir," the clerk said.

"I've been on the trail for almost two weeks. I need a room and bath. I see you have a barber on the premises. I'll require his services after the bath." Hand pulled out two gold double eagles and dropped them on the counter. "This should take care of at least that much."

"Well, yes, sir," the clerk said. His attitude changed subtly at the sight of specie. Hand suspected that the turn in his disposition also rested on how Hand spoke. He was obviously an educated man.

"I need to send a boy to the Western Union office. There might be a telegram waiting for me to inform me of the arrival date of a package from New Orleans." Hand wanted the added weight of a second Lefaucheux in his pocket. The Thornberry brothers were near. He could feel it.

"Right away, sir." The clerk looked at the precise signature in the register and sent a bellboy hurrying off. "Would you require anything else?"

It took Hand a few seconds to realize what the clerk was offering. He curtly shook his head and spun away.

Laura's memory still burned too brightly for him to even consider another woman, much less a soiled dove supplied by a hotel clerk.

Three hours later, Sebastian Hand felt worlds better. He had changed his dirty trail clothing for his more usual attire—with one exception: the swallowtail coat he wore had a leather pocket sewn into it also. The six-shooter rested comfortably in the pocket, ready for instant use. He stood in front of the full-length mirror in his room and drew the Lefaucheux a few times. The heavy French pistol comforted him. If felt a part of his arm now—and his speed was improving, in spite of what Drew Claggett had said. He might never be able to take the fastest of the men on the frontier, but he didn't intend to.

He wanted only four of them.

Satisfied that he was sartorially perfect and ready to join polite society. Hand went to the hotel dining room and feasted on squab, three different fresh vegetables, and finished with peach cobbler that reminded him of that his mother used to make. He leaned back, more content than he had been in weeks.

He looked past the blue velvet plush seats and out the beveled glass windows into the hotel lobby. Two men argued with a third. When the third man turned, Hand saw a marshal's star pinned on his chest. The marshal gestured and ran the men off.

Hand dropped a pair of greenbacks on the table and hurried out to speak with the lawman. Of all the people in Denver he wanted to see, this was the man.

"Marshal," he called.

"What is it?" the lawman snapped. From his attitude, he was not having a good night.

"I need to speak to you about a bank robbery that occurred a week or more ago."

"The Denver National holdup?" The marshal cocked his head to one side and peered quizzically at Hand. "What do you know about it?"

"I understand the robbers got away and you were unable to track them down."

"It happens." The marshal's walrus mustache twitched and his muddy brown eyes took on a drier, harder appearance, as if they had been left under the burning sun for a summer.

Hand blinked, waiting for the man's eyes to show the telltale cracking lines that formed when Kansas mud turned to dust. He shook himself. That was ridiculous. The marshal's demeanor was one of complete hostility. "I am not blaming you. I need to know if you have descriptions of the men."

"What do you know of it, Mister . . . ?"

"Sebastian Hand. I am—was—the district judge over in Ellsworth, Kansas."

"You're a mite far from home, aren't you, Judge?"

"I have reason to believe the robbers are three brothers from Texas and their cousin."

The marshal stared at Hand and then smiled crookedly. The corner of his mouth had been cut away with a knife, giving him the appearance of a perpetual leer. "You got a personal stake in finding them, don't you?"

"I do," Hand said stiffly. He hadn't realized how obvious his involvement with the Thornberry brothers was.

"That's a good way of getting killed. Don't let your personal feelings get in the way of the law. Why don't you go on back to Ellsworth and let me do the criminal chasing in Denver?"

"Sir, I am not impugning your ability. You obviously have more to deal with than you can handle. I want only to bring these men to trial for their crimes."

The marshal's brown eyes drifted to Hand's heavy right coat pocket. "I think we both know how you intend bringing them to justice."

"I will prosecute them if you arrest them, Marshal. I have warrants for them, also." Hand touched the inner pocket holding the warrants he had issued for the Thornberrys and Marshall Aylesworth.

"We got lawyers for that. We got lawyers coming out our ears. The railroad brought in more of the damned shysters than I can abide by." He took a deep breath and got himself under control. "I've got to make the rounds. You keep yourself out of trouble, Judge, and let me go after the robbers."

"Do you know who they are?"

The marshal's crooked grin widened. "Reckon I might.

The descriptions we got on them make 'em out to be three yahoos going by the name of Thornberry.''

Hand sucked in a breath and held it. His heart raced. The Texas drovers had robbed the Denver bank. He was only a week behind them.

"Your hands tremble, Judge. That's no good if you go against a man wanting to ventilate you. Let me keep the peace. You just stay out of trouble."

The marshal swung around and strode out of the Palmer House lobby, head high and walrus mustache bobbing with every step. Hand saw for the first time that the marshal wasn't very tall. When speaking with him, though, he had the impression of a much larger man. The marshal dominated when he spoke, a necessary advantage when dealing with the rowdies likely to infest a boom town like Denver.

Hand hesitated to follow, then decided that he must. If he wanted the marshal's cooperation, he dared not leave the man angry or suspicious about his intentions. He wanted the lawman's full concentration turned on finding the Thornberrys.

He stepped into the Denver night. The cool air struck him like a blow to the face. The seasons had passed him by and he had hardly noticed. Autumn winds blew off the Rockies and across the bricked streets of this city. The heavy snows of winter wouldn't be far away after the leaves on the many trees dotting the city streets dropped.

Hand looked both ways, trying to find the marshal. A dozen saloons were just coming alive toward the west, on the far side of Larimer Square. He turned in that direction, thinking the marshal would patrol through them giving a cursory once-over before looking in other quarters for lawbreakers.

Halfway to the Big Nugget Saloon, Hand paused. He stared down a dark alleyway. Curious sounds came from the depths. Hand almost walked on. The glint of a stray light beam off a marshal's star caught his attention. He reached into his right pocket and pulled out his pistol. Finger curled around the trigger, ready to use the six-shooter for the first time against another man, Hand entered the alley.

"This is the last time you'll throw me out of a club,"

snarled a tall, thin man. A silver-toed boot cocked back and launched itself, burying deeply in the fallen marshal's side.

The lawman grunted and recoiled, taking the full force of a second blow in the pit of his stomach. "You're going to pay for all the misery you brought me."

"And you're going to jail for attacking a peace officer," Hand said, his voice steadier than he would have believed possible. He sighted along the Lefaucheux's barrel. He had filed off the front sights to prevent the pistol from becoming tangled as he drew it. At this range he didn't need the sights. He had the man attacking the marshal dead to rights.

Faster than a striking snake, the man with the silver-toed boots ducked into a shadow. Hand almost fired but stopped, not having a good target. The tongue of flame that would leap from the muzzle of his .44 might blind his opponent—it might also betray him to return fire.

"Don't," croaked the marshal. "Let the son of a bitch go."

Hand pressed his back against a wooden wall and edged closer. The sound of running feet came to him. For the briefest instant he saw the man's back silhouetted at the far end of the alley. Then the man vanished into the cool Denver night.

"Are you all right?" Hand asked, helping the marshal to a sitting position.

The lawman spat blood from a split lip and rubbed his belly. "I'll live. Lovejoy sucker-punched me. That's the only way he'll ever take me—and he just used his trump card. The man's dead meat. He's gone too far for his pa's money to save him." The marshal groaned as he tried to stand. Hand helped him.

The short man doubled over and vomited in a corner. Gasping, he forced himself erect. "Don't like for any man to see me like this."

"He was going to kick you to death," Hand said incredulously. In spite of his time in Ellsworth and the vicious customers he had seen paraded before him—in spite of the Thornberrys—such mindless violence still shocked him.

"Hell, he wouldn't have done that," the marshal said,

sounding stronger. "That might have got blood on his fancy-ass boots. No, he'd have rolled me over and shot me in the back of the head. He'd have wanted to see my blood and brains on the ground. He's a nasty one, that Jeffrey Lovejoy."

"You know him?"

"Yes."

"What's wrong?" Hand asked. "I saw him. You know who he is. Get some deputies and go arrest him. Or don't you do things like that in Denver?"

"You don't know for spit, Judge," said the marshal. "It's not that easy."

"If you want help, I'll gladly give it."

"And?" prompted the marshal. "I know when I hear a bargain being struck."

"You know my conditions. I help you track down this miscreant and you help me get a line on the Thornberrys."

"You surely do want them bad, Judge. Then again, you might not know what you're getting yourself into offering to help me arrest Lovejoy." The marshal brushed dirt from his mustache and then thrust out his calloused hand. "Let's shake on it."

"Then it's a deal?" asked Hand, beginning to worry about what he had gotten himself into.

"A deal. You help me get Lovejoy locked up and I'll find the Thornberry brothers for you—for *us.*"

Hand experienced an odd combination of thrill and dread at the marshal's words. But to get revenge on the men who had ruined his life, he'd walk though hell barefoot.

13

"I reckon you're dressed good enough for the types of places we'll have to go to find Lovejoy."

Hand stared down at his clothing. He didn't understand what the marshal meant.

"We're going into some fancy clubs. Private clubs," the marshal explained. "You won't get let in, no matter what, Judge, unless you look right. Or smell right." The marshal made odd snorting noises and smiled his quirky smile.

"Do I smell all right?" asked Hand.

"You got the reek of money about you, but you don't carry it like most of them. I suspect you live within your means, which sets you apart from the lot of them."

"They're all profligates?"

"Most are like Jeffrey Lovejoy. They live beyond their means, but then they've mostly got rich papas behind them so it doesn't matter too much." The marshal walked into the street and looked around, as if expecting to find lawbreakers everywhere.

Hand followed more cautiously, his six-shooter still firmly in his grip. He had hardly realized he had drawn the pistol. Now he wasn't so sure he would have fired at Lovejoy unless the other man had threatened him directly. That worried him.

How was he going to be sure Claggett hadn't been right about him not being a killer? He dared not freeze when he faced the Thornberry brothers. The worry gnawed at his gut and made his hand tremble more than he liked.

Finding this Lovejoy, the man who had attacked the marshal, might not be such a bad idea. It might give him a taste of blood and determine his fitness for facing down the Thornberrys.

"The name's Leon Pevsner," the marshal said unexpectedly. He thrust out his strong, calloused hand and crushed down hard on the judge's.

Hand winced at the pressure applied to the handshake. He returned it the best he could. He knew the marshal was sizing him up and trying to determine if he would be able to help him out.

"I got deputies, but I don't think they're likely to find Lovejoy as easily as you could. You have the look about you, all except for the way you carry that fancy pistol in your pocket. Where'd you learn that, Judge?"

Hand didn't answer, nor did he think Pevsner expected one. The lawman headed north, making several quick turns and thoroughly confusing Hand.

"Where are we going?" Hand finally asked.

"Not much farther." Marshal Pevsner opened the gate on his Peacemaker and checked the load. Satisfied, he thrust it back into his holster. "There are any of a half-dozen private clubs where Lovejoy hangs out. We check them one by one until he shows himself."

"What's the problem with him?" asked Hand, wanting to know exactly what he had become embroiled in.

"Bad debt, mostly. He reneges on his gambling debts—and he gambles bad. Never seen a man who took such chances and lost as much. Downright destructive, it is. Can't figure him. Lovejoy gets into fights all the time over not paying."

"Why do the clubs continue to allow him inside?"

"His father is rich. The club owners know that, sooner or later, he'll cough up the money his deadbeat son owes. If he doesn't do anything too ornery, they don't much care who he cheats or loses to."

Hand shook his head in disbelief. Simply having money did not permit anyone to welsh on debts. From what Marshal Pevsner hinted at, Lovejoy's crimes went beyond simple larceny.

"He gets mean drunk, too," the marshal supplied. "I've been riding him hard and threw him out of several places—not the private clubs. Those are usually away from my usual grazing grounds."

"You're using me to gain entry?"

"That's about it. I want him for what he did to me

tonight. And I'd just as soon get to him without having to gun him down. Outside the clubs, he's likely to go down fighting. His pa wouldn't like having a dead boy to bury, mark my words.''

They trudged along in silence, each wrapped in his own thoughts. The marshal stopped and checked his six-shooter again. Hand stared at the front of a building a few blocks away from the city's heart in Larimer Square. It hardly looked like the sort of place a rich man's son would come to gamble.

''It used to be a whorehouse,'' the marshal said. ''The madam moved on to better quarters over along Colfax. Two Easterners set up a gambling club well nigh a year ago.''

Pevsner knocked on the front door. A small window opened. Hand saw an eye looking them over.

''What do you want?'' came the curt question.

''A few minutes' talking to the owner might be nice,'' said Marshal Pevsner. ''My friend here wants to do some gambling while I'm palavering with your boss.''

Hand saw that this was the magic ticket to get inside. Heavy bars slid away and the door opened on well-oiled hinges. As he passed into the club, he saw that a battering ram would have been required to force the door.

''You run along and play some cards,'' said the marshal, ''while I talk with Mr. Abbots.'' Pevsner gave Hand a broad wink.

Hand knew what was expected of him. If he found Lovejoy, he had to keep him occupied until the marshal got permission from the club owner to arrest the man on the premises. And if Lovejoy wasn't here, the marshal expected Hand to ask around and find where he might be.

Hand realized how much rested on him if he wanted to bring Jeffrey Lovejoy to justice.

And not for the first time, Hand also knew how much the law meant to him. It offended him that any citizen could beat up a city's marshal the way Lovejoy had. He didn't even know the man, and yet he wanted him caught, convicted, and imprisoned. Only through law and order could there be civilization.

Not for the first time, he remembered how Laura had said the same thing to him.

Marshal Pevsner and the doorman turned left down a long, narrow corridor and left him staring into the main gambling casino. A dozen tables filled with poker and faro players did not attract him. Two at the far side dealt blackjack. One had three men playing Spanish monte. The roulette wheel caused him to pause.

A few desultory players placed their bets. He ignored them. An empty chair made him wonder about its occupant. A tall, red-haired woman hovered behind it, her hand resting on a cushioned arm. The jacket draped over the back held Hand's full attention.

The collars sported silver tabs similar to the boot-toe protectors Lovejoy wore. Hand remembered little about the man from the alley. There had been time only for fleeting impressions and quick decisions. He realized that he hadn't gotten that good a look at the marshal's attacker.

The redhead caught his eye and winked broadly. He knew she had not come with anyone. She worked in Abbots' casino to keep the customers happy and betting.

"Good evening, ma'am," he said politely.

"My, what a refreshing change," she said in a voice a touch too strident for Hand's liking. "A true gentleman. We see so few of them here. Fred, give this man some chips. I do believe he wants to chase the wooden ball around the wheel a mite."

"Thank you," Hand said. He passed over two rumpled ten-dollar greenbacks, not knowing what amount he should furnish. As a judge, he had never engaged in gambling. As a lawyer in Chicago, it had never interested him, either. This was virgin territory to be explored.

"Don't bet it all on one number," the redhead said.

Hand tried to find a hint of sarcasm in her voice and failed. She seemed to be giving honest advice.

If so, that was all that was honest in the casino. The jerky motion of the wooden ball as it spun and banged against tiny metal posts in the roulette wheel convinced Hand that some type of mechanical brake determined the ball's eventual resting place. The croupier chose the winner, not chance.

"May I sit here?" he asked, indicating the chair with the dress coat draped over it. The indecision fluttering on the woman's face told him she expected the coat's owner back soon.

"Never mind," he said. "I can see much better from this side." Hand placed alternating bets on red and black, winning twice more than he lost.

"You're lucky this evening," she said, turning her attention to him.

"I might be," Hand said, letting her determine exactly where she thought his luck lay. He looked past the painted woman at a small door decorated with inset wood pieces. The door opened and Jeffrey Lovejoy came through it.

Hand had not seen the young man's face clearly in the alley, but knew instantly who he was. The silver toes on his boots, the silver cuff links on his dress shirt, and the arrogant gait all condemned him as the man who had attacked Marshal Pevsner.

"Is this your companion?" he asked the woman.

She looked over her shoulder and nodded.

"Sorry to be so long, my darling," Lovejoy said, settling back into the chair, "but you know how tedious money talk can get."

"Did Mr. Abbots approve your credit, Jeffrey?" she asked in her unpleasantly shrill voice. This confirmed Hand's quick identification of the man.

"Of course. He always does. He knows who his good customers are. Don't you, my darling?"

She shuddered lightly.

Hand wondered what went on between them. Whatever it was, the woman didn't like it. She worked here and must endure much that a more moral woman would never condone. The hint of cruelty in Jeffrey Lovejoy's eyes hinted at a relationship based more on fear and pain than love.

"Do hurry and bet," she said to Lovejoy. "Fred is about ready to spin the ball again."

Hand hung back and watched Lovejoy place a hundred-dollar bet on red. The ball landed on black. Lovejoy increased his bet and lost more and more heavily. A thousand dollars went on a single number. The croupier made no effort to hide how he used the mechanical brake to prevent the ball from landing anywhere near the number.

Lovejoy seemed not to notice. If anything, he became more flushed and animated. He drank heavily and began to wobble, even when seated. Hand hoped that the marshal had convinced the club's owner that Lovejoy could be taken out without too much commotion, which would be bad for business.

The redhead alternated between an increasingly drunk Lovejoy and Hand, who bet modestly and won slowly by going against Lovejoy's bet. He had started with twenty and now had fifty dollars in chips before him on the table.

"Do bet more," the woman urged. "It's more fun!"

Hand looked up and saw the marshal standing at the entryway. The lawman shook his head slightly to indicate that Abbots refused to allow him to arrest Lovejoy on the premises.

"I'd rather spend the money in other ways," Hand told the woman.

Her eyes widened and she smiled in honest pleasure. "I'm glad, but you'll have to offer more than him." She indicated Lovejoy, gesturing cautiously.

"You misunderstand," Hand said. The woman tensed. "No, wait. Get him outside and this is yours."

"All fifty dollars?" Her eyes widened even more, this time with greed. Hand had no idea what she earned in a month, but the money he offered far exceeded it.

"Just get him outside—after I leave."

She nodded briskly, all business.

Hand left his chips on the table and quickly joined Marshal Pevsner.

"The owner refused to let me take him out, and we won't pry him loose," grumbled the marshal. "I've seen that son of a bitch stay in here for days."

"He'll be out in the alley in a few minutes," Hand said.

"You think you bribed the red-haired whore?" Pevsner snorted in disgust. "You've got a lot to learn about the lowlifes in Denver, Judge. She took your money and then she'll take his."

"There's no other way, is there?" asked Hand. He had

read the woman right. She had no love for the drunken profligate at the table. Even if the club's owner protected his patrons, the woman wouldn't. Not this time. The expression on her face had told Hand Lovejoy was not a gentle master.

"Reckon not. I got other business to tend to and I'm not going to put a deputy on Lovejoy full-time, as much as I want to nail the son of a bitch."

"Just a few minutes, Marshal. I don't think we have long to wait."

Hand began to get impatient when Lovejoy hadn't appeared in ten minutes.

The marshal grumbled under his breath and shifted his weight from one foot to the other. "If Abbots wasn't such a powerful man, I'd say the hell with him and drag that rounder Lovejoy out by the scruff of his neck."

Hand knew the marshal was talking himself into doing just that. He held the lawman back when a slice of yellow light showed at the side of the building. An argument reached across the street to where they stood in deep shadow.

"You worthless whore," Lovejoy shouted. "You spend my money, then you refuse me. I'll beat you good!"

The sound of a fist striking soft flesh sounded. Pevsner and Hand raced across the street in time to keep Lovejoy from hitting the woman a second time.

The redhead held her cheek where she had been struck. Fire and hot hatred blazed in her eyes. "Take him. I hope he rots in prison!"

"He won't be out any time soon. Not even his pa is going to get him out," Pevsner declared.

"You worthless slut," raged Lovejoy. He spun and reached for his pistol. A sick crunch echoed through the night. He toppled to the ground, unconscious.

Hand had drawn his six-shooter and clubbed him with it in one smooth, quick motion. He stood over Lovejoy and stared at him, realizing how easily he had drawn. If he had thought about it, he could have pulled the trigger and killed the man as easily as he had laid him out in the dusty alley.

"Thanks, Judge," the marshal said.

"Are you a judge?" asked the woman.

Hand fumbled in Lovejoy's pockets and found the man's wallet. He passed it to the woman. "Take this. You've earned whatever's in it."

She didn't bother examining the wallet. She threw it into the alley. "I already got every cent he had on him," she said contemptuously.

Hand shrugged it off. He helped Pevsner get the man to his feet and walking away from the building. The peace had been maintained inside Abbots' club. No matter how powerful Lovejoy's father, he could have no dispute with the club's owner. Jeffrey Lovejoy had been arrested outside, on the street, broke and drunk and disorderly.

"I'm going to keep this son of a bitch locked up until his balls turn blue," Pevsner declared. "Thanks for the help, Judge. I'd've got him eventually. You made a touchy situation work for us. I appreciate it."

"You owe me," Hand said.

"You still want to find the Thornberry boys? You're a damned fool." Marshal Pevsner heaved a deep sigh as he dragged his prisoner along. "A promise is a promise. I'll do what I can when I get this owlhoot put away for the night."

Hand's heart almost exploded in his chest. At last he would get even with the men who had murdered his family.

14

"Get on back to your hotel and rest up," said Marshal Pevsner. "I'll keep this yahoo on ice for the night and do some askin' around about the Thornberry boys."

Hand started to argue. The marshal had said he would help, but Hand wanted him to do the questioning now. He paused when he saw the expression on the lawman's face. It had been a long, difficult night, and locking up Jeffrey Lovejoy counted as a fulfilling task for the marshal.

"All right," Hand said. "I'm feeling tireder than I'd thought."

"That red-haired whore back at Abbots' club had a thing for you. I saw it in her eye," the marshal said. "You could do a lot worse than her."

"I'm going back to the Palmer House to sleep," said Hand. "Just sleep."

Pevsner stroked his thick mustache and eyed the judge curiously. "That's part of what's eating at your innards, isn't it? You got to find the Thornberrys because of something they did to your woman."

"Here are copies of their arrest warrants. Read them for yourself, Marshal." Hand dropped a handful of papers onto the lawman's desk and left, not trusting himself to say anything more. From the corner of his eye he saw Pevsner poking through the stack to read the charges filed against the Texas drovers.

The tiredness evaporated when Hand stepped outside onto the rickety boardwalk. Cold wind blew from the mountains and erased all thought of sleep. He started for the saloon district with half a thought to doing what the marshal had promised—he had questions to ask. Hand realized that he was new to Denver and didn't know the right people to ask or the right places to go. He could only end up in trouble.

Yet he hated the inactivity. Every instant he waited allowed the murdering Texans to get that much farther away. Pevsner seemed to know them and wanted them for bank robbery. Hand wondered what he would do when he caught up with the murderous Thornberrys. Could he draw the pistol riding high in his coat pocket? Could he pull the trigger that would end a life?

His fingers traced the raw scar around his neck. Without even conjuring up the memory of his raped and dead wife, he knew he could. Some men deserved to die like rabid animals. The Thornberrys and their worthless cousin counted among those the world would be better off without.

Hand wandered the streets of Denver, feeling separate from the activity of the boom town. Plays went on behind doors fitted with elaborate beveled-glass windows brought across the country by rail. Men drank in saloons. Others gambled and whored. He saw it and floated away, a solitary leaf caught on a flood and unable to change his destiny.

Fatigue again seized him after hours of pointless wandering. Once he stopped outside Abbots' gambling club just beyond Larimer Square. He thought about what Pevsner had said, about the red-haired woman, about the hollow ache inside him. Hand made a decision and turned for the railroad yards and the Palmer House situated near them. There would be another woman for him one day. Not now. And not a woman who sold her body to any man with two coins to rub together.

Troubled sleep and haunted dreams caused Hand to thrash about until the first pearly fingers of dawn appeared above the eastern horizon. The knock at his door brought him bolt upright and reaching for the six-shooter stashed under his pillow.

"Hand, it's Pevsner. You in there? You alone?"

Hand wiped the sleep from his eyes and rolled to the floor. He put the Lefaucheux back into the special pocket on his coat before opening the door.

Marshal Pevsner stood outside, impatiently rubbing his

bushy mustache. "I got news for you. You want to hear it?"

"Yes, what?" Hand was still partially asleep. "Where are they?"

"Get your drawers on and meet me downstairs. You can buy me some breakfast. I'll tell you then." A wicked gleam came into the small man's eyes. "You're quite a sight in your long handles. You didn't go find yourself that redhead, did you?"

"No." Hand came fully awake and knew the marshal poked fun at him. It was good-natured, but Hand could think only of the information about the Thornberrys.

"Don't mind if I see how she thinks about a peace officer, then?"

"No. Do as you will. I'll be down in a few minutes." Hand closed the door and organized his thoughts. Dress. Be sure the pistol was placed properly in his pocket. Get his boots on. Go down and find the marshal. As he went through the routine of climbing into his clothing, he reflected on what the marshal said about the whore. He pushed it from his mind. Pevsner only joked.

The marshal sipped at a cup of bitter coffee when Hand entered the restaurant.

"Sit down. This isn't going to take too long." Pevsner motioned for the waiter to bring a cup of coffee for Hand.

Hand hadn't realized that he was still not awake until the hot coffee puddled in his stomach and brought him to full consciousness.

"Where are they? I want them, Marshal."

"I reckon you do. Names weren't mentioned in the warrant you showed me, but I reckon the women raped and killed were some relation. What was the man to you?"

"A brother. And one of the women was his pregnant wife."

"And the other woman was your wife." Pevsner shook his head and sipped at his coffee. Droplets dotted his mustache. He shook them free and added more sugar to his coffee.

"I want them. They did this to me." Hand pulled his collar away and showed the scars left by the rope.

"Wondered how you'd come by that. Seen a man or

two with similar rope burns, but they weren't like you."
He chuckled. "Fact is, one of them I caught and sent to
the Territorial Prison down in Cañon City. He was all set
to have his neck stretched when the governor comes
through with a pardon. Big mistake, that."

"Why? What happened?" Hand impatiently waited for
the marshal to have his say and get on to the reason he
had helped the man the night before.

"He ended up killing the governor's business partner
in a robbery less than a week after he got out. So much
for leniency."

"The Thornberrys," Hand said. "Jake, Matt, Ben.
And Marsh Aylesworth."

"Don't get your dander up. I'm a mite slow in getting
around to finding out about them, but I will." Pevsner
pulled out a pocket watch and studied it as if it told him
everything he needed to know. He snapped shut the case
and returned it to his vest pocket. "Time's about right."

Hand reached for the Lefaucheux in his pocket.

"You won't be needing that. We're not cornering the
Texan bastards. We're just going to find out about them
now."

"How?"

"A man of few words. I usually appreciate that,"
Pevsner went on, his voice cheerful. "There's a rumor
that the 7:05 train to St. Loo will have a passenger who
might know something about their whereabouts."

"Who is he?"

Pevsner grinned crookedly. "It's not a he. The Texas
lads cut a big swathe through Denver in the few days they
were here. They're quite the ladies men." Pevsner heaved
himself to his feet and dropped a nickel on the table.
"Let's go talk to the lady, if you can call her that."

Hand found himself hard-pressed to keep up with the
bandy-legged marshal. The man's legs pumped briskly as
he crossed the street and mounted the steps to the railroad platform. In the distance a column of smoke appeared and grew.

"Coming down from the pass," said Pevsner, not
looking at either Hand or the approaching train. "It's
only supposed to stop a few minutes for passengers and
to take on some water. Looks as if there's going to be

one passenger less." He pointed to a petite, homely young woman sitting nervously at the end of a hard wood bench. She worked a lace handkerchief back and forth between her fingers. Now and then she dabbed at her running eyes.

"Who is she?" Hand was startled to see her so conservatively dressed. She looked far too respectable to be a friend of the Thornberrys.

"She was a teller in the bank they robbed. I suspect she gave them information they needed for committing the robbery. It went too smoothly and they got too much money on just the right day without someone giving them details of how the bank was protected and when money came in. They took out a guard with a shotgun and another in the back room and never worked up a sweat."

"Why haven't you questioned her before?"

"Judge, you think I don't know my job? She went to ground, and it's taken this long to find her. People in her class don't peach on each other like most of the folks I know." The marshal stopped in front of the woman.

She looked up at him, her eyes wide with fear. "No," she said in a trapped-animal voice. "I didn't mean to . . . I didn't know Jake would do it. Honest!"

"Calm down, ma'am," the marshal said. The woman looked toward the slowing train. Pevsner moved to block her view. That simple shifting told the woman everything. She was in deep trouble and wasn't going to be allowed to run away from it.

"I didn't know Jake was going to rob the bank. You've got to believe me."

"That's a mite hard," the marshal said, "since you upped and disappeared after the robbery. I figure you and Jake were holed up somewhere."

Hot red spots appeared on her pale cheeks. Hand saw indignation stiffen her entire body.

"Mr. Thornberry and I were *not* together, Marshal," she denied hotly. "He . . . I never saw him after the robbery."

"He used you, didn't he?" Pevsner said quietly. "He's a real son of a bitch. Excuse the language, ma'am. That's the way I see him."

Hand admired the skillful way Pevsner interrogated the

woman. He put her at ease with his manner and then fed her indignation at the conniving outlaw.

The train came to a screeching halt at the platform. The conductor bellowed, "We're leaving again in ten minutes. Ten minutes!"

Pevsner shifted again and blocked the woman's direct view of the train. "I reckon most of what you did was innocent-seeming at the time. You told him about the bank guards, didn't you?"

She nodded and lowered her eyes in shame.

"But you couldn't have known he and his brothers were going to rob the bank. Did you love him?"

"I thought so. I thought he loved me. He swept me off my feet. He seemed different from other men."

Hand said nothing. Jake Thornberry must have taken up acting to convince this poor, somewhat plain woman that he had eyes only for her. He tried to make up his mind how he would rule if her case had come before him in a court of law. Could he send her to prison for her part in the robbery?

"He is different. He's one mean son of a bitch." This time Pevsner didn't bother apologizing to her for his vulgar language. He looked over his shoulder at the train. The conductor was waving passengers aboard. "You plannin' on going back East?"

"To my family in Decatur. I'm so ashamed of what I've done."

"Trusting a man isn't a crime, ma'am." This caused the plain young woman to look up. Tears welled in her eyes and threatened to overflow at any instant. "I reckon Denver isn't the place for you right now." Pevsner heaved a deep sigh and looked at Hand. "What do you think, Judge?"

"She did aid and abet the Thornberrys in a felony crime," Hand said, seeing his role in this small drama.

"This here's Judge Hand, come all the way in from Kansas after those scalawags."

"A judge? From Kansas?" The woman's eyes widened even more. Tears seeped out and ran down her pale cheeks. She dabbed gently at the salty, wet streaks.

"He's on their trail. He doesn't want a poor bank teller who made a mistake, do you, Judge?"

Hand paused dramatically as if going over the ramifications of the law in his own mind, then shook his head slowly. "I want Jake and the others."

"See? I reckon we'd both let you get on that train and go back to your family if'n you'd help us."

"You want to know where they are, Marshal?"

Pevsner said nothing. The woman had to come to grips with her own guilty conscience. From what had been said, Hand saw that the decision to turn the Thornberrys over to the law wasn't a difficult one for her. She had been used, and she knew it. The hardest part—and the part that had kept her silent to this point—was the humiliation of being duped by the outlaws.

She straightened and clutched hard at her handkerchief until Hand thought it would turn to liquid.

"I don't know for certain where they are. I heard the one who worries all the time—"

"Matt Thornberry," Hand supplied.

"Yes, Matt Thornberry. I heard him talking about heading south. They didn't know I overheard, but I did. They were going to Manitou Springs."

"They're going to Manitou Springs," Pevsner said, mulling over what this might mean. "And you, ma'am, are going to Decatur, if you want to get on board that train."

"Thank you, Marshal. I appreciate this."

"Be more careful in your selection of men," the marshal said. He helped her onto the train.

Less than a minute later, the engine's smokestack belched ash and sparks and the heavy train began to move ponderously. In less than five minutes it was out of sight. Not until it vanished did Marshal Pevsner speak.

"I can't go after them. Manitou Springs is out of my territory, a good two days' ride to the south."

"You've done what you promised, Marshal. Thank you."

The marshal ignored the outstretched hand. "I don't want you crossin' those owlhoots. They're mean sons of bitches. You find them, you get a lawman and get them arrested properlike. Do you understand, Judge?"

"Thank you for your concern, Marshal Pevsner. You've been a great help to me."

"Go find them, then," Pevsner said angrily. "Get yourself killed. See if I care. Damn. New warrants to issue for them. Got to telegraph and—" He stalked off muttering to himself.

Hand returned to the hotel to pack. He had a two-day ride ahead to reach Manitou Springs and his quarry.

15

Sebastian Hand worried that the winter snows would come early. He had left Denver immediately after Marshal Pevsner had learned of the Thornberrys' intention to go to Manitou Springs. The wind whipped past him off Pikes Peak and turned his face to leather. The coat he wore with the Lefaucheux riding in the pocket proved scant protection against the cold working into his bones.

Only the hatred burning brightly inside kept him moving into the teeth of the canyon winds. He passed Colorado Springs and worked his way past incredible varicolored stone arches in what the local residents called the Garden of the Gods. More than once he wished he had taken the train to Colorado Springs and then ridden up toward Ute Pass. He had been too eager to find the men who had ruined his life to wait for any train. Hand patted his horse's neck and decided to get down and walk a spell. The climb had become steeper and the animal strained with every step into the wind.

The canyon was dotted with small ranches. He didn't bother stopping to beg a meal or shelter. The wind had yet to become unbearable. He had a hint of what winter in the Rockies would be like, though, from the biting edge.

"There," he said to his horse at the end of the second day. "Down in the canyon bottom. We can get somewhere nice to hole up and rest." Hand patted his coat pocket to assure himself of the six-shooter there. The gunsmith in New Orleans had been contacted. The shipment of Lefaucheux pistols from France had been delayed. A spare pistol would be shipped to Denver and would await him at the Palmer House within a month.

Hand worried over the lack of that second pistol. Drew Claggett's advice had been specific.

More than that, he would have felt better having another pistol balancing him in his left pocket.

"One's all it will take," he muttered to himself. "And when I find them . . ."

He rode slowly into the small town, expecting to see the Thornberrys at every turn in the winding road. Hand wasn't sure if he was disappointed when he failed to sight even one of the treacherous Texans along the way. He needed some time to compose himself and overcome the doubts Drew Claggett had put into him.

Could he kill a man if he had a chance? He knew he could never shoot anyone in the back, even Jake Thornberry. But to face him, six-shooter in his grip? Hand thought that he could. And that worried him. He thought he could. He lacked real experience. Sentencing a man to hang had put a great strain on him when he'd been on the Ellsworth bench. The Thornberrys and their cousin had deserved the sentence he handed down, but it had still gnawed away at him.

"Shooting a mad dog isn't a crime. It's a duty," he said aloud, trying to convince himself he was able.

A man coming out of a general store stopped and stared at him, wondering about a stranger who talked to himself.

Hand had to smile. He must be a sight. Two days of hard riding through wild and beautiful land had taken its toll on him. Every bone in his body ached. He longed for a hot bath, a shave, and the chance to sleep in a soft bed. The brief stay in Denver at the Palmer House had spoiled him for life on the trail.

"Can you recommend a hotel?" he called to the man standing in the general store's doorway.

The man scratched himself, then pointed farther down the street. "The Manitou House is the best you can do in these parts, mister."

"I need to find the sheriff, too," said Hand.

"What's your need with him?" This sparked hot interest that had only been smoldering before.

"I'm looking for some men."

"You don't look like a bounty-hunter."

"I'm not. I was a judge. They got away from the Ellsworth marshal and fled to Colorado."

The man's attitude hardened. "You're looking for them Texas bastards, ain't you?"

"I need to talk to the sheriff about it," insisted Hand. He didn't want to waste his time informing everyone in Manitou Springs of his mission. In a place this small, word might get to the Thornberrys and make finding them even harder. He didn't want them to split up. Taking all four of them at once might be hard. Tracking them down one by one would be the work of a lifetime.

"You're talkin' to him," the man said. He came out to the edge of the boardwalk and pulled back his vest. A seven-pointed star clung precariously to his dirty green-and-black-check flannel shirt.

Sebastian Hand dismounted and tethered his horse to a post supporting the roof over the store's boardwalk. He used the time this took to get his thoughts into order. He didn't want to step on the lawman's toes needlessly. Finding the outlaws would go quicker with the sheriff's co-operation.

"Marshal Pevsner up in Denver telegraphed you about me," he said. "Sebastian Hand is the name."

The sheriff made no move to take the proffered hand and shake it. "You was a judge over in Kansas? They're stupider out on the plains than I thought," the sheriff said, spitting into the street. "You can't just come over here and think you got any authority."

"I've got the authority," Hand said. He pulled out copies of the arrest warrants he had issued for the Texas drovers. The sheriff waved them aside.

"Those don't mean squat out here. What do you know about those boys?"

"I know they're cold-blooded killers." In spite of himself, Hand couldn't keep back the image of his dead Laura. His voice almost cracked.

"You said a mouthful. And they're *my* business, after what they done here."

"They robbed a bank in Denver. Marshal Pevsner wants them for that. And my warrants are for murder."

"That's still nothing compared to what they done here. I want them bad, mister."

"Hand. Sebastian Hand."

"Well, then, Mr. Ex-judge Sebastian Hand, you ride on up to the Manitou House and get yourself a square meal, take a bath in the mineral waters if that suits you, sleep till noon tomorrow if you like, then get on that horse of yours and get the hell out of Manitou Springs." The sheriff spun and stalked off without another word.

Hand watched him go, wondering what the Thornberrys had done. He would find out.

Unless he missed his guess, the outlaws had committed atrocities here that matched those in Ellsworth. The sheriff's family might have been involved, too.

He walked slowly down the main street in Manitou Springs and saw few people. Those that ventured out carried rifles or shotguns at ready in the crooks of their arms. The town had prospered under the direction of General Palmer and Doctor Bell, who had not only built the Manitou House but also the soda springs bottling plants. Everywhere Hand looked he saw the evidence of thriving business. Shoshone Springs, Ute Chief, Magnetic Springs, Navajo Springs, three others—all operated at full capacity from what he could see.

Yet Manitou Street was virtually deserted. He wandered down by the Denver and Rio Grande Railroad depot. The pleasant little station house showed five trains a day came into Manitou Springs. Finding the railroad agent proved impossible. Like the others in the town, he conducted his work behind closed door and drawn shade. Poking around a little did not reassure Hand.

Inside the lobby of a large hotel, the Mansions, Hand found a plaque proclaiming this to be another of Doctor Bell's hotels and only recently opened in June. But the clerk glared at him, and the men idling away their time in the lobby all had six-shooters close by. The entire town had turned into an armed camp. Being an outsider meant suspicion flowed toward him like an icy cold river. He shrugged it off the best he could. He wanted to be one with them—not their enemy. He left the Mansions in favor of somewhere else.

Hand considered the sheriff's recommendation of the Manitou House and discarded it. Both the Mansions and Manitou House were on the main street. From all he had heard, he didn't think the Thornberrys were likely to ride down Manitou Avenue.

Turning toward the steep cliffs, he spotted another large hotel looking over William Valley. He rode up Canyon Road to the Cliff House, another spa.

He took his horse behind the Cliff House and left it for the stable boy. When he entered the large lobby, he couldn't help remembering how lavish and extravagant the Palmer House had seemed. This country hotel was more modest—but only by the thinnest of margins.

"Heard tell the sheriff wants you to get on out of town tomorrow morning," the clerk said without preamble. Hand's eyes widened. Manitou Springs was a small town but news shouldn't have traveled from one end to the other this fast.

"He mentioned it," Hand allowed. "I'll be willing to go in the morning, but I need information."

"We aren't too talkative, 'cept about the mineral waters here. You might try a sulfur soda. Smells terrible but tastes real good," the clerk said. "It cures what ails you."

"Later," said Hand.

The clerk shrugged this off. "It'll be two dollars for you, half that for your horse. Your animal'll get curried and fed grain and your tack will be polished up real nice."

"Sounds fair," Hand said. He peeled off three greenbacks and pushed them across to the clerk. The man's lips curled. Nobody liked getting worthless pieces of scrip when hard currency was to be had.

"You a gunfighter?" the clerk asked suddenly.

"No," Hand said. Not everything had reached this man's ears. "I'm a judge—used to be, at any rate."

The clerk cleared his throat loudly. Hand wasn't sure if it was meant to be a derisive noise or if the man had medical problems. The answer came quickly.

"We don't need no judge in these parts. The springs bring in a good international trade. The soda water from all six springs is good to drink and bathe in. The General likes this place. So do we. The Fontaine qui Bouille lets you bathe for fifty cents. Best bargain in the Rockies."

The clerk cleared his throat again. "But the last thing we need is a judge."

"Every county needs a judge," said Hand. "The law is important, even if the town isn't too large."

"When we catch those bastards, we won't need no judge. String 'em up, I say. So does everyone else." The clerk's sudden change of topic didn't surprise Hand. The man had been edging toward a dislike of strangers, in spite of the town's reliance on them for the baths. Whatever the Texans had done had blighted the town of Manitou Springs.

"The Thornberry brothers and their cousin?" Hand tried to keep the tension from his voice.

The clerk was so het up talking about the Texans he didn't even notice. "Who else? They raped and killed and done horrible things in Manitou Springs. The sheriff couldn't get 'em. He was out serving process for the damned judge over in Colorado Springs when they blowed through here."

"Where did they go?"

"If any of us knew that, we'd be after them in a flash."

Hand said nothing about the sheriff's bravery or the townfolk's dedication in tracking down the killers. The instant the Thornberrys got beyond the sheriff's jurisdiction, he'd gladly forget all about the drovers. He hadn't struck Hand as a man intent on chasing felons to the ends of the earth.

Hand silently climbed the broad stairs and found his room halfway down the hall. He dropped his gear on the bed and stared out the window. He had not only a good view of the city but also the stable to the south. There a young boy began working on his horse. On impulse, Hand left the room and went to the stable. The clerk had vanished from behind the small desk. This suited Hand just fine. He didn't need to be told to bathe in mineral water or drink the bubbling soda water.

"You're doing a mighty fine job," Hand complimented the boy working on the horse. The boy was dark-haired, with big, wide eyes, and looked to be around eight years old.

"You the owner of this horse? You must be. No one else

is in town. The sheriff's run everybody off ever since . . .''
His voice trailed off and his face turned somber.

"What happened was quite a shame," Hand said, pretending he knew it all.

"Some of the womenfolk'll never get over it. My sister's only twelve." A catch in the boy's voice told Hand that the Thornberrys were even worse than he had thought. He touched the bulge in his coat pocket without consciously realizing it.

"The sheriff knows where they went, I reckon," he said, trying to draw the boy out.

"Everybody knows they hightailed it up the pass."

"Ute Pass?" Hand asked as softly as he could. His heart began to race. If the outlaws had gone back toward Colorado Springs, they might be anywhere now. But the pass acted like a funnel. Even if they had reached the far side of the Rockies, there weren't too many places they could have gone. That section of Colorado Territory was thinly populated.

"Where else?" the boy asked. He wiped a solitary tear from his eye and turned back to his work on the horse.

"I'd heard they'd gone south, toward Cañon City."

"Doubt that. Nobody around here thinks they did. No money there—and why would they want to go toward the territorial prison? No, sir, they'd hightail it away from the penitentiary." The boy pronounced the last word carefully.

Hand asked him questions about Manitou Springs and how he liked it here before getting back to the Thornberrys. "They'd most likely get to the other side of Ute Pass and head north, then?"

"The only thing worth mentioning on the other side is Leadville," said the boy, "and it's petered out. California Gulch was mined clean well nigh ten years ago—that was before I was born."

"A ghost town, is it?"

"Not that," the boy said. "There's enough crazy old prospectors in the area. Some of the folks here even talk about pulling up and moving there. Not my pa. He's too smart. He knows we can do all right selling goods to the damn-fool prospectors heading that way. You'd be surprised how much soda water we can sell. He gets it from Cheyenne Springs.''

Hand had to laugh. Those were words the boy had heard his father say and he only repeated them. ''Think what Leadville would be like with outlaws like the Thornberrys in it,'' he said.

''There's no sheriff over there,'' the boy said. ''Wide-open town. A real bad place, my ma says. Our sheriff rides over now and again, but he don't like it much. He says Manitou Springs is his home and he wants to keep it that way.''

''He probably knows Leadville is where the Thornberrys went when they left here,'' Hand said grimly.

''Yes.'' He was startled when the fierceness of his own words was matched by that from the eight-year-old boy. ''Wish I could go over there. They'd pay for what the did to Sarah. They'd really pay.''

''Be sure my horse is ready at first light,'' Hand said. He gave the boy a gold double eagle. The boy's eyes widened and he tried to thank Hand but no words came.

For what the boy had told him, this was small-enough payment. Sebastian Hand knew where his quarry had gone—and they had no idea that their nemesis was so close behind.

16

The unpredictable Colorado weather changed from burgeoning autumn to summer once more. Sweat poured down Hand's face as he guided his horse down the far side of Ute Pass from Woodland Park and north and west toward the Leadville mining district. He reined in and hooked his leg across the pommel as he studied the lay of the land. The area had been a booming gold-mining town once, back immediately after the War. California Gulch had been pillaged of every ounce of the precious metal, and the entire district had fallen on hard times.

A few miners' ramshackle shacks dotted the main street. A general store run by someone named Tabor had seen better days but clung on to life by the thinnest of threads. From the pathetic trickle of dusty men going and coming from the store, Hand saw that the store catered to the prospectors trying to duplicate the golden bonanza of the 1860s. No one got rich in Leadville; it had seen better days that might never return.

Two saloons, a Marx Brothers clothing store, and an improbable three-story hotel misnamed the Grand filled the muddy street well. Hand knew where he was most likely to learn about the Thornberrys. He rode toward the nearest saloon and dismounted. From inside, even though it was hardly past noon, came the raucous sounds of a piano player and men laughing.

He entered, aware of the weight in his right pocket. Since he had started carrying the Lefaucheux, he had found himself anticipating its use, wondering if the Thornberrys would pop up unexpectedly and force him to gun them down. Just inside the door he paused to let his eyes adjust to the dimmer light. Not for the first time he wished he had the other six-shooter he had ordered from New Orleans. The men in the saloon were the types he had most often sentenced to prison for their misconduct.

Silence fell as all eyes turned on the stranger. Then the jokes started and the piano player started another off-key, bawdy song. The patrons of the Gored Ox Saloon had looked him over and found him acceptable. Hand went to the long wood bar and leaned against it. This simple act felt better than he would have ever thought possible. Riding up into the high-altitude Ute Pass and back down had taken a considerable amount of the stuffing out of him.

"You look tired and thirsty," the bartender said. "More thirsty than tired, if I read you rightly," he amended.

"What kind of whiskey do you have?"

"Trade whiskey. Make it myself. A bit of gunpowder, some rusty nails for body, and the best damned almost Kaintucky whiskey we can get in from Denver."

"Beer," Hand decided.

The barkeep's face drooped, as if he took this as a personal affront. He served up the mug of foaming, hot beer without comment.

Hand dropped a dime on the counter and wasn't surprised when he got no change. Everything was expensive at the edges of civilization—except life.

The fight broke out and rapidly turned into a gunfight. The two prospectors dragged out old black powder pistols and started shooting at each other. Hand scrambled over the bar and landed flat on his belly beside the barkeep.

"This happen often?" he asked.

"Be over soon," the man said, his face pale. "They can't hit the broad side of a barn—leastwise, they never have before this." He cowered down when a stray slug blew apart an empty bottle on the bar.

Hand tried counting the rounds fired and lost track. Even though he wasn't on the receiving end of the barrage, it frightened him more than he would have thought.

When the firing was over, one prospector bellowed, "That surely does work up a man's thirst. Buy me a drink. And one for my friend here!"

The barkeep scrambled to his feet and gave both men, again friends, shots of his murky trade whiskey. They drank as if it were good. Draining their glasses, they left the saloon.

"Quite a bit of excitement," Hand remarked, returning to the front of the bar and his warm beer. "From the sleepy look of Leadville, this must be about it, though."

"Hardly," the barkeep said. "We got damn fools riding through all the time shooting the place up. And ever since them Texas bastards came into town, robbery's become well-nigh commonplace."

"You don't say," Hand remarked, fighting to keep himself under control. "Why's the sheriff allow them to stay if you think they're responsible for thieving?"

"What sheriff?"

"Sounds as if Leadville needs a lawman."

"You asking for the job, mister?" The bartender laughed. "You don't look to be that stupid. The Gallagher boys are doing all right protecting their silver shipments into Denver. They ain't lost but one or two."

"The Gallaghers?"

"Three Mick brothers, John, Charlie, and Patrick. You must be new around here if you ain't heard of their luck. They came to town a couple years back and asked Uncle Billy Stevens where to dig. He pointed them as far away from his own claim as he could. They started Camp Bird up north of town. They're going on rich now and Uncle Billy's still eking out a poor living on his claim." The barkeep shook his head, as if saying Irish luck was everything.

"They haven't been bothered by robberies?"

"Didn't say it don't trouble them, but they can take care of themselves. Most folks around here can." The barkeep looked significantly at the holes in the walls left by the two would-be gunfighters. "Some just don't have a good eye for shootin'," he concluded.

"You might just be putting all the thieving on the Texas boys because you don't like them."

"They're mighty easy to dislike," the barkeep said. He stepped back a half-pace when it occurred to him he might be talking to another from their camp. "Don't mean nothing by it, mister. They're good men. I'm only repeating what I heard others say.''

''Where might the Thornberrys be?''

''Back toward the mountains, back in the direction of Mosquito Pass, if I heard right.''

''Much obliged,'' said Hand. His innards shook in reaction. The Texans had a camp nearby. He had chased them a quarter of the way across the West. Now he had them.

He went outside and rested his head against his saddle. His horse shifted uneasily. Hand looked up, seeing nothing of the town. Attention focused on his Winchester. He drew it from the saddle sheath and made sure it held its full complement of shells. Shaking fingers closed around the Lefaucheux as he drew it. The gate opened and he found all six rounds ready to fire.

''Rifle, pistol, the Thornberrys. I don't need any more than that,'' he said to himself. He vaulted into the saddle and rode back toward the mountains.

A crudely lettered sign in the fork of the road showed where one trail came over from Manitou Springs and the other from Mosquito Pass. Hand didn't hesitate as he turned his horse in the direction of the other pass. Chance might work against him. One of his quarry might happen by the saloon and find someone had inquired after them.

Hand wanted to take them by surprise. Getting all four would be hard. He didn't doubt that. He went over in his mind what would happen, acting it out as if he were on a stage and the outlaws were mere props to his leading role.

He would dry-gulch them. He would shoot them down where they stood. No quarter. They hadn't given him or his family a chance. He wouldn't give them one, either.

The road turned rocky and showed signs of heavy wagons coming down from the high country. Hand got off the road and paralleled it for a mile before reining back. The sounds of horses came to him and turned him wary. He dismounted and edged back toward the road to look.

His heart almost exploded in his chest. Not fifty yards away he saw Smelly Ben and Matt Thornberry. What they said vanished in the distance, the wind smothering their voices. Hand saw that Matt complained and Smelly Ben objected to something. From the look of it, Matt wanted to ride in a wide circle and the burly younger Thornberry wanted to make a beeline for camp.

Hand slid down behind a rock and waited a few minutes. He was sure they could hear his heart beat, his lungs strain, smell the sweat popping up on his forehead. He was so close!

After what seemed a fair time, Hand peered back over the boulder. The men had vanished. He cursed his anxiety. He'd have to track them now, and he wasn't sure his skills were up to that. The outlaws were edgy and knew the law might be after them—even here, where there were no lawmen. They wouldn't leave a good spoor for him to find.

Still, Hand had to look. He was too close to their camp to call off his manhunt now. On foot, he went to look at the rocky ground where he had seen them. He could hardly believe his good luck. Deep, shiny scratches in the hard granite showed the direction the two men had taken.

Rifle clutched grimly, Hand started in the direction of the scratches. A turn took him into the mouth of a canyon. He inhaled deeply and caught the barest hint of wood smoke.

He took to the high ground, knowing he couldn't hope to get off a good shot upslope. If he got above them, sighted in on them as they ate, he might be lucky enough to wing two or more of them before they knew what was happening.

Ten minutes of strenuous climbing brought him to the top of a rise that gave him a perfect view of the Thornberrys' encampment. Hand dropped to his belly to keep from being silhouetted against the late-afternoon sky. His black shadow fell long and cold on the rock. He didn't want to alert the men by a careless movement any greenhorn might avoid.

Flat on his belly, he lost sight of the camp. Cursing softly, he wiggled around trying to get a better view of what went on below him. A tiny cascade of stones tumbled away. He froze, sure that the Thornberrys would hear and know he was after them.

". . . more silver than we can spend in a lifetime," bragged Jake Thornberry.

"It's gettin' too dangerous," complained Matt. "Those Irish brothers are guarding their shipments back to Denver too good. We can't open up one of them iron-plated wagons without dynamite."

"So we steal some," Jake argued. "We can open those wagons up like tin cans."

Hand worked around to get a good shot at the four men. Matt continued to argue the point of moving on while Jake insisted they had a good chance to get rich off the sweat of the few prosperous silver miners in the area.

"There's not much silver being moved," pointed out Marsh Aylesworth. "We might shake our asses into richer country if we go over to Battle Mountain in Nevada."

"This is prime country," Jake insisted.

The men stopped talking. Hand kept crawling until he pushed past a piñon and rested his Winchester on a gnarled scrub-oak branch. The sights lowered and centered on Jake Thornberry.

Hand's entire body shook uncontrollably. He thought of Laura, of Randolph and Frannie and their unborn child. He remembered the atrocities these men had committed in Manitou Springs and elsewhere. They were wanted for more than simple robbery in most places where they passed through.

He had it in his power to end their crime spree and bring justice to the territory.

He shook so hard he had to pause to collect his wits.

"What's that noise?" demanded Matt Thornberry. "I heard something moving up in the rocks."

"You hear every damned snake that slithers by. I never seen a man so spooked all the time as you, Matt."

"I heard something. There's somebody up there, I tell you." The soft gliding of metal against leather sounded. Hand knew the outlaw had pulled out his six-shooter and was ready for a fight. He could have retreated and bided his time. Another opportunity would have presented itself after those in the camp quieted down.

His nerves broke and he scooted forward even more, the rifle barrel finding a target below. Hand wasn't even sure which of the Thornberry brothers he saw. The sight picture was what Drew Claggett had taught. The spasmodic jerk of the rifle's trigger wasn't. The slug went ricocheting off a boulder above and to the right of his startled, unwitting target.

Pandemonium broke loose below. A hail of bullets answered his single shot.

"I told you, I told you," screamed Matt. "There's a whole damned posse up there, and they got us trapped in this damned box canyon!"

Hand forced himself to look over the oak limb and seek out another target. He saw Jake Thornberry running for his horse. He fired four times; each shot missed. He knew now what Claggett had meant about it being harder to hit a moving target than it was to potshot an empty bottle.

Even more to the point, Hand knew the cattle rustler had been right when he declared that Hand didn't have the guts it took to kill another man. He could have at least winged one of the outlaws. He had seized up, panicked, pulled his shot. He'd gotten buck fever.

He fired twice more and emptied the rifle's magazine. By now the Thornberry brothers had climbed into their saddles. Hand drew his six-shooter and fired at their backs, but the range was too great and the Texans were fleeing for their lives.

They thought an entire posse had set up an ambush. They couldn't have known it was a single man—and one who hadn't the mettle to kill from hiding.

Sebastian Hand sat on the boulder and stared at the empty camp. The four men had escaped. He doubted he had done more than scare them—and he had wanted to kill them, each and every one.

He had a considerable amount of thinking to do before he faced them again. Could he kill? Even after what they had done to him?

17

The next four days brought Sebastian Hand to tears. The Thornberry brothers had vanished from the face of the earth. He had had a chance to stop them—and he had failed.

Hand stood in a gully miles away from the Leadville central district and stared at six empty tin cans sitting on rocks. He drew the Lefaucheux in a smooth, easy movement, pulled back on the double-action trigger, and loosed a round. A tomato can flew into the air. He spun, crouching, and fired twice more. Two more cans whined off their perches. With easy contempt, he finished off the last three cans.

Then he stood and stared, empty inside once more. Men weren't tin cans. He could blast away accurately at lifeless targets all he wanted. He had faced a man, a living, breathing man, and he had gotten a bad case of buck fever. He had been unable to kill Jake Thornberry.

Hand went limp, the six-shooter dangling in flaccid fingers at his side. He could be the best shot in the entire West and it meant nothing. He had to use that skill—and he had to use it to slay.

Looking around the deserted terrain did little to reassure him of his mission and its likely successful completion. Since he had spooked the Thornberrys, they had hidden beyond his efforts to find them. He had tried tracking them and had failed. Quiet inquiries in Leadville had gotten him nowhere. Even posting a reward for them had failed to bring forth any information on them.

Hand had pulled down the posters after two days, fearing the Texans would leave the Leadville district and give him an even longer hunt to bring them to justice.

"To justice," he said softly. "Where's the justice? The law can't stop them. I've got to. I've got to!"

Frustration and anger built within him. He had failed his wife again. He hadn't been at home to protect her, to defend her from the Thornberrys when they had raped and murdered her. Now he had washed out again. Again, again, again.

He shouted in rage and clapped his hands over his ears. Guilt burned in him and he knew he could run a thousand miles and never be free of it. He had faltered for a split second and it had cost him the chance to end this madness.

Reloading, he considered a few more practice rounds. He dropped the Lefaucheux into his pocket and stalked off. Searching for the Thornberrys had been futile. He had to find a new way of getting to them. If he couldn't find them, he'd have to lie in wait and let them come out of their hidey-hole. It might take a while, but he dared not frighten them off. This had to come to an end now, or he would lose his nerve once and for all.

Sebastian Hand returned to the Leadville district and found the saloon where he had first gotten information about the Texans. Not for the first time in the last five days he entered and looked around, hoping against hope to see one of the outlaws. Hand had worked it out in his mind what he would do.

Confronting the murderer would not do, even if it happened to be Jake Thornberry. He needed to be sure he ended the miserable lives of all four men. Hand would slip out of the saloon and wait until the man rode off. He would trail him through the hottest hell, the deepest snow, across the tallest mountain. Once he found the others' camp, he would kill swiftly and surely.

Hand's entire body shook as he entered. He almost feared finding one of the Thornberrys as much as he did not finding one. The nervous release nearly made him collapse.

Only three men drank in the saloon—and none was a man he sought.

He made his way to the bar and ordered a beer. He had come to like the weak, watery brew—almost.

"Haven't seen you in here for a while. What you been up to?" asked the barkeep.

"I'm thinking about staking a claim," Hand said, more to hear himself talk than for any other good reason.

"You're not the only one. The Gallaghers just hit a new silver vein. They're braggin' on how this is going to make each of them a millionaire. They already got more money than they can spend in a lifetime. Now them damned Irishmen're going to be able to buy the whole damned town."

"Is that so bad?" Hand asked, not caring one way or the other.

"Not really. There's others around I'd as soon see rich. You, for instance. You're a likable sort, even if you don't know spit about mining."

"What makes you think that?"

"Your hands don't have the dirt crusted on them. Hell, mister, you look to be a gunfighter."

"What's that?" came a bellow from across the room. "Who's a gunfighter?"

"Not me," Hand denied, not even turning to face the man who had accused him of being a gunfighter. "The barkeep was just mouthing off. He didn't mean anything by it. I intend to file a claim in a day or two."

"You ain't a miner."

Hand turned and saw a huge mountain of gristle and ugly lumbering in his direction. The miner's eyes were bloodshot and the stench was enough to knock over a civilized man. Stale sweat and spilled beer made Hand's nose twitch. Without realizing it, he moved so that his right coat pocket was free.

"I'm new at prospecting," Hand admitted. "I'm lucky, though." Even as he talked, a seedling of an idea began to grow and burst into full bloom.

"Your luck just ran out," the miner said. He towered above Hand and peered down at him through bleary eyes. A heavy hand rested on the judge's shoulder and forced him back into the bar. "I think I'm going to enjoy taking you apart."

Hand's reaction came quickly and startled him as much as it did the miner. He slid along the bar until the man's arm straightened. He slapped the palm of his hand against the miner's stiffened elbow and batted his powerful arm away.

In the same movement, he drew his six-shooter and thrust it directly between the man's eyes.

"I could blow your brains out," Hand said in a voice that sounded as if another spoke. He tried to decide what was going on, then realized *he* was talking. It was as if part of him had slipped free and left his body to fend for itself. Detached, he watched and listened to the events unfolding.

The miner stepped back and grinned. Crooked black teeth showed through his cracked lips. "Go on. I seen how you pantywaists use your guns. You couldn't hit anything with that hunk of iron if you tried."

"Mister, wait . . ." the bartender started.

Hand, still detached and watching himself as if he had become another, shifted his sights slightly and fired. The newel post on the staircase leading to the second-floor cribs exploded into splinters. Not stopping, Hand swung the pistol around and shot out a coal-gas mantel on a light next to the stairs.

"Don't do this, mister. That costs money! The owner'll take it all out of my pay."

Hand ignored the barkeep. He said to the miner, "Either of those could have been your head." The part of him that watched from afar recoiled in horror at what the body did next.

"I've heard it said that even a .44 slug will bounce off the thick skull of a grizzly bear. You're about the size and pretty near as stupid. I know you sure as hell smell as bad as one."

The miner growled but did not advance.

"I don't reckon a bullet between your eyes would do much of anything." Hand dropped the six-shooter onto the bar and shucked off his coat.

For a few seconds the miner simply stared. It slowly dawned on him that Hand invited him to battle it out with bare knuckles.

"You just earned yourself a grave in the potter's field, mister," the miner said. He doubled up fists the size of quart jars and tensed his powerful shoulders. His shirt strained at the seams. The miner took an ungainly step forward, arms flailing. If either fist had struck Hand, he would have died.

Hand dodged quickly, moving on his feet as if he floated on a cloud. He cast one quick look at the Lefaucheux on the bar and knew he had made a decision that was likely to be fatal. Why he'd done this, he couldn't say. Part of him remained aloof and analytical. He tapped into the observations from that other self and did not panic.

Swinging as hard as he could, Hand drove his fist into the miner's midsection. He might as well have struck a slab of granite. The shock rolled all the way back to his shoulder and rattled his teeth. The blow ought to have felled ten men. All it accomplished was bruising Hand's knuckles.

The miner grunted and brushed it off as if a gnat had landed on him. "You're mine, you little wart. I'm gonna bust your head wide open!" He rushed forward.

Hand knew he couldn't let the man grapple with him. Those powerful arms would make quick work of him if they locked around his waist in a bear hug. He sidestepped and landed another powerful blow to the side of the man's head.

It staggered the miner enough to drive him to one knee. He shook his head, then roared like a bull and charged again.

Hand slipped in the sawdust on the floor. More in desperation than by design, he turned this to his advantage. He kicked out and tangled his legs between those of the giant miner.

The miner bellowed and toppled facedown onto the floor. Hand rolled over and smashed his elbow into the miner's neck. The rabbit punch dazed him.

"Kill you," the miner mumbled.

Hand was panting too heavily to answer. He came to his knees and saw a ring of people around him. Money changed hands. He knew they bet against him. If he had been with them, he would never have backed the slender, almost fragile judge over the muscular miner.

A fist crashed into his shoulder, off-target but still powerful enough to send him sliding across the floor. The miner got back to his feet. He wobbled as he walked;

Hand took scant consolation in that. Even a blow from this weakened giant could kill if it landed on his head or belly.

Hand rolled and rolled again. He crashed into a table. Using it to get to his feet, he knew the fight wasn't going to last forever. His arms had turned to lead. The spot where the miner had hit him smarted. A bruise already turned green and purple and made him wonder if he'd ever use the arm again.

"You've got spunk," the miner said. "I hate that!"

The burly man charged again, arms outstretched. They caught Hand and scooped him up into the bear hug the judge had feared most. Air gusted from his lungs as iron arms circled his waist. Hand screamed when his feet left the floor. He instantly regretted it. He needed the air for simple survival. Every breath he let out was a mistake; the miner tightened that much more and prevented new, healing air from entering his tortured, straining lungs.

The saloon turned black around him and the world spun in wild and crazy circles. Hand clapped his palms over the miner's ears. It took several seconds of frantic gasping for breath to realize this had worked and the miner had dropped him.

"My ears. He busted my goddamned ears," the miner roared.

Hand knew it wasn't fair. He didn't care. His arms were useless for fighting now. His strongest punch would bounce off the miner. Hand widened his stance, judged the distance, and waited. As the miner blundered toward him, still roaring in pain, Hand rocked back and got his weight on his left leg. His right foot shot out and drove straight into the miner's crotch.

He lifted the man a foot off the floor. The miner dropped to the sawdust-covered floor and lay there, twitching feebly and sobbing like a small child.

"He won," came a surprised voice from the back of the saloon. "As I live and breathe, he won! You owe me a hundred dollars, Clay."

The others in the saloon let out a shout that deafened Hand. They clapped him on the back and almost knocked him over.

"Let me buy you a drink, mister. I never seen fighting

like that. You took out Mountain Sid. Nobody's ever done that before. Nobody, and I been in Leadville almost two years now.''

Hand didn't know how he kept from shaking as he took the shot glass of trade whiskey and downed its contents. For the beat of a heart, nothing happened. Then the potent liquor exploded in his guts. It burned worse than anything Mountain Sid had done to him.

''Give me another. I need it,'' Hand said.

Everyone in the saloon laughed and crowded close. They wanted to be near the fighting phenomenon. The one who had won the bet from his friend Clay pushed through and said, ''Have you ever fought fisticuffs professionally?''

''Fisticuffs?'' asked Hand. He shook his head. He winced. Something felt as if it had come loose inside. He took another drink of whiskey. It burned worse than those preceding it, but they did give him a semblance of stability.

''We can arrange a match,'' the small man rushed on. ''There's enough fighters touring out West and calling themselves champions to make it interesting.'' He rubbed his hands together as if already counting the take from betting.

''I'm not a fighter,'' protested Hand.

''Any man who can deck Sid is one hell of a fighter,'' the small, weaselly man countered. ''I'd like to be your manager. We can make a fortune!''

''Get on out of here, Roy. You can't be a manager. Not for him. He needs someone like me.'' Another man pushed up beside Hand and poured a drink into his glass.

Hand knocked this back, too. The buzz from the fight left his ears and was replaced by the hum of too much powerful whiskey.

''I said I'm not a bare-knuckles fighter,'' repeated Hand. ''I'm going to stake a claim nearby. I want to be a prospector.'' No one was listening to him. They were caught up in the momentary excitement of a heavyweight champion from Leadville.

He let the others argue over who would manage him. He bent and picked up his coat. He winced as he put it on. The miner hadn't connected often, but when he had, the results had been devastating. Hand settled the coat on his shoulders with a sigh of relief as the pain from the effort faded.

He reached for his six-shooter, only to find it gone. The initial flash of anger at the theft was replaced by cold, gut-wrenching fear. He stared down the barrel of his own pistol. The .44 caliber had turned into something larger than the entrance to a large cave.

"Do you want to do this?" Hand asked softly. He stared into the miner's bloodshot eyes. A trickle of blood ran from the corner of Mountain Sid's mouth, and he gasped for the thin air like a straining locomotive.

The miner took a half-step forward, the Lefaucheux wobbling in his grip. Pain still etched the man's features. Hand was sorry now that he hadn't finished Sid when he had the chance.

"I never been whupped like that before," the miner said. The gun waved around wildly. The others in the saloon had fallen silent and drifted away from their new-found champion. Hand heard the one named Roy starting to make bets on how long he would live after Sid plugged him.

Hand started to argue and then stopped. He had no idea what would convince Sid not to kill him.

"Nope, no one's ever beat me up before. Especially not a little runt like you." Sid smiled broadly, his black teeth wet with blood from the fight. "I want to shake your damned hand, mister!"

Mountain Sid shoved the Lefaucheux toward Hand, who took the pistol and dropped it into his pocket. Then he yelped when the miner's hand engulfed his and crushed down.

"This here fella's my friend," Sid bellowed. "Anybody who messes with him's got to mess with me, too!"

"It's nice to have a friend," Hand gasped out.

"What's that?" demanded Sid.

"I said," Hand gulped, "drinks for everyone. A gift from my friend Sid and me!"

Sebastian Hand left the saloon hours later on shaky legs—but he left alive and with the respect and rough friendship of many in Leadville.

Finding the Thornberry brothers would be that much easier now, he thought. He had two dozen sets of eyes looking for them and that many tongues willing to wag when they sighted the outlaws.

18

Sebastian Hand sweated more than he had ever thought possible. He had found a small patch of land outside the official Leadville district and had filed a claim on it. He had no intention of actually mining. Finding silver or gold as they had done years earlier along California Gulch did not appeal to him.

He wanted to establish himself as a miner with a reason to ship huge amounts of silver to Denver. When word of his shipments got around, he knew it would draw the Thornberrys like flies to shit.

The sun beat down on him as he struggled to dig enough of a hole into the side of the hill to make it look as if he had a real claim on the mother lode. Not for the first time he was happy he had the money from the sale of his brother Randolph's store. In an instant he would have traded every cent for the return of his brother—in a way, he was using the money to get back at the men who had robbed him of his family. Sebastian Hand couldn't think of a better way to spend it.

When he had ''worked'' his claim a few more days, he would announce a huge discovery. He would flash money around Leadville and make everyone believe he had struck it rich like the Gallagher brothers over at Camp Bird, not ten miles distant. A strongbox loaded down with worthless rock would be sent to Denver.

And he would wait for the Thornberrys to hijack the shipment. When they did, he would have them. This time he wouldn't freeze up. His finger would pull back on his six-shooter's trigger, and he would end their spree of cruelty and death.

Hand wiped more sweat from his face and returned to his work with pickax and determination, if not skill. He had a great deal left to do if he wanted others to believe he had mined even a speck of silver from this claim. Timbers went up in the shallow hole to reinforce the shale and dirt roof. A path was cleared away to make a short runway for tracks. A single ore cart was all he could find, but it would be enough if he left it on the tracks just inside the mine entrance.

Appearance mattered more than practicality. From a distance he wanted his Lorelei Mine to look like any other—and no one would be allowed inside. Not until after it no longer mattered. Not until Jake, Matt, and Smelly Ben Thornberry and their cousin Marsh Aylesworth had been put into their graves.

"A miracle," the bartender said in awe. "You knock down Mountain Sid and we all thought that was just luck. But finding silver out there goes beyond mere luck."

"Right," cut in the weasel-faced Roy Fredericks. "This is superb. You've got an angel sitting on your shoulder, showing you what to do. You're one in a thousand, Sebastian."

He slapped Hand on the back. The former judge grinned widely, playing his role of successful miner to the hilt. "Drinks are on me. Drinks for everybody. Compliments of the Lorelei Mine's foot-thick vein of pure silver."

This bit of munificence didn't amount to a hill of beans. Hand had chosen a time when there were fewer than a dozen men in the saloon. One of the whores from upstairs offered herself to him. He gently told her he wanted to celebrate in more public ways. The hundred-dollar bill he carried soon evaporated as more miners came in and learned of his success.

He replaced the scrip with a pair of battered twenties. He didn't think about how much he spent. He worried more about getting the word out of a big strike. And he needed to let everyone know it came from the Lorelei. The Thornberrys might turn tail and run if they heard the owner's name.

A shot of whiskey rested on the bar in front of him as he thought about the outlaws. Did they even remember his name? Did they care who they slaughtered? As a judge, they might remember him, but the name "Laura Hand" would mean nothing to them. Randolph Hand was less than a memory, he was sure. Men like the Texans slept easily at night because they didn't know who they killed.

Sebastian Hand never slept well. Memories of his loss were everything to him. He needed to replace them with the sight of four graves on some windswept hill.

"You're one lucky son of a bitch," Mountain Sid said, sidling up to the bar. "You knock me silly and then you go out and find the richest damned claim since the old days along California Gulch."

"Barkeep," called Hand, "Bring a bottle. Sid's thirsty. Isn't that so, Sid?"

"It surely is, Sebastian. Thank you." The huge miner expertly flipped the cork out of the bottle of trade whiskey and took a long swallow that emptied a full quarter of the bottle. He coughed and wiped his lips. "Good whiskey."

"I need to know how to go about getting some of my silver to Denver. What can you tell me about shipping it?"

"Best to keep it buried somewhere and wait for spring," the big miner said. "No matter what's said around town, the only people getting their entire shipments through are the Gallaghers. And they spend a young fortune on guards."

"I want to get it to the big city," Hand argued. "Debts. The men who grubstaked me want some return on their money."

Sid nodded as if he knew all about this. "Tabor over at the store has been doing that to a lot of the prospectors. Heard tell he even gave those two deadbeats Augie Rische and George Hook enough to keep them looking. Money down a rat's hole if you ask me."

"It paid off in a big way for my backers. It might pay off for Tabor, too," Hand allowed.

"Reckon so, but I doubt it. You don't know them two deadbeats like I do." Sid took another long drink from the bottle and belched. "But you say you want to move a bit of silver out. You got it smelted down already?"

Hand cursed to himself. Simply finding the telluride of

silver wasn't good enough. He had to justify a box filled with ingots when he hadn't mined the tons of ore required to smelt down to a few ounces. If the Thornberrys asked around, they would know he hadn't kept the local smelter busy reducing the ore.

"About ready," Hand said. "I've been working day and night. I tell you, Sid, this is almost pure." He lowered his voice to a conspiratorial whisper. "I don't need to smelt this. It's that good. Pure nuggets the size of your fist!"

The miner's eyes widened. "Even over at the Gallaghers' claim, it ain't that good. They're even talking about bringing in a hydro mining rig to get into the pay dirt faster. I tell you, Sebastian, you're one lucky son of a bitch. I admire the hell out of you, I truly do."

Hand let the burly miner drift off with the bottle in his dirty grip. By the end of the night, every telling of Hand's find had magnified and become even more amazing. Hand overheard two men talking about the Lorelei as if it were El Dorado itself.

". . . the silver oozes down the walls, I tell you. He's dug so far down it's hot in there—and the silver is molten. All he does is put out buckets and collect it as it drips!"

". . . more than a mule can pull in a single day! Richer than California Gulch!"

Others offered less lofty appraisals of the amount of silver Hand had discovered, but no one doubted he had hit the mother lode. The money he had spent lubricating their voices had been well spent. Wherever the Thornberry brothers had holed up, word of such a mine would get to them quickly.

Word that there'd be a shipment back to Denver would certainly attract them.

"You going so soon, Sebastian?" Sid asked.

"Got to get back to the Lorelei. Hate to leave the little lady when she's been so good to me," Hand said. This sentiment was something the miners understood. Even though their faces fell when they realized they'd be paying for their own drinks, they wished him well.

Hand went outside to stare up at the stars peering down at him like thousands of tiny, spying eyes.

He heard movement behind him. He reached into his

leather-lined pocket and found the Lefaucheux. His finger curled around the trigger as he prepared himself for a fight.

"Got a second, Sebastian?" asked Mountain Sid.

"I reckon I do. What is it?"

The burly miner shifted uneasily from foot to foot. "I ain't liking working for the Gallaghers a whole lot. They're tight-fisted penny-pinchers. They don't pay a decent wage and I got to work twelve hours a day."

Hand sucked in his breath. He knew what was coming and he hadn't foreseen it when he had fabricated his story of a rich claim.

"I don't mind the work. Twelve hours a day is fair enough. You might even say the Gallaghers pay fair, too, but I don't cotton to them much. If'n you offer me the same as I'm gettin' over at Camp Bird, I'd be pleased as punch to work for you. The Lorelei is the talk of Leadville."

"Thanks, Sid, but I don't—"

"I'd even consider working for less. You ain't dropped as far down as the Gallaghers. I don't like working the lower stopes. Being all closed in gets to a man."

"I can't go hiring anyone right now, Sid," Hand said, thinking up a lie quickly. "I have to get permission from my backers in Denver. I'm only one-third owner. It'll make me rich, but there's two others with a say."

"You'll ask?" Sid sounded hopeful.

"Of course I will. I can see you're a fine worker. We'd be stupid not to hire on a man like you. But it can't be until after they see the first shipment of silver."

"I understand. You're sending it on the next stage, right?"

"That I am. Good night, Sid. And thanks for coming to me like this. I'm going to need men—and maybe even a foreman."

The huge miner went off whistling to himself, content that he might see a promotion to foreman. Hand hated to lie to him. He was a good sort and had heart. But it was necessary. Finding the Thornberrys meant everything to him.

He mounted and rode back toward his fraudulent mine. The night had turned cold as new hints of winter blew off the Rockies. Hand hoped that he could smoke out the Texans soon. He didn't want to spend a winter in Leadville, especially after he had announced such a rich strike. The men here were honest and hardworking. They weren't likely to take to him lying for any reason.

The road split toward the foothills. Hand reined in and sat stock-still in the saddle. Some hint of unidentifiable noise echoed down to him from his mining site. He'd had too much to drink and wasn't sure if the sound was only the liquor buzzing in his ears. Hand rode for another few minutes, then stopped when he heard a faint curse on the wind blowing downhill toward him.

He dismounted and drew his Winchester from its saddle scabbard. Taking a deep breath, then sniffing quickly at the wind told him of men upwind.

He cursed constantly now. He hadn't thought out his trap too carefully, he now realized. He should have known men like Mountain Sid would ask for jobs. He had neglected to take care of the detail of bribing someone at the smelter to claim he had brought in enough ore to reduce to a strongbox filled with silver bars. And he had completely overlooked the notion that the Thornberrys would hear of his strike and go directly to the mine.

Stealing ore wasn't their style, but he had been throwing around money as if it meant nothing. To Hand it didn't. The Thornberrys would interpret that spendthrift spree in another way: they'd think he had money to burn. He had played his role too well.

Hand approached the Lorelei Mine on foot. At first he thought whoever had been rummaging around in his camp had fled. Then he saw two horses tethered near the mine opening. He had dug only ten feet into the hillside before shoring up the fake mine and laying the ore-cart tracks to give the illusion of activity.

The outlaws were inside the mine's entrance.

Sebastian Hand's mouth turned dry. Two of the outlaws had come to rob him. Where were the other two? And was Jake Thornberry inside the mine? Of the Texans, Hand knew Jake was the leader, the worst, the one who had dropped the noose around his neck. He touched the scars on his throat and remembered the piercing terror of being left to sit on the horse, wondering if it would spook and race off to leave him dangling and dead.

He hoped Jake was inside the fake mine. He wanted him bad.

Hand levered a round into the Winchester's chamber. The sound ripped through the still night as loudly as if he had pulled the trigger.

"Somebody's outside," came a whispered voice.

"You're imagining things again, you fool. Keep looking. There's got to be silver around here somewhere. He didn't get rich off just granite."

Hand tried to calm himself. He started to shake, just as he had before when he'd come on the Thornberrys in their camp outside town. He vowed not to freeze as he had then. He had to pull the trigger when he got Jake Thornberry in his sights. For Laura, for Randolph and Frannie, he had to!

Circling, he swung around the mouth of the mine and went to the tethered horses. He pulled out the outlaws' rifles and carried them off. If they got to their mounts, he didn't want them enhancing their firepower. The two inside the mine might have only their sidearms; this gave Hand a decided advantage.

"There's someone outside, I tell you. The horses are whinnying!"

A dark form filled the mouth of the mine shaft. Hand lifted his rifle and aimed, centering on the darkness. His finger refused to curl. He still couldn't kill in cold blood.

Tears streaming down his face, he advanced until he could hide behind the ore cart. His movement attracted the man's attention. The shadow within a shadow moved. Iron hissed as it drew across leather. The foot-long tongue of orange flame that leapt from the outlaw's six-shooter almost blinded Hand.

He cowered behind the ore cart, clutching his rifle to him.

"There *is* someone out there. It must be the owner," the man just inside the mine's mouth shouted. "Get your butt out here. We got to get away."

"There's silver here somewhere. You saw how he was spending money tonight. I want it!"

"He was spending scrip, not silver. We got to get out of here."

"If there's anyone out there, why ain't they firing at you?" demanded the second man.

Hand swung around the side of the cart and leveled the rifle. "I've got you covered. Give up!"

The outlaw's six-shooter again spat flame. The leaden slug whined off the cart just above Hand's head. More from reflex than intent, his finger tightened on the rifle's trigger. The Winchester bucked and sent death flying into the mine.

One man grunted. The other cursed. Then the night filled with blazing pistols. Hand ducked back behind the ore cart, not sure if it would give enough protection. When one slug penetrated its wood side and almost took off the top of his head, he knew it wouldn't.

His best defense rested in his hands. He swung around again and fired slowly into the mine, measuring the shots, striving to hit the constantly moving forms he saw. Once he heard an outlaw grunt, but he wasn't sure he had even winged him.

"Surrender," he yelled.

"Go to hell," came the hoarse voice from inside.

Hand reloaded his rifle and continued firing. When he came up empty again and started to reload, the men in the mine made their bid for freedom. They erupted from the dark mouth, pistols blazing. Hand squinted and tried to get a good look at them.

"Run for it. Get to the horses," one ordered.

Hand reached into his pocket and drew his pistol. The double-action Lefaucheux barked once, twice, three times. An outlaw fell facefirst into the dirt. The other cursed and came back for him. Hand missed with his last three shots.

He reloaded as fast as he could, only to find both men had reached their horses. The one he had hit was only wounded. From the way he wobbled in the saddle, Hand guessed he had hit him in the thigh. The other man cursed when he discovered his rifle gone.

Hand fired at him. For a heart-stopping instant, Sebastian Hand thought he had blown the man's head off. A dark, round mass sailed into the night, then floated down.

By the time he realized he had only shot the man's hat off, both outlaws had wheeled and put the spurs to their horses' flanks.

Firing the remaining rounds at the fleeing outlaws did little to relieve the feeling of desolation building inside Hand. Again he had let the Thornberrys escape.

He went downhill to where their horses had been tied. He found the large brown Stetson. A single bullet hole—put there by his .44 slug—adorned the brim. Hand turned the hat over and over as he examined it. Sewn in the sweat brim was a name.

He carried the Stetson back to his small camp and lit a coal-oil lamp and confirmed what he had already guessed.

The name inside the hat was that of Roy Fredericks. Hand hadn't chased off the Thornberry brothers. One of the men in the saloon had come to rob him.

Hand sighed. He'd discovered still another flaw in his plan. The Thornberry brothers weren't the only crooks in Leadville. He hadn't thought that other thieves would be out to rob him blind.

Disheartened, he didn't even bother going after the sneak thief and his companion. Hand turned in for the night.

His nightmares were even worse, peopled with crowds of Texas drovers and weasels ripping at his flesh.

19

Sebastian Hand awoke in the middle of the night, bathed in sweat from his nightmares and worrying about Roy Fredericks. He pushed aside the thin wool blanket covering him and rose, hand on his six-shooter. Its presence did nothing to reassure him of his safety—or the workability of his mad scheme to catch the Thornberrys. Pacing up and down the hillside near his fake mine failed to work off the nervous energy he had built up.

If anything, his agitation grew.

Fredericks knew firsthand there wasn't any silver in the mine. What would the man say when he returned to Leadville? The same grapevine that had spread the word of a huge strike would quickly carry the truth. Hand might never trap the Thornberrys if Roy Fredericks told them of the fraudulent claim. They might turn tail and leave the district if they thought anyone had come after them expressly.

Hand's only advantage lay in surprise. The Thornberry brothers didn't know he was in Leadville and hot on their trail. For all they knew, he had died back in Ellsworth. Their brief encounter outside town had been a disaster, but they had no inkling who it had been shooting at them.

"Damn him," grumbled Hand. "He ruined it all trying to rob me. He ruined my plan." Hand paced for a few minutes more, letting the cold mountain winds erase the sweat from his body. Only then did he come to a conclusion: bluff wouldn't work if Fredericks insisted there was no silver.

Or would it? Hand smiled slowly, then returned to his thin bedroll. The weasel-faced thief and his friend might have played into Hand's ill-conceived plan. All it took to make the plan work even better was another, bigger lie.

In the morning Hand rode into Leadville and went straight to the saloon where he had spent so many hours drinking the night before. Another bartender was on duty, although the whores still worked into the early hours. The one who had offered herself to Hand could barely lift an eyelid in his direction; for the cribs upstairs, it had been a busy night.

"I'm looking for Roy Fredericks. I got some money for him for the job he's going to do for me," he told the bored barkeep.

The man shrugged. Nothing mattered to him right now. All he had to do was clean the glasses left filthy from the night shift.

"Can't say I've seen him around. Roy made himself scarce last night when him and me was over at the Full Keg Saloon. He and that good-for-nothing friend of his just upped and vanished."

"Oh?" asked Hand, knowing full well where they had gone. He wanted to hear if the bartender also knew.

"He left the faro game owing me damned near a dollar. I'm looking for him, too. If you see him, tell him he owes me and I intend to collect."

"No longer. Here." Hand passed over a crumpled greenback. "I'll take it out of what I owe him."

The barkeep looked at Hand, skepticism etched on his lined, weathered face. "What do you owe Fredericks a plugged nickel for?"

"As I said, he's doing a job for me. See you later on." Hand left. Standing on the boardwalk outside the saloon, he considered his best course of action. He looked up and down the street, past the Clarendon Hotel and to the line of shoe, book, and general stores. He went directly to Tabor's store, knowing it was the busiest in Leadville.

" 'Morning," greeted Horace Tabor when Hand marched in. "What can I get for you?"

"Nothing today," Hand said. Tabor had the reputation as the local easy touch for money. He grubstaked more than one prospector and had yet to see a penny in return for his generosity. Hand found himself liking the man and his good-natured behavior. Tabor had ended up in Leadville after coming to Colorado from Vermont. He had taken a fancy to Hand because of his short stay over in Manhattan, Kansas, and considered him a colleague. At the very least, he thought they were the only two in Leadville who came from Kansas.

Hand knew better. The Thornberry brothers had come to the district through Kansas.

"You didn't drop in to chin with me. I know you. I know a hard worker when I see him. And the word's out. You struck it big over by the Gallaghers' claim."

"Keep it under your hat," Hand said. "I'm getting a mite edgy about claim jumpers."

"Don't think of it," Tabor said. "We know who's where. There aren't enough of us in the district. Nobody'd believe for an instant you didn't have clear title to your claim. Old Johanssen in the land office might be deaf as a post, but he's not blind. He knows what's going on in these parts."

"I came by to see if Roy owed you anything."

"Roy?" Tabor frowned, as if the name didn't mean anything to him. He eyed Hand suspiciously and asked, "You don't mean Roy Fredericks, by any chance?"

"None other." Hand peeled off a twenty from the roll of greenbacks he carried. "I want to take care of any bill he has with you. It's part of his payment for doing me a favor."

"He owes me better'n fifty dollars. I thought he was a deadbeat." Tabor's eyes widened when he saw that Hand intended to pay the full amount. From the back room came a stout, stern woman dressed in a severe black dress with a high collar.

Tabor held up the money and looked at it as if he thought it might be counterfeit. "Look at this, Augusta. This man's paying off Roy Fredericks' account for him."

The woman took the bills and gave them the same scrutiny her husband had. She sniffed. "Whatever can that disagreeable man have done to earn this much money?" She fixed her coal-black eyes on Hand, as if demanding that he answer.

Hand was only too happy to. In his conspiratorial whisper he said, "Roy's doing me a big favor. He's going to tell everyone there's no silver out at my claim."

"Why ever would you want him to do that?" Augusta Tabor asked.

"Robbers. I'm getting ready to ship a strongbox filled with silver ingots to Denver and I don't want the robbers to think there's anything inside."

Augusta Tabor sniffed and turned, not wanting to hear any more of such a harebrained scheme.

Her husband frowned even deeper and shook his head. "I don't know what you're doing, Mr. Hand, but taking Roy Fredericks into your confidence isn't the wisest course. He has a reputation for being unreliable. Mean, too. In fact, there're rumors to the effect that he might be responsible for more than one theft himself. As I said, he's downright unreliable."

"He's a good man, Horace," Hand said earnestly. "The highwaymen plaguing the shipments to Denver can't be caught, but they can be decoyed away."

"There's been a mite more thieving than I remember in the past," Tabor allowed. "But, then, there's more silver coming out of Leadville than there has been in the past."

"I want mine to get to my Denver bank. Mining is hard work and I aim to retire a rich man."

"Luck to you. You're a good and decent fellow." Tabor hesitated, then added the piece of advice, "Just don't go trusting Roy Fredericks too much."

Sebastian Hand laughed and waved good-bye to the shopkeeper. He felt he had accomplished a good deal toward scotching anything Roy Fredericks said about the lack of silver in the Lorelei Mine. The rumors would fly, Fredericks claiming it was a salted mine and the others in town winking broadly. They would all think they and they alone knew Roy was working for Hand to ensure a safe shipment to Denver.

He went over to Chestnut Street and ate a hearty breakfast in the Grand Hotel's surprisingly good restaurant. After finishing his steak and eggs, he walked down Harrison Avenue and greeted everyone he saw, often inquiring after Roy Fredericks. The weasel of a sneak thief would hole up somewhere, thinking Hand was after blood. By the time the strongbox was on its way across Mosquito Pass, the Thornberrys would be lured out.

What Roy Fredericks did or said then wouldn't matter to Hand.

He still worried that the Thornberrys might be scared off. He had to do something to ensure their attack on the wagon shipment. Hand went to the assay office over on East Main near the Starr Ditch and looked around. Several suspicious fellows lurked outside, looking more like vultures waiting for dinner to die than prospectors bringing in ore for assay.

Hand touched the six-shooter resting in his pocket and reassured himself that he could use the pistol if he had to. He had fired at Fredericks and his cohort. He had even wounded one of the men. Being in a position of having to defend himself made it easier to use his weapons, he decided. When the time came to settle accounts with the Thornberrys, he could do it.

He *would* do it.

Sven Johanssen looked up from his pans filled with dark, gritty dust. When he saw who had entered his office, he covered the balance pans with a dirty cloth and wiped off his hands. "How can I help ya, Mr. Hand?" he asked.

"I need a favor," Hand said. "I can pay for it," he added quickly when Johanssen scowled mightily and started to shake his balking, gray-haired head.

"There's all the time prospectors coming in asking for free assays. It don't work that way. I got a family to think of. I could starve if I did everything on credit, like Horace does over at his store. Don't know how he lives. Don't know how Augusta puts up with his so-called charity."

"I can pay," Hand assured the man again.

"Been wondering when you'd come calling. Ya got one hell of a claim, or so they say. Why haven't ya had me assay it yet?" He cocked his head to one side and smiled slowly. "Ya got a sample in your pocket and want me to do it straightaway. All right, but for a price. I got the griddle hot. Plop your telluride down and let's see the silver dance out of it." He pointed to a potbellied stove in the corner of the cramped office. Even though it was warm, Johanssen had the stove fired up.

Hand had seen the process of assaying the black telluride of silver. Heat boiled out the silver. The amount of silver beading when compared with the size of the original sample gave a good indication of the richness of the pay dirt.

"I want to buy some silver, not have an assay done."

"What you up to, boy?" demanded the old man. "You're not saltin' that claim of yours to make some damn-fool Easterner think it's worth more than it is?"

"Nothing like that," he reassured Johanssen. "The silver is flowing from the mine just as I anticipated."

"Then why do you need more? Don't have enough of your own?"

Sebastian Hand flashed the greenbacks. The assayer's eyes widened slightly, then he squinted once more. "I get my fill of silver and the occasional gold nugget. What does scrip mean to me?"

Hand dropped two of the large-denomination bills on the counter. A third one moved Johanssen to drag out a box filled with silver scraps. He pawed through the old dynamite crate and found several medium-sized pieces of raw silver.

He placed them on the chemical-stained counter for Hand to examine.

"Any bags of silver dust?"

"It don't come like that. Not usually. Well, there might be some," Johanssen admitted. "I get this from the assay process." He dropped a small leather pouch on the counter.

Hand added a fourth greenback and dropped both dust and the silver nuggets into his pocket.

"This isn't anything illegal you're doing?" Johanssen asked as Hand was leaving. "I don't want any part of it if you're out to rook some greenhorn."

"Quite the contrary," Hand said. "With any luck, I'll be serving justice."

Johanssen waved him away, not wanting any more to do with Hand.

For his part, the judge was happy with the transaction. The silver had cost him more than it was worth, but Johanssen wasn't likely to brag about how he had suckered him. The silver had come from assays. According to law and custom, the silver belonged to the prospector bringing it in. Johanssen had kept it for himself after running the chemical tests to determine ore grade.

Hand waited until a small crowd had gathered near the shipping company before going into their office. He asked the clerk, "What's the commotion?"

"Stage is coming in from Denver."

"When is it returning? Soon? I've got a box I want to get to a bank back there."

"You getting ready to 'port some silver, Mr. Hand? Heard tell about your good fortune. Who'd've thought there was anything in the ground out there?"

"Silver?" Hand said too loudly. "I'm not shipping any silver. Just some personal things of mine." When he knew he had attracted attention, he reached into his pocket as if to pull out some papers. With his hand came the bag of silver dust. He had left the pouch open the slightest amount. As he moved, a trail of silver dust filled the stagecoach office.

A half-dozen people turned and pointed. Hand looked sheepish and shrugged at the clerk.

"You're *not* shipping silver, is that right, Mr. Hand?" asked the clerk.

Hand gave him a broad wink and put the pair of silver ingots on the counter. The loud click as he slapped them down drew even more attention.

"That's right. All I want to ship back on the stage is a box of personal belongings. For my family."

"Whatever you say. Can you get your box here by noon? The driver is all het up to get back into the mountains. He wants to make the first way station before sundown. If you ask me, that's straining his team way too much."

"I'll have it here." Hand strained to hear what the others in the office were saying. They whispered about his good fortune at the Lorelei Mine and speculated on how heavy the strongbox of silver was likely to be. Hand aided them in their guessing. "My box'll weigh in at close to eighty pounds. Is that any problem?"

"Eighty?" The clerk let out a low whistle. "I reckon not. It's a mite heavier than we usually carry. The pass is steep, you know."

"I'll pay extra, if I have to," said Hand. "And I want to know what security you provide."

"There's the driver and an armed guard. He carries a

sawed-off shotgun and is one mean hombre. You don't need to fret none on that score, Mr. Hand. We've got a good record for getting across the Rockies with our cargo.''

''Road agents have been working the area, or so I'm told,'' said Hand.

He hesitated after he spoke. He had flushed out Roy Fredericks and his cohort. How many other highwaymen were there likely to be, other than the Thornberry brothers? He didn't want to draw all of them—he wanted only four.

''We'll get your silver—your personal belongings—to Denver for you,'' the clerk assured him. ''We charge a dime a mile. It's steep, I know, but we've got a good record for getting through. Even in the dead of winter, we can get through.''

''All right,'' Hand said, putting extreme reluctance into his voice. He scooped up the nuggets from the counter and tucked them into his pocket. He trailed silver dust onto the floor as he left and pretended not to notice.

He heaved a sigh of relief when he got into the street. Enough people had seen him with silver to spread the word. No matter what Roy Fredericks said or did, no one would believe him. Everyone in Leadville was convinced he had found a rich vein of silver and was ready to send some of it back to his bankers in Denver.

Hand had only one more chore to do before saddling up and following the stage: he had to find a strongbox and load it down with worthless rocks.

20

"Don't you fret none, Mr. Hand," the shipping clerk said. "That strongbox will get into Denver just fine. We're takin' special care with this shipment."

Sebastian Hand looked at the driver and guard and nodded. Both men had a no-nonsense air about them. Both looked as if they could kill without a qualm in defense of their cargo and passengers.

Hand turned from the stagecoach company's employees and studied the two passengers. He had seen one man around Leadville but didn't know his name. The other had the look of a preacher about him.

"He's given up. Said we were godless heathens and too hard to convert." The clerk spat accurately into the brass cuspidor at the corner of the office. "If you ask me, he's just lookin' for a handout. He never done a lick of work after he got here. He expected us to build his damned church for him."

The clerk rattled on, but Hand barely listened. His mind raced ahead as he tried to cover every possible attack the Thornberrys might make on the stage. He had done all he could. He had baited the trap with what they would find irresistible: silver. Hand still worried. The murdering brothers and their cousin weren't the only crooks in these parts. How many others might his bait attract?

"Thanks," he said suddenly. "I've got to go talk to a friend." Hand spotted Roy Fredericks across the street. The ferret-faced sneak thief was talking to a miner and gesturing toward the stage. Hand didn't have to read lips to know what Fredericks was saying—and that the miner already knew everything he was telling him.

"Roy," Hand called out. The small man darted away.

Hand paused for a moment, then raced after the fleeing thief. He caught him when Fredericks stumbled over a rain barrel and had to regain his balance. He grabbed the man's collar and lifted enough to keep Fredericks from getting good purchase in the soft dirt.

"Don't kill me," Fredericks whined.

"Why should I do that, Roy? What have you been telling people around Leadville?"

"I don't know what you're doing out at that worthless mine, Mr. Hand, and I don't want to know."

"But you have been telling anyone who would listen there's nothing but drossy ore in the Lorelei."

"All I know's what I saw."

"Did you tell Jake Thornberry what you saw?"

"Thornberry? No, I don't know any Jake Thornberry. Or any of his brothers!"

Hand smiled. Fredericks had been spreading the word, and he hadn't figured out what Hand had done to make it seem that they were working hand-in-glove together. "Did Thornberry believe you?"

"He called me a liar. Me! I don't know why he said that. I just told him what . . ." Fredericks' voice trailed off. He realized he had just contradicted himself. "Don't kill me!"

"When did you talk with Thornberry?"

"Not more than two hours ago. He said he was leaving town. What's Jake Thornberry to you?"

Hand didn't want the weasel he held so easily talking with Thornberry again. If Jake had left Leadville, that might mean he and the others were planning on robbing the stage. Hand's heart raced at the thought of getting another chance at the men who had so thoroughly destroyed his life. Fredericks yelped. It took Hand a few seconds to realize he had lifted the man entirely off the ground and was shaking him like a terrier shakes a rat.

"You made a big mistake, Roy. There is silver out there. Tons of it."

"No . . ."

"Is your friend badly hurt?"

"Lloyd's hobbling around. Might for the rest of his life. You did something to the bone in his thigh."

Hand wanted to tell Fredericks that he'd blow his head

off if he saw him again. He refrained. That might send him scuttling out to find the Thornberrys and warn them off.

"I've been telling folks around town that you're working for me. Why don't you go over to the saloon and have a drink?"

"I owe money to the bartender," Fredericks said.

"I paid him off for you. Have a drink. On me." Hand thrust a dollar bill into Fredericks' pocket.

"You're a strange one," Fredericks mumbled. He got his feet under him and backed away. Then he ran as if all the demons of hell were nipping at his heels. As Hand watched the man go, he hoped Fredericks wouldn't tie up with the Thornberrys. If Jake had left Leadville hours before, the chance seemed slim.

Still, Hand knew his plans had seldom worked the way he had hoped. He had been too eager to find the murdering swine who had killed his wife and brother and had repeatedly overlooked important details. He touched the six-shooter in his pocket to reassure himself, then spun and hurried to his horse. He had work to do.

Killing work.

Hand sat astride his horse for several minutes, watching as the stage driver and his guard loaded the strongbox containing the worthless rock. The driver helped the two passengers into the Concord and then went to check the horses. The cursory inspection finished, the driver swung up into the high box and left Leadville without further ado.

Hand galloped for less than a mile, then reined in and let his horse walk. He didn't want to tire the animal needlessly. He might need the horse's full endurance later. For the moment, he was content to ride along parallel to the road and keep a sharp eye out for the Thornberrys. Trying to decide where they would hold up the stage had only made his head ache.

There were too many likely places. Hand decided their best choice was the first long incline leading into Mosquito Pass. The driver would slow there or kill his horses. The Thornberrys might even wait until the stage was a mile or two up the grade to ensure the team being as tired as possible.

He shook his head. Trying to figure out how an outlaw thought was beyond him. For all he knew, the Texas outlaws might just hold up the stage a mile or two outside Leadville and let the devil take the hindmost. After all, there wasn't a sheriff in the district. It would take an outraged citizenry forming a posse to stop the thieving along the roads. Hand wasn't sure anyone in Leadville cared that much—except for mine owners such as the Gallaghers. And they took care of their own shipments and didn't care what happened to the stagecoach.

Hand settled into the easy rhythm of riding. The stage rumbled past in the distance, raising a column of dust as it went. He kept up his steady pace, then cut back toward the road and followed a mile behind the stage. It startled him how fast the driver went. The horses would be dead by the time they reached the mountain passes.

An hour later Hand saw why the driver wasn't chary with his whip. A small way station along the road had a corral with six foam-flecked horses in it. The driver had changed teams and continued into the mountains with a fresh team. Hand didn't even slow. He kept after the stage, certain that the lure of the silver in the strongbox would draw the Thornberry brothers.

The longer he rode, the more disheartened he became. He barely walked his horse to maintain distance between him and the stage. The steep grade caused the driver to proceed so slowly a walking man could outrace the Concord. Hand began to worry that the driver and guard had spotted him and thought he was a problem waiting to happen. If they stopped and waited for him, he wasn't sure what he'd do.

To show himself might scare off the outlaws he wanted so badly. Yet if he did not, the guard might take it into his head that a robbery was in progress and demand that they return to Leadville.

Better to be on the rocky plain west of Mosquito Pass than along the narrow canyon roads through the Rockies during a holdup.

Hand reined in and waited for the driver to get his coach moving again. The judge couldn't tell what the problem had been; it might have been nothing more than an exceptionally rocky section of road. When the stage rounded the bend, Hand rode forward. He studied the roadbed and nodded to himself. He was getting better at reading signs. A deep rut had stymied the stage for a few minutes. The driver had placed medium-sized rocks behind the wheels to keep the stage from rolling backward as the horses strained uphill.

In the still mountain air, he could hear the clatter of the wheels and the loud protests of the horses as they pulled the stage ever higher into the Rockies. It took him several seconds to realize the loud report echoing through the hills wasn't a natural sound.

He'd heard a gunshot!

The pistol shot was followed by the bull-throated roar of a shotgun. He couldn't tell but thought that the second discharge from the shotgun followed quickly on the leaden heels of the first. The guard was defending the passengers and eighty pounds of worthless rock.

Hand experienced a pang of conscience. If he hadn't weighed down the stage, they might have a better chance of getting away from the highwaymen trying to rob them. He shook off such guilt. If he hadn't put the strongbox on the stage, he might never have flushed the Thornberry brothers.

If the road agents responsible for the ruckus ahead were the men he sought so desperately . . .

Sebastian Hand put his heels into the horse's flanks and urged the beast onward at a faster pace. The horse responded. It had been walking most of the day, except for the brief period of galloping outside Leadville. It responded well. Hand rounded the bend in the road to see that a small avalanche had blocked the path.

High above on the side of the mountain was the source of the rock slide. Smelly Ben Thornberry stood with a rifle raised to his shoulder. He shot wildly at the driver and guard. Both of those men had abandoned the high driver's box and had taken refuge behind a boulder beside the road.

"Give up, damn your eyes," came a voice all too familiar to Hand.

Jake Thornberry was leading the holdup. Hand sucked

in his breath and tried to calm himself. He had frozen once before when he had the outlaw in his sights. He didn't dare get buck fever twice.

He reminded himself of the gunfight with Roy Fredericks and his cohort at the worthless Lorelei Mine. He had been frightened then but had come through well and defended himself adequately. Drew Claggett had trained him well, too. He could knock out Jake Thornberry's left eye at this range, if he had to.

He pulled out his Winchester and swung it up to his shoulder. Aiming uphill took a considerable bit of skill. The bullet's trajectory was tricky, he knew. Complicating the shot even more, he fired from horseback.

Smelly Ben yelped when the leaden slug ripped away at his feet. Hand cursed. He had shot too low, trying to correct for the slope and the arc of the bullet. Still, the shot had its effect. It took some of the pressure off the driver and the guard.

"Who'n the bloody hell's comin' up the road at us?" came a loud voice. He thought he recognized Marsh Aylesworth's strident tones.

"I told you we should have let it go," came another voice from farther up the road he recognized as Matt Thornberry's. Hand rejoiced. All the brothers and their cousin were here.

Now all he had to do was kill them.

He levered another round in the Winchester's chamber and waited for a target. Ben gave it to him. He squeezed off the round, knowing that he had a man in his sights. Smelly Ben yelped like a scalded dog and dived for cover again. Hand couldn't tell if he'd winged him or if the bullet had gone astray.

Hand found little time for wondering. He had been able to approach and attack without reprisal because his presence hadn't been expected. Now that they knew he had joined the fight on the side of the stage driver and guard, the Thornberrys opened up on him. Hand dived for cover, almost falling from the saddle. The horse reared, then trotted away.

Hand didn't want to lose the animal, but he thought it was for the best if the horse went back around the bend in the road. The bulk of the mountainside would protect it from the bullets filling the air.

"I want that strongbox," Jake Thornberry bellowed. "Give it to us and you can ride on out of here."

"Go to hell, you damned son of a bitch," roared the driver.

Hand scooted on his belly, narrowly avoiding chunks of rock flying all around him. He pulled up beside the guard. The man's left arm dangled limp at his side. The amount of blood he had already lost was enough to make Hand worry he might bleed to death.

"Let me tend it," he offered.

The guard shook him off. "We got to worry about those road agents. They'll kill the lot of us. You shouldn't have joined in like that, mister. They'll kill you, too."

"I want them," Hand said with such intensity both driver and guard stared at him.

"You're the miner what gave us the strongbox, aren't you?" the driver asked. "You didn't trust us to get your silver to Denver safely."

"There's no silver in the box. It's worthless rock. Give them the box and get on out of here."

"It doesn't work that way," said the guard. "They don't want witnesses."

"Give them the strongbox. I'm not lying. There's nothing of any value in it. If nothing else, you've lightened your load by eighty pounds."

"Do it," said the driver. The guard hesitated, then shouted, "We're dropping the strongbox. Give us a second to get it out."

"Cover him," said the driver. "They might decide to reduce our numbers by one."

Hand found himself firing steadily as the guard fumbled one-handed to get the box free from the boot. The two passengers inside the stage shouted constantly for the driver to do something. Hand was amazed at the curses the preacher knew and used to express his disdain for the stage company and its personnel.

"You get on out of here," Hand told the driver. "Leave them to me."

"You're crazy as a stewed hoot owl, mister," the driver said, "but I'm not arguing. This has put me an hour behind schedule. I get a bonus if we arrive on time in Denver.''

"Tell them we're all getting into the coach," Hand ordered. The driver did as he was told. The guard even opened and closed the passenger door to make it look as if Hand had entered.

"You got the silver. Let us go," cried the driver. He whipped the frightened team into motion, slowly at first, then with greater speed and determination. Within minutes they had vanished around the next bend in the rocky road.

Sebastian Hand settled down in the small depression beside the road and waited. He didn't know how long it would be, but the Thornberry brothers weren't likely to let the box roast in the afternoon sun too much longer.

Even as the thought crossed his mind that they were gathering their courage to come and open the box, he spotted Smelly Ben slipping and sliding down the rocky slopes beside the road. He let out a tiny sigh. He had hoped to wing the man with an earlier shot. The way Ben scampered about, he hadn't been touched by any of Hand's shots.

"Here it is. I got it, Jake. I got it," Smelly Ben crowed. He bent over and touched the brass lock, then dropped it with a clank. The loud report of his six-shooter blowing off the lock made Hand wince. He summoned up his courage and peered up at the outlaw.

Ben was digging through the rocks inside. The scowl on his face told Hand that he had to act quickly.

"Jake, we been snookered. There's nothing but granite in this here box!"

Hand fired a single shot that caught Smelly Ben high on the shoulder and spun him around. The burly man dropped like one dead. Hand moved as fast as he could.

The ground around him puffed up with tiny dust devils—the other Thornberrys had opened fire at the most likely spot for a sniper to hide.

Hand rolled and rolled and finally came to his knees behind a large boulder. Smelly Ben had wiggled off the road and had found cover. Hand cursed. He hoped he had killed the man.

"Get the hell out of here. It must be an entire posse come for us," cried Matt.

Hand fired in the direction of the man's loud voice. He didn't want them to flee. He wanted them to stand and fight—and die.

For several seconds there was no sound. Then Jake yelled, "Get on out of here. There's no silver. They tricked us. Marsh, you take care of Ben. Matt, bring the horses around."

Hand waited for someone to show enough of a target to make firing worthwhile. The outlaws had retreated around the bend in the road, sheltered by the stony bulk of the mountain.

He cursed long and hard when he heard the clatter of horses' hooves on the roadbed. Letting them escape again wasn't in the cards. He wanted them—and he'd run them to ground.

Cautious, suspecting a trap, Sebastian Hand made his way back down the road toward Leadville, found his horse, and mounted. Then he retraced his steps and came to the place where he had hit Ben Thornberry. The trail of blood was likely to be the best spoor he could find. He set off tracking, using the drops of fresh blood as his signposts.

The road came to a three-way branching. He couldn't tell which of the three paths the outlaws might have taken. He dismounted and studied the ground closely. Possible blood drops showed that Ben had gone up the left canyon. But he wasn't sure. Fresh chips out of the rock hinted that someone had gone up—or come down—the right canyon.

And the road? The trail was confused with the recent passage of the stage. He couldn't tell if the outlaw band had gone this way or not.

From ahead he saw the flash of sunlight glinting off metal. He squinted and made certain that he wasn't seeing things. And old tin can catching the rays of the late-afternoon sun might have produced the same reflection. He was sure that it hadn't. Someone moved up the right-hand canyon.

Hand mounted and followed the sandy-bottomed arroyo up into the canyon until he found a bit of cloth dangling on a thorn bush. He smiled grimly. He hadn't been deceived. The Thornberrys were ahead.

This time he would have his revenge.

He rode to the top of a small rise and peered ahead. In the distance a solitary rider struggled to get his mount up a rock fall. Hand dismounted and took his Winchester from the saddle scabbard. Dropping to his belly, he sighted carefully at the distant outlaw. He exhaled just as he pulled back on the trigger.

He tried to keep the thought of killing another human being from his mind. The buck of the rifle startled him, just as Drew Claggett had taught him. The far-off horse stumbled, took a step, and then fell, sending its rider tumbling. Hand had missed the man and destroyed his steed.

Hand waited for a second shot at the man, but the opportunity never came. He mounted and circled, to cut off any retreat. Whoever he had put on foot, he wanted to finish off.

Cautious of an ambush, Hand rode up to the dead horse. The animal lay on its side, tongue lolling. Already a glaze formed over the sightless eyes. Rifle resting in the crook of his arm, Hand stood in his stirrups and studied the terrain. The rider had to be around somewhere.

"I don't believe it. You a ghost?" came a gravelly voice.

Hand swung around, rifle coming up. Jake Thornberry stood beside a small scrub oak. The branches obscured his face and partially protected his body, but Hand knew the voice.

"I've come for you," Hand said.

"Then take me in a fair fight." Jake Thornberry moved out. His six-shooter was stuck in his belt. He planted his feet wide and waited. "It is you, Judge Hand? I swear I thought we done you good."

Sebastian Hand was aware of the weight of the Lefaucheux in his leather-lined pocket. He dismounted cautiously, stood less than twenty feet from the outlaw, and just stared at the man.

"I can see the rope burns now. Must have scared you shitless being all trussed up like that. But you always was a lucky man, Judge. That was one fine woman you had. We enjoyed her several times 'fore we killed her.''

Thornberry tried to provoke him, to make him lose his temper. Claggett had warned him of this. Hand concentrated on why he wanted the outlaw dead. The law had been ineffective. The Texan had escaped his sentence. Until now.

The judge now became the executioner.

"You can't shoot me, can you, Judge Hand? It's different sitting on a fine bench and telling someone else to kill a man. When you got to do it yourself, you get all nervous inside, don't you?''

Hand remembered how he had lined up the outlaw in his sights once before and had failed to kill. Claggett had been right about this, too. It was hard to face a man and then kill him.

Jake Thornberry saw the doubt flicker across Hand's face. "You *are* having second thoughts, aren't you?''

Hand drew the six-shooter in his pocket with blinding speed. Thornberry started to reach for his pistol but got only halfway. The shock on his face faded.

"You should have killed me when you had the chance, Judge. You outdrew me. But you can't gun me down. I see it in your eyes. You can't do it.''

Jake's hand crept toward his pistol.

"You're wrong," Sebastian Hand said as he pulled the trigger. The Lefaucheux bucked and a .44 slug ripped through the outlaw's chest. Like a marionette with its strings cut, Jake Thornberry collapsed.

Hand walked over and stared at the dead outlaw.

He wasn't sure who was the deader. Thornberry would never rape and kill again; Hand felt hollow inside, stripped of all emotion and humanity.

He dropped the Lefaucheux back into his pocket and went to find the other three. Revenge had turned to ashes in his mouth, but he had a duty to the memory of his wife and brother.

He had a duty to himself to finish what he had started.

21

"Package for Mr. Hand. Package for Mr. Hand," cried the bellman.

Sebastian Hand motioned wearily from across the lobby of the Palmer House. The young man hurried over and gave him the package. Hand dismissed him with a dime tip for his trouble. From the weight of the parcel, he knew what was inside.

The spare Lefaucheux 1870 six-shooter had arrived from the gunsmith in New Orleans.

"Didn't expect to see you again," came a familiar voice.

Hand looked up to see Marshal Pevsner. "I had to come back."

"Heard tell three of the Thornberrys came tearin' through these parts less than a week ago. Don't know what happened to the fourth one." Pevsner cocked his head to one side and worked at his walrus mustache, waiting for Hand to give him a good answer to the unspoken question.

Sebastian Hand had faced Jake Thornberry. Never had his reactions been faster, never had he pulled his pistol quicker. Drew Claggett had warned him of this moment. Killing another man was not a task lightly taken for a man with a conscience. The outlaw had mistakenly assumed Hand had a conscience left.

The single shot had settled one-quarter of the score Hand had with the Texans. Seeing Jake dead on the ground had left him empty inside—and worse. He had no sense of triumph. He couldn't gloat. He couldn't even feel that he had accomplished anything worthwhile.

Three of the Thornberry clan were still free and on the run.

"They took a different path from Jake," he said, more to himself than to Marshal Pevsner. "Smelly Ben was injured, but not too badly from the speed they made getting back here."

"A doctor just outside of Larimer Square patched him up. A rifle slug took him in the shoulder. The doc said Ben isn't going to have full use of his left arm again. That bullet really tore up his muscles something fierce."

"I was aiming at his head," Hand said.

Pevsner laughed harshly. "That's always a bad shot. The head bobs around too much. Go for the body. Bigger target. Better."

"I know. I shot Jake through the heart."

Pevsner's muddy brown eyes widened. "You don't say. Hand, I reckon I misjudged you. I didn't think you had it in you."

"I cut their head off, but they're still kicking," he said. "Ben, Matt, and their cousin are still alive."

"Killing him makes you feel a sight better, doesn't it?" Pevsner asked.

Hand looked at him sharply.

"Killing makes you feel important, good, like a real man."

"Marshal, I didn't enjoy cutting him down. But I can't forget what he and his family did to me and mine." Hand tried to conjure up a mental picture of Laura or Randolph. He failed. More than Jake Thornberry had died on the road through Mosquito Pass. His wife and brother had become names to him rather than living memories.

Hand wasn't sure what drove him on now. Revenge wasn't much of an answer. He felt too drained for further killing to be a goal.

"I don't have anything left in my life but to hunt them down," he told the marshal.

"There can be more for you, Judge, if you let it."

Hand shook his head. There would never be more for him until he had put the Thornberrys behind him once and for all.

"Have it your way," Pevsner said. He fiddled with his thick walrus mustache for a moment, then added, "I shouldn't be telling you this, but I owe you for all you did."

"Lovejoy?"

"He broke out of jail. Killed a deputy and tried to bribe a judge to get him off scot-free. Lovejoy's pa finally decided his son was a ne'er-do-well and not worth the powder it'd take to shoot him. We caught him a day after he killed Joe."

"And?"

"Justice came fast when his father wasn't standing there to protect him."

"Justice can be served in many ways, can't it, Marshal?"

Pevsner grunted. "I owe you, but I'm not sure I wouldn't be doing you a bigger favor by keeping my fat yap shut."

"So don't tell me." Sebastian Hand felt as if he carried the world on his shoulders. Seldom had he been this tired, even though he had slept well and rested after coming back to Denver. Something vital had vanished from inside, and he couldn't put into words what it was.

The marshal stared at him for a moment, then said, "I got word that they split up. The three each went in a different direction, probably with the intent of losing you and joining up again later."

"Where?"

Pevsner shrugged. "Don't rightly know that. Don't know where two of them went, either, but the third headed out for Santa Fe. Reckon he might be tryin' to get on back to Texas and his kin."

"Which one headed south?" asked Hand. To his surprise, it didn't seem to matter who he brought to justice next.

"Ben Thornberry." Marshal Pevsner waited a moment, but Hand stared off into the distance, seeing nothing. The lawman sighed and left without another word.

Sebastian Hand opened the package he had received and took out the six-shooter. It fit his grip well. Having a spare pistol would serve him well when he tracked down Smelly Ben Thornberry.

And the other two outlaws who had killed his soul.

ABOUT THE AUTHOR

Karl Lassiter is the author of over fifteen Western novels. A Southwesterner for nearly thirty years, he was born in Mineral Wells, Texas, and lives in Albuquerque, New Mexico. Lassiter is a full-time writer and is presently studing the tongs, organized Chinese street gangs that operated in San Francisco from 1875–1906.

⊘ SIGNET (0451)

UNTAMED ACTION ON THE WESTERN FRONTIER

☐ **THE TERREL BRAND by E.Z. Woods.** Owen Terrel came back from the Civil War looking for peace. He and his brother carved out a cattle kingdon in West Texas, but then a beautiful woman in danger arrived, thrusting Owen into a war against an army of bloodthirsty outlaws. He would need every bullet he had to cut them down.... (158113—$3.50)

☐ **CONFESSIONS OF JOHNNY RINGO by Geoff Aggeler.** It was a showdown for a legend: Johnny Ringo. Men spoke his name in the same hushed breath as Jesse and Frank James, the Youngers, Billy the Kid. But those other legendary outlaws were gone. Only he was left, and on his trail was the most deadly lawman in the West. (159888—$4.50)

☐ **FORTUNES WEST #2: CHEYENNE by A.R. Riefe.** A spellbinding series! As the Civil War ended, cattlemen, sheepherders and farmers in Wyoming vied for the land against the fierce Cheyenne and Sioux. Dedicated officer Lincoln Rhilander had to defy his superiors to rout the redskins ... and had to choose between duty and desire in the arms of a beautiful woman. Stunning adventure! (157516—$4.50)

☐ **THE SAVAGE LAND by Matt Braun.** Courage, passion, violence—in a surging novel of a Texas dynasty. The Olivers. Together they carved out an empire of wealth and power with sweat, blood, bravery and bullets.... (157214—$4.50)

☐ **THE BRANNOCKS by Matt Braun.** They are three brothers and their women—in a passionate, action-filled saga that sweeps over the vastness of the American West and shines with the spirit of the men and women who had the daring and heart to risk all to conquer a wild frontier land. (143442—$3.50)

☐ **A LAND REMEMBERED by Patrick D. Smith.** Tobias MacIvey started with a gun, a whip, a horse and a dream of taming a wilderness that gave no quarter to the weak. He was the first of an unforgettable family who rose to fortune from the blazing guns of the Civil War, to the glitter and greed of the Florida Gold Coast today. (158970—$4.95)

Prices slightly higher in Canada

Buy them at your local bookstore or use this convenient coupon for ordering.

NEW AMERICAN LIBRARY
P.O. Box 999, Bergenfield, New Jersey 07621

Please send me the books I have checked above. I am enclosing $_____ (please add $1.00 to this order to cover postage and handling). Send check or money order—no cash or C.O.D.'s. Prices and numbers are subject to change without notice.

Name_____

Address_____

City _____ State _____ Zip Code _____
Allow 4-6 weeks for delivery.
This offer is subject to withdrawal without notice.